MW00619985

# THE UNITED STATES OF ENGLISH

# THE UNITED
# STATES
# OF ENGLISH

## THE AMERICAN LANGUAGE FROM COLONIAL

## TIMES TO THE TWENTY-FIRST CENTURY

ROSEMARIE OSTLER

OXFORD
UNIVERSITY PRESS

# OXFORD
## UNIVERSITY PRESS

Oxford University Press is a department of the University of Oxford. It furthers
the University's objective of excellence in research, scholarship, and education
by publishing worldwide. Oxford is a registered trade mark of Oxford University
Press in the UK and certain other countries.

Published in the United States of America by Oxford University Press
198 Madison Avenue, New York, NY 10016, United States of America.

© Oxford University Press 2023

CIP data is on file at the Library of Congress

ISBN 978-0-19-764729-5

DOI: 10.1093/oso/9780197647295.001.0001

Printed by Sheridan Books, Inc., United States of America

# Contents

# Acknowledgments

Many thanks are due to the following: my long-time agent, Janet Rosen, for her enthusiasm and expert work on my behalf; my Oxford editor, Meredith Keffer, for her excellent editing and ideas on how to make this a better book; my friend and fellow linguist Joe Emonds, for his careful reading and good advice; two anonymous reviewers, for their thoughtful comments; and my husband, historian Jeff Ostler, for his invaluable guidance through the ins and outs of American history, his many insightful comments and suggestions, and most of all, his unstinting support and encouragement over the years.

# Introduction

## One Country, Many Englishes

American English should really be called American Englishes—there isn't just one version. In 2013, *The New York Times* published an interactive map outlining the dialect regions of the United States. The map was accompanied by a quiz that consisted of twenty-five multiple-choice questions about people's word uses and pronunciations, for example, "What words do you use in casual speech to address two or more people?" "What do you call a carbonated beverage?" "How do you pronounce *caramel*?" "Do you pronounce *cot* and *caught* the same?"[1]

Many questions had a long list of possible answers. The question about addressing two or more people offered eight choices, not counting "other": *you all, youse, you lot, you guys, you'uns, yinz, you,* and *y'all.* People who answered *y'all* or *you all* were probably identifying themselves as Southerners, especially if three of their other answers were *coke* as a generic term for a carbonated beverage, *caramel* with three syllables, and *cot* and *caught* pronounced differently. Someone from the Midwest would most likely have answered *you guys, pop,* and *caramel* with two syllables. That person would probably pronounce *cot* and *caught* differently, too—but not necessarily.

The dialect map probably did not hit the bull's-eye every time. Americans move around a lot and sometimes they adopt words and even pronunciations that go with their new location. (For instance, somebody might start saying *spendy* instead of *pricey* after moving to the Pacific Northwest.) People can also pick up words and usages from parents or grandparents who grew up in a different part of the country (so they might say *teeter totter* even though most people where they live say *seesaw*).

Still, enough patterns exist to make the dialect quiz more than a game of random chance. Many of us can be connected with our home regions fairly accurately by the way we say our words, and which words we say. Furthermore, in spite of the fact that Americans watch the same television shows and movies across the country, follow the same blogs and comment boards, and relocate to different regions in large numbers, America's Englishes aren't getting any more alike.

On the other hand, Americans as a group sound distinctively different from other English speakers, most obviously in their pronunciations. *Cot*, *caught*, and *caramel* would all sound different from any American dialect if said by someone from England. The English omit the *r* sound in places where most Americans pronounce it, so *heart* sounds closer to *hot*, and instead of the typical American pronunciation of *bath*, they say something more like *bahth*. They use words differently, too. For instance, they use *shall* more often, as in *I'll sit here, shall I?*

This book tells the story of how Americans got from the British version of English (the only version until English speakers settled in North America) to a form of the language that is easily distinguished from other Englishes, and yet is itself full of variety. Part of the story has to do with natural linguistic processes. Like all languages, English is constantly evolving and adjusting to meet the needs of its users.[2] Most of these changes occur very slowly, so speakers of the language don't consciously notice them, but over time, they can lead to significant variation.

A version of a language that identifies its speakers as being from a specific location or group is called a dialect. Dialects arise when there is little or no contact between different groups of speakers, either because they are separated geographically, or because they belong to communities that don't mingle. All languages are made up of dialects. People sometimes think of a dialect as a degraded version of the "real" language, but in fact, everyone speaks a dialect. One dialect may be singled out as the "best" or most acceptable form of a language because the people who speak it have economic power and social prestige, but in reality, all varieties of a language evolve in the same way and are equally effective forms of communication.

Given enough time, distance, and isolation, dialects can grow so far apart that their speakers no longer understand each other at all.

For instance, the Germanic language, spoken in northern Europe a few thousand years ago, split into dialects that eventually became German, Norwegian, Swedish, Danish, Icelandic, Dutch, and English. Nothing so drastic has happened to the English language yet, but there has been plenty of time for multiple dialects to arise. As we'll see, the first colonists were already speaking different Englishes when they arrived in North America. Separated from the home country by thousands of miles of ocean, their speech continued to evolve in innovative ways and take on the characteristics that made it clearly American, while at the same time retaining some of their original differences.

The most obvious part of language change happens in the vocabulary. Words enter and exit the language, or simply change their meanings or how they're used. When speakers of different languages come into contact, they often borrow words from the other culture, especially if their situation calls for new terms that don't exist in their own language. Word borrowing was the first step in reshaping English for American uses. The earliest colonists adopted Algonquian terms to name the unfamiliar plants and animals of North America. The American lexicon has continued to evolve throughout the country's history and is still growing and changing today.

Changes in pronunciation are another big part of how American English took its current shape. Sound changes are almost always small and incremental and happen below the level of consciousness, but they can eventually result in speech that sounds very different from that of a few generations back (or different from speakers in other places). In American dialects, variety mostly comes down to how people pronounce their vowels.

Vowels are shaped by moving the tongue forward, backward, up, or down in the mouth, and pursing or widening the lips. When we speak, we don't think about the shape of our mouth or the position of our tongue, but that is how we create different sounds. Language change (and hence, language variety) happens when a subgroup of speakers starts shifting the place in the mouth where a vowel is typically articulated. For instance, *bait* has a long vowel that is pronounced with the tongue about midway in the mouth. If speakers of a certain dialect start pronouncing the vowel of *bait* slightly higher in the mouth, it starts to sound more like *beat*. This change happens across all, or at least most, words using that vowel.

Having *bait* and *beat* (and other word pairs using these vowels) sound almost the same is not optimal for communication, so those speakers will probably start to pronounce *beat* differently as well, to differentiate the words. For example, they might keep the vowel high, but start to push it farther back in the mouth. Eventually, a whole set of vowels will shift so the words they appear in continue to sound distinct from each other. Vowel shifts have happened several times in English over the centuries. As we'll see, regional vowel shifts, which are still happening around the country, are a large contributing factor in keeping American dialects distinct. If you hear someone speak and know they are from the Northeast, or the Midwest, or the South, most of what you're hearing is differences in vowel sounds.

Because vowels are important for following language change, vowels in this book will be illustrated with an example word that represents the sound in most dialects, as well as described by the place in the mouth where the vowel is typically articulated. Because dialects do differ, this system can only be approximate, but it allows readers to follow along without any technical linguistic knowledge. For those who want more precision, most examples will also include a symbol from the International Phonetic Alphabet (IPA), a system used by linguists to uniquely identify sounds. The Appendix lists American vowel sounds with their description, a keyword, and their IPA symbol, as well as a chart of vowel articulation in the mouth.

Unconscious linguistic processes are only one part of the story of how English Americanized. Languages don't exist in a vacuum. They are interwoven with society, affected by events in the world and by the behaviors and attitudes of the individuals who speak them. For that reason, this book covers a certain amount of American history as well as American speech. The two track closely together. As already mentioned, the English language started changing as soon as colonists arrived on North American shores and encountered the Algonquian speakers whose homeland it was. Later, speakers of other languages arrived and contributed their own words and ways of talking. (It should be noted that the population of the United States includes native speakers of hundreds of languages besides English. Not all of them speak English as a first language or at all. Their languages are also part of the rich tapestry of American speech, but because this book is about English, it will mostly touch on those languages as they relate to American English.)

As Americans spread out across the continent, people from different regions and social levels mingled in new configurations and affected each other's speech in novel ways. Every major facet of American life—politics, social movements, scientific inventions, wars, popular cultural trends—has played a role in forming the American language and differentiating it from British English. This book will show how those threads intertwined over time.

Americans themselves also guarantee that the language continues to be full of variety, partly through linguistic creativity and partly through their own self-awareness as speakers. The early chapters show how Americans, eager to separate themselves culturally from England, struck out on their own linguistically. They unapologetically adopted new words and usages (like Thomas Jefferson's invention, *belittle*). At the same time, they preserved some words and sounds that the English had abandoned, such as the expression *I guess* and the pronunciation of *r* after vowels.

The book's later chapters explore how Americans have continued to keep the language fresh by embracing innovative ways to express their identities through language. Slang and colorful colloquial speech have been part of the language since early times. The earliest slang arrived with the convicts, indentured servants, and others outside the mainstream who brought their vernaculars and jargon, but Americans soon began inventing their own. One major source of linguistic creativity is the generations of young people who have adopted their own in-group language. Another, more recent, source is found online, ranging from teenage texters who use abbreviations and typographical symbols to express their feelings, to political discussion groups that invent code words to keep their conversations secret.

Shifts in societal attitudes have also affected the language and how we use it. The landscape of pronoun use is constantly shifting. The growing trend of using *they* to refer to a single individual is one example, as are suggestions for new pronouns like *ze* and *hir*. Americans are also engaging in discussions about how they want to be identified and appropriate ways to refer to each other. For example, Americans have shifted from *stewardess* and *mailman* to *flight attendant* and *mail carrier*. They are investigating inclusive abbreviations such as *LGBTQIA+* and new inventions like *Latinx*.

Given the myriad influences that have shaped American English, it's hardly remarkable that there are eight (or maybe more!) ways to address a group of two or more people. American English started out as a collection of Englishes and its speakers have continued to build on that foundation, both consciously and not, while at the same time contributing material to the language as a whole. Languages never stay static. As the Afterword explains, American English is still evolving and taking off in new directions. Where we are going starts with where we came from—a group of immigrants finding its footing, and a new nation finding its identity.

# I

# The Beginnings of American English

## English Americanized

In the preface to his landmark 1828 dictionary, *An American Dictionary of the English Language,* the lexicographer Noah Webster made a bold prediction about English in the United States. "Our language, within two centuries," he wrote, "will be spoken by . . . *three hundred millions of people* [italics in original] who are destined to occupy . . . the vast territory within our jurisdiction."[1] As the Anglo-American population of the time was about 12 million, mostly clustered around the Eastern Seaboard, many might have seen this claim as extravagant, but Webster was not far wrong. Over 330 million people now live in the United States. While many languages are spoken around the country, most people speak some English, and for a large majority it's their first language.[2]

The English they speak is recognizably distinct from other Englishes of the world. American English features its own vocabulary, its own identifiable pronunciations (some common throughout the country, others specific to a region or group), alternative spellings, and ways of constructing sentences that are different from the British "mother tongue." Besides that, Americans have novel ways of expressing themselves. They use figures of speech that grew out of the landscape, culture, and history of the United States—*blaze a trail, pass the buck, step up to the plate*—and a constantly evolving collection of slang terms that range from colonial expressions for drunkenness (*in liquor, stiff as a ringbolt*) to the latest buzzwords of Gen Z (*extra* for over the top, *salty* for irritated).

When Webster's dictionary appeared in 1828, the United States had been an independent country for less than forty years, but English had been Americanizing for centuries. Out of the 70,000 or so words in *An American Dictionary,* 12,000 had never been recorded in a dictionary before.[3] Many, if not most, were American inventions. These named physical features of the continent (*swamp, cane-brake*) and native plants and animals (*raccoon, persimmon, cranberry*). They also included a large number of words that covered various aspects of American life— *congressional, electioneer, barbecue, land office, corn-mill, deputize, caucus.*

Webster also introduced several spelling changes that Americans would eventually adopt. These were meant to make spelling simpler and more consistent. Changes included dropping the *u* from words ending in *-our* like *colour* and *honour,* changing the *-ise* in words like *organise* to *-ize,* dropping the *k* from the end of words like *musick* and *physick,* switching *-re* to *-er* in *theatre* and *centre,* and replacing *qu* with *k* in words like *musquet.* Spelling thus became another way that American English distinguished itself from the British variety.

The language had grown apart from British English in other ways, too, although these were less easily captured in a dictionary. By the early nineteenth century, Americans were beginning to develop a discernibly different accent from the British. For instance, in most parts of the country, Americans pronounced the *r* sound after vowels and at the end of a word (as earlier English speakers had done), while the English were beginning to drop it. They also pronounced the sound of *a* differently in many words. The English said *bath* with the same vowel sound as in *hot,* but Americans pronounced it as they do now, with the same vowel as in *hat.* Different regions had their own speech patterns as well. New Englanders said 'wite' (without an *h* sound) for *white,* and backcountry Virginians said 'cheers' for *chairs.*

Americans even composed sentences differently. They often used *will* with *I* and *we,* where the English used *shall* (*I will do it* rather than *I shall do it*). Some speakers left out the *to be* in compound verbs like *ordered delivered,* or said *I want in* rather than *I want to come in.* On the other hand, Americans preserved some words and usages that had become obsolete in England, such as *fall* for autumn and *I guess* to signify agreement or certainty. While American speech was still obviously English, it encompassed a unique set of words, pronunciations, usages, and expressions that differentiated it from the language as spoken in England.

# The English of the First Colonists

The language that Americans speak today was built on a foundation of seventeenth-century English, which is noticeably different both from present-day American speech and present-day British speech. Here is a sentence from a 1612 description of Virginia, written by Captain John Smith, leader of the Jamestown colony: "Virginia doth afford many excellent vegitables and living Creatures, yet grasse there is little or none."[4] This sentence is easily understandable, but no English speaker today would say it. *Doth* is no longer in use, and *living creatures* instead of *animals* sounds stilted. The second half of the sentence would probably be written now as *there is little or no grass*. Besides these issues, the spelling seems quirky (*vegitables, grasse, Creatures* with a capital).

As described in the book's Introduction, English, like all languages, is constantly evolving. Words come and go, and pronunciations change over time. Sentences also get structured differently, so *Grass there is little or none* shifts to *There is little or no grass*.

Even before the first colonists carried English to North America in 1607, the language had already undergone several major evolutions.[5] It would continue to evolve in both the British Isles and in North America, with myriad changes accumulating in both places over the centuries.

English emerged sometime in the mid-fifth century, when waves of Germanic tribes began invading southeastern Britain, gradually settling throughout the southern part of the island. It grew out of the version of Germanic that these tribes spoke. Old English, as the earliest form of English is called, resembled present-day German more than modern English. The language was well established by the beginning of the eighth century, when the first Old English poems and stories began appearing in writing.

Old English started to morph into Middle English sometime in the twelfth century, partly from the impact of the French-speaking Normans, who invaded England in 1066 on behalf of their leader, the Duke of Normandy (also called William the Conqueror). The Duke defeated the English King Harold in battle, seized the throne, and installed his followers as the new ruling class. The French language became the language of the Court and officialdom. Gradually, a large number of French words infiltrated the English vocabulary. At the same time, English itself was changing in various ways that made it seem less like German and more like modern English. For instance, the word endings that identified subjects and objects in Old English were disappearing. Middle English is the language of Chaucer and *The Canterbury Tales*—more familiar than Old English, but still hard to read without a glossary and some practice. This stage of the language lasted until around 1500.

English shifted from Middle to Modern during the sixteenth century. The Jamestown colonists spoke Early Modern English, the language of Shakespeare and Queen Elizabeth I. Although far more intelligible to present-day English speakers than previous stages of the language, Early Modern English is clearly different from the English of today. That's why Shakespeare's plays now come with glosses defining all the words that have changed meanings or are no longer in use.

Besides the vocabulary, the biggest difference between early and later Modern English lies in the vowel sounds. The sixteenth century brought a series of changes known as the Great Vowel Shift.[6] Its main feature was that the long vowels of English began to be pronounced with the tongue held higher in the mouth. ("Long" vowels are pronounced with a tense mouth and are of longer duration than "short" vowels, which are pronounced with the mouth more relaxed. An example of a long vowel is the sound in *boot* [u]. A short vowel is the sound in *book* [ʊ].) At the beginning of the seventeenth century, when the Jamestown settlers first arrived in America, English was still at the tail end of the Great Vowel Shift.

Because sounds typically change in sets rather than one by one, as one long vowel began to be pronounced at a different place in the mouth, it pushed the vowel that had been previously in that spot into a new place, at the same time leaving a spot for a new vowel to move into. Each shift in pronunciation triggered another one, as though the first vowel to move was nudging the next one into a new position. This pattern of sound change is called a chain shift. Since spelling was beginning to be set, the result was that many words spelled the same (or nearly the same) as they were during the Middle English period are pronounced differently in Modern English. For example, *meat* [i] would have been pronounced the way we now pronounce *mate* [ei], while *mate* would have been said using the vowel that we now use in *hot* [ɑ], so it would have been pronounced something like 'mott'.

When people said *boot* [u], it would have sounded like the way we say *boat* [o], and *boat* would have been pronounced with a rounded 'aw' [ɔ] sound, almost like 'bo-aht'.

Other vowel sounds were also in flux. Short *e* and short *i* alternated, so *spirit* and *little* were sometimes pronounced 'sperit' and 'lettle', while *get* and *devil* might be said 'git' and 'divel'. *Boil* and *roil* were pronounced more like 'bile' and 'rile'. Also, many words spelled with an *er* had the sound of *ar*, such as 'marcy' for *mercy* and 'sarve' for *serve*. (Although this sound has mostly died out in the United States, it's still heard in England in words like *clerk* and *derby*, which are pronounced something like 'clark' and 'darby'.)

Other sounds were slightly different, too. For instance, words that end in *-ure* were pronounced without the gliding *y* sound, so *creature*, *pasture*, and *nature* were said 'creater', 'paster', 'nater'. A *gh* before *t* was pronounced like *f*, so *daughter* and *brought* were 'dafter' and 'broft'. (This pronunciation still exists in a few words like *laughter* and *enough*.) Final consonants were sometimes dropped, as in 'wep' for *wept*, 'nex' for *next*, and 'respec' for *respect*. Word-final *-ing* was often reduced to 'in' as well, for instance, 'stockin' for *stocking*, while a *g* was inserted in other words, such as 'sudingly' for *suddenly*.

How it is possible to know how people sounded in the seventeenth century? We can get a fair idea of early colonial pronunciations because spelling was much less standardized than it is now, particularly among the less educated. Although spelling conventions were hardening, aided by the introduction of the printing press in 1476, seventeenth-century spelling was still fluid. The result is that many people spelled words the way they sounded. Even among the more literate, whose spelling didn't particularly reflect their pronunciation, there was still plenty of room for personal choice. For instance, many people added extra "silent" vowels or spelled the same word more than one way at different times.

Records from the Salem, Massachusetts, witchcraft trials of 1692, written by various members of the community, offer many examples of spelling by ear. Spellings that reveal the writer's pronunciation include (in bold):

- I have warned the **parsons** above-named **accorden** to tenor of their Summonse.
- Sarah Good did most greviously **torter** me . . . severall times **sense** [since].

- There was a **lettell** black **menester** that Lived at Casko bay . . . and s[ai]d that he had kild 3 wifes . . . and had made nine **weches** in this plase.
- She said the **divel** carried the poole [pole].[7]

A 1675 description of conflict with the Wampanoags of New England shows many such examples, including the two below:

- If it wer so they wold have **broft** him.
- [They] Came **sudingly** upone the indians.[8]

Grammatical differences from modern speech are also apparent in seventeenth-century writings, especially in the verbs. The infinitive form of *be* (called invariant *be*) was used in some places where mainstream speakers today would use a tensed form of the verb, almost always *are*. *Be* usually appeared in the subjunctive mood (following *if*, *whether*, *although*, and similar words, to indicate a situation that might be counterfactual). It also sometimes showed up in declarative statements and typically indicated a habitual or ongoing state:[9]

- If ther be not some other dispossition setled unto . . . we . . . shall be examples.
- If the trees be very great, the ashes will be good.
- The younger provide . . . for those that be aged.
- Others there be that doe beare fruit much bigger.

Many verbs had past tenses that are now archaic, for example, *climb/clomb*, *help/holp*, *rise/riss*, *speak/spake*. *Have* could be followed by a simple past verb instead of the past participle, as in *I have spoke*. The most common third-person singular ending was *-eth*, although *-s* was making some headway. *Dost*, *hast*, and *durst* were also used with the second or third person. *Not* usually appeared after the main verb rather than between an auxiliary and a verb. Typical examples include:

- They **durst not**.
- This he **spake** onely to win time.
- Where, or how, none **doth** know.
- ...the first New-England water that they **drunke** of.
- It **seemeth** no fitt opportunity was offered.
- A vagrant **sayeth** hee is a Broomeman and **dwelles** in kent.[10]

The first English colonists also employed other grammatical structures that are seldom or never heard today. Multiple negatives in one sentence, such as *nor there are not none*, were often used for emphasis, as were double comparative adjectives like *most unkindest* and *more sadder*. More than one modal auxiliary could appear with a main verb, where most modern dialects allow only one. (The modals are *can, could, shall, should, will, would, might, must*, and *may*.) Typical combinations were *shall may* and *would might*. The phrase *fixin(g) to* before a verb and verbs prefixed with *a-* (*a-hunting, a-singing, a-shouting*) were also common. Measurements such as *pound, mile*, and *pair* were used without a plural *-s* ending: *three pound, eight mile*, and the like.

As English evolved in America, some features from the earliest colonial language would drop out (*-eth* and *-est, not* following the verb). Others would linger in one region while fading elsewhere (multiple modals, *a-* before a verb). Those that survived might be labeled folk speech or simply considered incorrect. At the same time, American English would continue innovating, as would British English, and the two forms of the language would inevitably grow further apart.

Language change happens at uneven rates and is often partial. Even within a dialect region or group, language use is varied and fluctuating. As the next chapter shows, the early colonists did not all speak alike. Their pronunciation and usage depended on where they were from, their level of education, personal history, and other factors. Linguistic changes did not come to every part of the American colonies at the same rate or all at once. Nonetheless, we can trace a broad trajectory from the first word adoptions to the accumulation of changes that put American and British speakers of English on clearly diverging linguistic paths.

## English Comes to America and Vice Versa

American words started trickling into the vocabulary during the sixteenth century, although it's doubtful that the English recognized them as such, since they came indirectly by way of Spain. More than a century before the British had any presence in the Americas, waves of Spanish-sponsored explorers and conquerors invaded the region, starting with Christopher Columbus's 1492 arrival in the Bahamas. The resulting flow of goods, animals, and people between the Americas and Spain (sometimes called the Columbian exchange) included several American plants unknown to Europeans. Eventually, these made their way to England. Typically, the Spanish adopted a version of the Native name for these items, which the English then borrowed and anglicized.

New foods from the Americas included potatoes, tomatoes, and chocolate. The word *potato* comes from Spanish *patata*, probably modeled on a word from an Arawakan language. (Arawakan languages are spoken in South and Central America and the Caribbean.) Until sometime in the late seventeenth century, *potato* without a modifier referred to sweet potatoes (*Ipomoea batatas*). White potatoes (*Solanum tuberosum*), which appeared on the scene later, were known as *Virginia potatoes*. The words *chocolate* and *tomato* (Spanish *chocolate* and *tomate*) both came from the Nahuatl language of the Aztecs of central Mexico. The Spanish also introduced a grain they called by the Arawakan word used in Haiti, *mahiz*. The English called it *maize*, but colonial Americans would later designate the plant *Indian corn* or just *corn* (more about that in the next section).

*Canoe, hurricane,* and *barbecue* were other early borrowings first introduced by returning voyagers. *Barbecue,* from Spanish *barbacoa* and the same word in Haitian, originally meant a frame for grilling or smoking meat. The verb *to barbecue* made its way into English in the late seventeenth century, and in the eighteenth century the noun expanded to encompass the meat cooked on a barbecue. Eighteenth-century Americans were the first to use *barbecue* to mean a social event that involved roasting meat. Several of George Washington's diary entries record his attendance at colonial barbecues.

*Tobacco* is another borrowing that came into the language during the sixteenth century, probably also from an Arawakan Haitian word by way of Spanish *tabaco*. The English enthusiastically embraced the pipe-smoking habit. A chronicler of English society writing in 1573 gives an early example of the word in print: "In these daies the taking-in of the smoke of the Indian herbe called Tabaco, by an instrument formed like a little ladell, wherby it passeth from the mouth into the hed & stomach, is gretlie taken-up & used in England."[11] Other early terms include *tobacco merchant, tobacco shop, tobacco breath* (possibly referring to lingering pipe fumes rather than smoker's breath), and *tobacco room*, a room set aside for smoking.

The first true Americanisms—that is, words and phrases adopted, created, or repurposed in America—entered the language when the English founded their first permanent North American colony. On April 26, 1607, a group of 104 men led by John Smith sailed into the Chesapeake Bay and established the Jamestown, Virginia, settlement. The colony was a commercial venture, financed by a group of shareholders called the Virginia Company of London. The colonists' main directive was to prospect for gold. As a secondary goal, they were to make contact with the Indians with a view toward establishing future trade relations.

When the English landed in Virginia, the Chesapeake region was home to between 14,000 and 21,000 Algonquians.[12] They grew corn, beans, tobacco, and other crops, which they supplemented by fishing, hunting, and gathering wild plants. The tribes were politically organized under the paramount chief, Wahunsonacock, known to the English as Powhatan. (His people were also called Powhatans.) The Powhatans spoke Virginia Algonquian, one of a family of languages then spoken all along the coast between Canada and present-day North Carolina.[13] The first words to be borrowed and naturalized into English all came from Algonquian languages.

The colonists needed to get on friendly terms with the Algonquians, not only for future trade relations, but also for immediate help. They were poorly prepared to survive on their own in an unfamiliar and challenging landscape. Most of the men, aside from a few carpenters and other skilled workers, were either gentlemen of leisure or their servants. They had no practical experience in planting and raising crops. The seeds they planted failed to sprout and the stores they brought from England soon ran low. This meant that to keep from starving, they would have to barter with the Powhatans for food—corn and venison in exchange for knives, hatchets, and other English goods.

Captain Smith lost no time in seeking out Powhatan and beginning negotiations for the needed supplies. His reports to the Virginia Company (and his later published descriptions of Virginia) include the first Algonquian borrowings to make their way into English. Whenever Smith wanted to describe a plant, animal, or cultural practice that had no equivalent in his own language, he reached for the Algonquian term.

One of the earliest word adoptions was *raccoon*, which arrived at its current form in stages. It appears in Smith's description of his first meeting with Powhatan. He found the great chief surrounded by courtiers, lying "uppon a Bedstead a foote high, upon tenne or twelve Mattes, richly hung with many Chaynes of great Pearles about his necke, and covered with a great Covering of *Rahaughcums*."[14]

Smith's spelling was obviously an attempt to represent Algonquian pronunciation. However, in later writing he simplified it to make the word more English-looking. In a description of animals native to Virginia he wrote, "There is a beast they call Aroughcun, much like a badger." Later, he streamlined the word still further to *Rarowcun*. By the late seventeenth century, other writers had standardized the spelling to *raccoon*. Words taken from Algonquian, and later from other Indigenous and European languages, frequently followed this pattern.

It's unclear exactly how Smith and Powhatan communicated, but it was probably some mix of English, Algonquian, and gestures. Smith's quotations make Powhatan sound like an Englishman (e.g., Powhatan's greeting on one occasion, "Your kinde visitation doth much content mee"),[15] but he was almost certainly paraphrasing or simply translating. Powhatan may well have known some English, however. English sailors had been making landfall along the North American coast since the mid-sixteenth century. Also, a dozen or more Algonquians had traveled to England by 1607, either willingly or as captives.[16] Typically, they learned English, then acted as interpreters, eventually returning to America on outbound English ships. Powhatan might have learned the language from either of these sources.

Smith evidently learned to speak Algonquian fairly well. According to fellow colonists, he was fluent enough to act as an interpreter during subsequent encounters with the Powhatans. Smith's "A Map of Virginia," written in 1612, includes a short vocabulary. It starts with a list of about three dozen Algonquian words for various items, followed by words for numbers and a handful of phrases such as "He dwels a great way hence."[17]

Most of the words in the vocabulary list never made it into English. Two that did are *tomahawk* and *moccasins*. These probably survived because, unlike most of the other words, they named things that weren't found in England. Smith also introduced several other Algonquian words to the English vocabulary. These include *opossum*, first spelled *opassom* or *apoussoun*, and *persimmon*, first spelled *putchamin*. While exploring New England in 1614, Smith picked up *moose*, *muskrat*, and *hominy*.

Besides describing the natural world in his reports, Smith recorded many Algonquian customs and ways of life. In one of these descriptions, he introduced a word that is the likely source of *caucus*. He wrote, "In all these places [tribal villages] is a severall commander . . . except the *Chickhamanians*, who are governed by the Priestes and the Assistants of their Elders called *Caw-cawwassoughes*."[18] The English form of the word first began appearing in print in the mid-eighteenth century, significantly shortened. Early mentions spell it *corcus*. By the nineteenth century, the spelling had standardized to *caucus*, and the word took on the current meaning of a group of legislators from the same political party who meet to plan strategy. It also spun off the verb *to caucus*.

In December 1620, thirteen years after the settlement of Jamestown, the second contingent of English colonists landed at Plymouth Rock, Massachusetts. These were a group of 102 Puritan Separatists, women and children as well as men, who later became known as the Pilgrims. Like the Jamestown colonists, they struggled to keep from starving in the months after their arrival. They also got help from the local inhabitants, including two who spoke English.

The Cape Cod region was home to several Algonquian nations, including the Nausets, the Wampanoags, and the Patuxets. When the Pilgrims arrived, the tribes were still trying to recover from a devastating epidemic that had swept through the area a year or two before, wiping out whole communities. Maybe for that reason, they avoided the colonists at first.[19] The first meaningful encounter between the two parties came in the spring of 1621. Some men of the colony were holding an outdoor meeting when a Native man walked up to them and, to their surprise, addressed them in English. His name was Samoset and he was an Abenaki from Maine, who now lived in a nearby village. He had learned English from the sailors who sometimes landed on the Maine coast. Samoset introduced the colony's governor, William Bradford, to Chief Massasoit, leader of the Wampanoag people.

He also introduced the colonists to Tisquantum, known to the English as Squanto, one of the few surviving members of the Patuxet tribe. Squanto had been kidnapped by a ship's captain several years earlier and taken to Spain. Eventually, he escaped to England, where he learned the language before returning to North America. Squanto was invaluable to the Plymouth colonists. He not only taught them what and how to plant and the best places to catch fish, but also acted as an interpreter between the colony's leaders and the surrounding tribes.

Access to interpreters might have been one reason why Governor Bradford, in contrast to John Smith, did not show much interest in Algonquian languages. His record of the colony's activities, *Of Plymouth Plantation*, makes little mention of Native words or customs. One word that he did use was an early version of *powwow*. Relating events that happened before and shortly after the Pilgrims arrived, he wrote, "Before they [the Wampanoags] came to the English to make freindship, they gott all the Powachs of the cuntrie for 3 days together."[20]

The word originally meant a shaman or healer. One early narrative described the main duties of the "Powah" as "calling upon the Divell, and curing diseases of the sicke or wounded." By the early eighteenth century, the English meaning had shifted to a tribal gathering, as in this example: "[T]he Indians at the Wigwams, near the Fort, had a *Powwow*, or sort of Conjuring."[21] The verb *to powwow* came into use at around the same time.

Bradford also recorded an early version of *wampum*, from a Massachusett word that he spelled *wampampeack*. Wampum were strings of beads made from shells, widely used as currency. Future writers quickly shortened the word to its present form. During the nineteenth century, Anglo-Americans used the word as casual slang for money, a usage that's now rare. Other words that entered early colonial English from New England languages include *wigwam*, from an Abenaki word for a dwelling; *hickory* (originally *pohickory*); *squash* (originally *asquutasquash*); *skunk*; *terrapin*; and *woodchuck*.

Other colonists and visitors occasionally recorded Indigenous languages of the area, but for the most part, these didn't lead to word adoptions. Roger Williams, the founder of Rhode Island, wrote *A Key into the Language of America* as a language-learning tool for missionaries and traders. The book is mostly a collection of practical phrases, greetings, or questions like "What is your name?" and "Where do you live?" The only word in *A Key* to be naturalized into English was *netop*, a Narragansett word meaning friend. According to Williams, New England colonists greeted the Natives by saying, "What cheare, netop?"[22] Then the colonists started addressing each other that way. *Netop* hung on as a casual greeting between Anglo-Americans until sometime in the nineteenth century, an example of a word that unpredictably becomes trendy, then just as unpredictably goes extinct.

# American English in the New Republic

Settlers faced with unfamiliar landscapes and previously unknown plants and animals had to find terms to name and describe them. As we saw in the previous section, they sometimes borrowed words from Native American languages. They also repurposed existing English words and invented new terms, as well as keeping words that had become archaic in British English. As non-English-speaking immigrants began to arrive during the eighteenth century, they accepted words from those languages as well. By the time of the American Revolution, English had been evolving separately in England and America for nearly 200 years, and the trickle of new words had become a flood.

*Corn* offers an example of how English words evolved in America. Before 1492, the plant that Americans call corn (*Zea Mays*) was unknown in England. The word *corn* was a general term for grain, usually referring to whichever cereal crop was most abundant in the region. For instance, *corn* meant wheat in England, but usually referred to oats in Ireland. When American corn came to Britain, it was named *maize*, the English version of *mahiz*. When the first colonists encountered it in North America, however, they almost always referred to it as *corn* or *Indian corn*, probably because it was the main cereal crop of the area.

Both John Smith and William Bradford nearly always called it *corn* in their writings, only using *maize* occasionally. Smith mentioned corn frequently in his reports of his dealings with the Powhatans. In 1607, he wrote, "Our provision being now within twentie dayes spent, the Indians brought us great store both of Corne and bread ready made." He also used the same word to refer to the seeds brought from England: "Our next course was to turn husbandmen, to fell Trees and set Corne." The seeds in question were probably wheat (or at any rate, not maize), suggesting that Smith still used *corn* as a general term for any staple cereal crop. Although Smith usually just said *corn*, Bradford and others often disambiguated with *Indian*, as in this example from *Of Plymouth Plantation*: "When they had maize (that is, Indean corne) they thought it as good as a feast."[23]

Corn was central to survival for the English settlers, so *corn* terms soon proliferated. In Webster's 1828 dictionary, the entries under *corn* cover two columns. These include the terms *corn basket, corn blade, corn cutter, corn flour, corn field, corn-mill,* and *cornstalk,* among others. Webster defined *corn* the way the English do, as a cover term for any grain, but noted, "In the United States . . . by custom it is appropriated to maize."

Other corn-related words that came into the language early on are *succotash, hominy,* and *pone,* all from Algonquian languages. In his narratives, Smith referred to "the bread which they call ponap," and also described "Homini" as "bruized Indian corne pounded, and boiled thicke."[24] The terms *roasting ear, johnnycake,* and *hoecake* (both cakes made from corn meal) were all in use by the eighteenth century.

Much of the landscape of North America was new to the English, so many early word inventions applied to the natural world. Often these simply combined a noun with an adjective: *back country, backwoods* (and *backwoodsman*), *back settlement, pine barrens, cane-brake, salt lick, foothill, underbrush, bottomland, cold snap.* Plants and animals were similarly named, for instance, *fox-grape, live oak, bluegrass, timothy grass, bullfrog, catfish, copperhead, lightning bug, garter snake,* and *katydid* (a grasshopper named for the sound it makes). All were part of the vocabulary by the mid-eighteenth century. Other descriptive landscape names included *clearing, rapids,* and *bluff.*

*Bluff* has the distinction of being the first word with a changed meaning to be noticed and criticized by a visiting Englishman. Writing about Savannah, he reported, "It stands upon the flat of a Hill; the Bank of the River (which they in barbarous *English* call a *Bluff*) is steep, and about 45 foot perpendicular."[25] A bluff in England denoted a high but rounded shoreline, while in America it was used to describe steep cliffs.

Americans repurposed other English words as well. For example, *bug,* which meant a bedbug in England, broadened to cover any insect, and *sick,* which referred specifically to a digestive upset, became a general term for any illness. What the British called *timber,* Americans called *lumber.* (In England, lumber is old discarded furniture and other items of the sort usually found in attics.) Americans called a shop a store, as in *grocery store* (perhaps from an archaic use of *store* to mean an abundant supply) and said *fall* for *autumn. Fall* was short for *fall of leaf,* once a common phrase in England, but becoming obsolete by the eighteenth century. Americans also said *mad* for angry, another English usage that died out in the old country.

The expression *I guess*, meaning that one supposes or agrees, is often used to stereotype Americans in British books and movies, but it was current in England during the seventeenth century, and was no doubt imported by the first North American settlers. Later, that usage went obsolete in England, but remained popular in America. An early in-print example comes from the *Massachusetts Spy* newspaper for February 2, 1798: "I guess my husband won't object to my taking one, if they are good and cheap." During the nineteenth century, it was a regionalism specific to New England, although it later became common everywhere. To quote the *Massachusetts Spy* again, for November 8, 1815, "You may hear [a Southerner] say 'I count'—'I reckon'—'I calculate'; but you would as soon hear him blaspheme as guess."

Americans sometimes misapplied names to animals and plants that looked like English species, but were not really the same, such as *rabbit* for American hares, *robin* for a kind of thrush, *butternut* for a variety of walnut tree, and *cottonwood* for a kind of poplar. *Huckleberry* is probably a corruption of *whortleberry* or *hirtleberry*, English regional names for the bilberry (*Vaccinium Myrtillus*), but in America, it refers to the species *Gaylussacia*.

Several words for bodies of water changed meanings between the old country and the new. In England a pond is artificial, but in America it is natural. *Creek* in British English refers to an inlet from the sea, while in American English it describes a tributary of a river. An English watershed is a line or ridge separating the waters that flow into different drainage areas, but in America it's a slope down which the water flows, or the catchment area of a river. Americans added the meaning of a small stream or brook to *branch*, and said *fork* to refer to one arm of a river as well as a fork in the road.

The word *buffalo* traditionally referred to any of several species of oxen such as water buffalo, but in America it expanded to cover the buffalo-looking bison. Most people now think of bison as an animal of the western plains, but in the seventeenth century its range covered most of North America. Bison were spotted in Maryland according to one seventeenth-century visitor to the continent, who wrote, "In the upper parts of the Countrey, there are Bufeloes, Elkes, Lions, Beares, Wolves, and Deare."[26] Early words to describe items related to bison or their environment include *buffalo grass*, *buffalo clover*, *buffalo hunt*, and *buffalo range*.

*Bee* took on the new meaning of a gathering where neighbors got together to help each other complete some chore, followed by eating, drinking, and socializing. Presumably, the idea was that bees are social creatures and they work as a team. Raising a barn, husking corn, and picking apples were made easier if tackled during a raising bee, a husking bee, and an apple bee. One of the first mentions of a work bee appeared in the *Boston Gazette* on October 16, 1769: "Last Thursday about twenty young Ladies met at the house of Mr. L. on purpose for a Spinning Match; (or what is called in the Country a Bee)." *Spelling bee* came into use sometime during the nineteenth century.

English speakers also adopted words from other colonial countries. The language that influenced early American English the most is Dutch. In 1609, shortly after the Jamestown colonists ventured into Virginia, an Englishman named Henry Hudson, who worked for the Dutch East India Company, landed on the island of Manhattan and claimed it and the surrounding territory for his employers. By the 1620s, New Netherland was the site of several Dutch settlements.

New Netherland changed hands in 1664, part of the English spoils of the Anglo-Dutch war. King Charles II handed it over to his brother the Duke of York, who renamed it New York. A substantial Dutch population remained, however, still adhering to their own customs and speaking their own language. Dutch could be heard in both New York and New Jersey until the late nineteenth century. Meanwhile, English speakers adopted several Dutch terms.

These include food words such as *cole slaw* (Dutch for cabbage salad), *cookie* (Dutch for little cake), *cruller*, and *waffle*. The words *scow*, *spook*, and *stoop* (the landing of the front steps) also came into the language in the eighteenth century. *Dope*, which is Dutch for a sauce, originally named a preparation of pitch and other ingredients that was applied to the bottom of shoes for smooth walking over softened snow. It had taken on its drug meaning by the 1870s. *Boss*, originally *werk baas*, or "work master," was used both to mean the man in charge and to refer to a master craftsman, for example, *boss carpenter. Bushwhacker*, from a Dutch term meaning forest keeper, made its first appearance in print in 1809, in Washington Irving's comic novel *A History of New York, from the Beginning of the World to the End of the Dutch Dynasty*, written under the pseudonym Diedrich Knickerbocker. He describes a gathering of prominent Dutch settlers as "gallant bushwhackers and hunters of raccoons by moonlight."[27]

*Yankee* is also almost certainly a Dutch contribution. Various theories have been suggested for the word's origin (for instance, that it's a Native American mispronunciation of *English*), but the most likely one derives the word from *Janke* (pronounced 'yan-kuh'), a diminutive of *John* that translates as something like 'little John'.[28] It may have been inspired by *John Bull*, a popular nickname of that time for a typical Englishman. Americans were "little John" Bulls. At first *Yankee* referred only to New Englanders, but by the time of the Revolution, when the song "Yankee Doodle" was first heard, the British applied it to all Americans. During the Civil War, Southerners adopted the term to apply to anyone from a Union state.

Other European languages also contributed words. French colonists were fewer in number and more scattered than the English. Most were itinerant trappers, traders, and missionaries, and the terms that entered eighteenth-century English reflect that. These include *butte*, an isolated hill; *prairie*, which meant marshy meadows in France, but rolling grasslands in America; *chowder*, from the French *chaudière*, the name of the pot that fish stew was cooked in; and *caribou*, which probably came originally from Mi'kmaq.

Although many thousands of Germans came to the British colonies during the eighteenth century, settling mainly in western Pennsylvania, they didn't have much impact on early American English. Most belonged to small religious sects such as the Mennonites, Moravians, and Amish, who kept to themselves and continued to speak German. The main German contributions to the vocabulary came from immigrants who arrived in the nineteenth century or later. However, a handful of earlier words and usages entered the language from "Pennsylvania Dutch" (so-named from *Deutsch,* the German word for German): *get awake* to mean wake up, *hex, spritz, flitch* for bacon, *sauerkraut, noodle,* and *pretzel.*

Africans were also a significant part of the population by the late eighteenth century, but because of the conditions of isolation and linguistic suppression imposed by their enslavers, few words from African languages entered the colonial vocabulary. The first Africans to arrive in British North America were twenty captive Angolans, brought to Virginia in 1619 by a Dutch sea captain. Over time, a regular slave trade developed, continuing until it was outlawed in 1808. By 1700, enslaved Africans made up about 10 percent of Virginia's population, and by the late eighteenth century, they formed nearly half the population of the Chesapeake region.[29]

Unlike other non-English-speaking residents of the colonies, such as the Germans in Pennsylvania and the Dutch in New York, captive Africans were not allowed to form linguistic communities. Most came from different parts of West Africa, which is home to over 1,000 languages and dialects, so many did not speak the same language. If they did, their captors deliberately separated them. That way, chances of organized escape or revolt were kept to a minimum. Once in America, enslaved Africans were dispersed to different places on the same principle. In order to communicate, they were forced to abandon their native languages in favor of English.

In spite of the suppression of African languages, colonial English did borrow several African words. Like many borrowings, they center around unfamiliar foods and cultural practices. The earliest came to English indirectly through other European languages. *Banana*, first noted at the end of the sixteenth century, is from Guinea by way of Spain or Portugal. (The word is the same in both languages.) *Gumbo*, an Angolan word for okra, probably came into the language through French. Other early borrowings are *yam* from the Fulani language, *goober* (peanut) from Kikongo, and *voodoo* and the related *hoodoo* from Fon. The major African American contributions to English emerged in later centuries (see Chapters 6 and 7).

Thomas Jefferson's purchase of the Louisiana Territory from the French in 1803 indirectly led to another rush of newly created words. This vast tract of land stretched from the Mississippi River west to the Rockies, almost doubling the area controlled by the United States. It was largely alien country to Americans, so President Jefferson appointed an expedition led by Meriwether Lewis and William Clark to explore the region and report back on what they found.

Jefferson's instructions called for copious details on every aspect of the territory. He wanted to gauge the possibilities of trade with the western tribes, so he asked the men to discover as much as they could about tribal life, ranging from population numbers to religious practices. He also wanted a complete and accurate picture of the natural world, including landscape and topography, climate statistics, and careful descriptions of plants and animals, in particular those not found in the East.[30]

Lewis and Clark took Jefferson's instructions to heart. Both wrote almost daily in their journals, collecting minutely observed details of the world around them over the course of their two-year trek. This meant that every time they met with an unfamiliar plant, animal, landscape feature, or cultural item, they had to find a word or words to describe it. As a result, their journals include hundreds of terms that are new to English or used in a new way. Not all of them made it into the permanent vocabulary, but many did.[31]

They often named things for what they looked like or some other salient feature. A journal entry by Lewis for May 10, 1805, illustrates their naming process. Describing a type of deer distinct from those seen in the East, he wrote, "The year [ear] and tail of this anamal . . . so well comported with those of the mule . . . that we have . . . adapted the appellation of the mule deer." Similar examples include *turkey buzzard*, *yellowjacket*, *sapsucker*, *red-tailed hawk*, *whistling swan*, *big horn sheep* (from the French trappers' name for it), *red elm*, and *snowberry*. The men named the grizzly bear for the "grizzled" (i.e., silver grayish) appearance of its coat only after studying several pelts closely to determine the exact color. At first, they referred to it as "yellowish" or "whiteish." They also named things for where they were found. Examples include *prairie dog*, *prairie lark*, *prairie hen*, *sand hill crane*, *Osage apple* (found in Osage territory), and *buffalo berry* (found where buffalo grazed).

Lewis and Clark frequently recorded Native terms, but very few of them entered English. One that did is *camas*, a lily-like plant whose bulb was used for food. Clark noted in his September 20, 1805, journal entry: "Those people [the Nez Perce] gave us . . . roots . . . Some round and much like an onion which they call Pas she co quamash." They also recorded the cultural terms *buffalo robe*, *council house*, and *sweat lodge*, as well as *medicine* in the sense of a magical power, likely a translation of an Ojibwe word. Terms in the journal include *medicine man*, *medicine dance*, *war medicine*, and *big medicine*.

## Changing Accents

For most of the colonial period, there were no obvious pronunciation differences that distinguished Americans from the English. That began to change during the late eighteenth century, when two sound changes occurred that would have a lasting impact on the language.

Both happened in England, and both have become widely recognized markers of British versus American speech.

One change affected the *r* sound. When the first English colonists came to America, English speakers pronounced the *r* wherever it appeared in a word. A minor exception was *r* before *s*, which started being omitted from words like *horse*, *curse*, and *burst* as early as late Middle English, making them sound more like 'hoss', 'cuss', and 'bust'. The colonists almost certainly brought that pronunciation with them. (And it can still be heard in some American dialects.) Otherwise, however, both the colonists and their compatriots in Great Britain said their *r*'s.

At some point during the eighteenth century, fashionable Londoners developed the habit of dropping the *r* sound after a vowel, before a consonant, and at the end of a word. One of the earliest mentions of the new trend comes from a guide to English pronunciation written in 1791: "In England and particularly in London, the *r* in *lard*, *bard*, *card*, *regard*, etc. is pronounced so much in the throat as to be little more than the middle or Italian *a* [like the vowel in *hot*] lengthened into *laad*, *caad*, *baad*, *regaad*." The author noted that *r* was "sometimes entirely sunk" except at the beginning of a word.[32]

This pronunciation change spread gradually into the greater London area and southeastern England. By the end of the eighteenth century, "*r*-lessness" was the norm throughout the southeast. More importantly, it was also a feature of the London-based prestige dialect that was beginning to emerge as the upper-class standard for educated people in all parts of England (known as Received Pronunciation), due to London's social and political influence. In the west and north of England, *r* remained (and still remains) part of the regional speech. (Irish and Scottish English speakers also say their *r*'s.)

The fashion for *r*-lessness never caught on with most Americans. They continued to articulate the *r* wherever it appeared in spelling, just as their ancestors had done. The only parts of the country where the new pronunciation took hold were eastern New England and the South, where evidence of dropped *r*'s appeared by the late eighteenth century. For example, Robert Treat Paine, a little-known Bostonian poet who was composing during the 1790s, rhymed *war* and *awe*, *morn* and *lawn*, *thorn* and *gone*, and *resort* and *thought*, among other word pairs. Noah Webster, writing in 1789, remarked that some Southerners, Virginians especially, "almost omit the sound *r* as in *ware*, *there*."[33]

*R*-lessness never expanded beyond these circumscribed regions, however. As the population grew and Americans spread into other parts of the continent, they carried the *r* sound with them. It became the default pronunciation nearly everywhere in the country. Today, *r*-lessness is found only in a few coastal enclaves, and its range is shrinking.

It's unclear exactly why New England and the South adopted *r*-lessness.[34] One possibility is that the new pronunciation entered through port towns such as Boston, New York, and Charleston, where British visitors were common, but didn't spread much beyond those areas. Most Americans of the time never heard British English spoken, and since the spelling of words with *r* didn't change, there was no written clue to the changed sound. Only people exposed to British English speakers would have become familiar with it.

An alternative theory is that the change was already happening in the popular speech of London and southeastern England when the first colonists from these places arrived. Many early Massachusetts settlers came from the southeastern counties of England, and many of the first Virginians were from the London area, both places where *r*-lessness appeared early on. Occasional misspellings like *woned* for *warned* and *fouth* for *fourth* occur in seventeenth-century colonial records, suggesting that the *r* was at least sometimes not pronounced. Later British immigrants, on the other hand, usually came from parts of Great Britain that were *r*-ful, such as northern England and Ireland. These groups settled west of the original colonists, mainly in the Appalachian backcountry. Their presence may have acted as a barrier to the expansion of *r*-less pronunciations beyond the coastal areas.

The retention of *r* in the speech of most Americans is an instance of linguistic "lag," the tendency of colonies to keep features of the language that have changed or disappeared in their original home. Another such instance for Americans is the British change in their pronunciation of the letter *a*. Before the late eighteenth century, there was no *a* sound like the one heard now in *hot* (sometimes called a "broad *a*" or an "Italian *a*," as mentioned previously). Both American and British speakers pronounced the letter the same way as the vowel in *hat*.

Once again, Londoners introduced the new pronunciation. They started saying the *a* before certain consonants with the tongue farther back in the mouth, approximately an 'ah' sound. For instance, *fast*, *dance*, *half*, *bath*, *glass*, and *aunt* were said as if they were spelled 'fahst', 'dahnce', 'hahlf', 'bahth', 'glahss', and 'ahnt'. Gradually, this pronunciation, like the changing sound of *r*, became widely accepted in England. Most *a* spellings in America, however, kept their colonial sound. The exceptions were *a* before *r* plus a consonant, as in *hard* and *part*, and *a* before *lm*, as in *calm* and *psalm*, as well as a few outliers like *father*, and borrowings like *garage* and *massage*, both from French. Even these few changes were slow in coming. The Founding Fathers probably said *father* with the vowel sound in *hat*.

Again, New England was more receptive to the sound change than other parts of the country. New Englanders adopted the new *a* sound in a number of words, for instance, *laugh*, *aunt*, *path*, and *chance*. This pronunciation later became a verbal hallmark of the countrified "Yankee" as portrayed in plays and novels. However, like *r*-lessness, it never spread beyond a limited area. As with the missing *r*, the 'ah' pronunciation was a noticeable enough sound change to become an identifying feature of British, as opposed to American, speech.[35]

## Talking like an American

By the mid-eighteenth century, American English was different enough from the British variety to prompt a London newspaper to plead for a glossary to interpret "the words, figures, and forms of speech" coming from across the ocean.[36] The article points to several Native American terms, such as *war hatchet* and *wampum*. Other writers of the time occasionally mention new American words like *maize* and *canoe*. Words like these were distinctive additions to the vocabulary, so it's not surprising that the English commented on them. Many other new terms slipped into the language unnoticed or at least unremarked on, including most words that named an object, animal, or landscape feature of North America.

Other types of American word invention triggered more discussion among both Americans and British, some of it in the form of complaints. New verbs came in for frequent mention. Among the American creations that entered the language in the eighteenth or early nineteenth centuries are *eventuate*, *locate*, *legislate*, *deputize*, *magnetize*, *revolutionize*, *antagonize*, *to table*, *to deed*, and *to progress*, as well as the more arcane *happify*, *retrospect*, and *citizenize*. Americans also broadened the use of the verb *fix*. The British author Frederick Marryat, writing of his travels around America in the early nineteenth century, reported, "The verb 'to fix' is universal. It means to do any thing. 'Shall I *fix* your coat or your breakfast first?'" He also noted the word *fixings*, meaning accompaniments to a main dish.[37] As mentioned above in "The English of the First Colonists," *fixing to*, meaning just about to, was part of English when the first colonists arrived. Americans retained that expression, so Marryat probably heard that form of the verb as well, although he didn't comment on it.

Turning nouns and adjectives into verbs is a very common, centuries-old way of creating new vocabulary in English. Nonetheless, newly coined American verbs were sometimes treated as nonstandard at first. Thomas Jefferson's invention, *belittle*, drew an unusually strong response from one British reviewer. In *Notes on the State of Virginia*, Jefferson commented on the idea of the French naturalist Buffon that animals of the same species were smaller in North America than in Europe. He described it as "the tendency of nature to belittle her productions on this side of the Atlantic." The reviewer was appalled by this new word. He accused Jefferson of trampling on the English language: "We forgive all your attacks . . . upon our *national character*; but for the future, spare—O spare, we beseech you, our mother tongue!"[38]

Adding *be-* to an adjective is a regular way to create a verb, which also gave the language *becalm*, *befoul*, *becloud*, *begrime*, and a number of similar words. However, because of the sharp criticism of *belittle*, it was treated as nonstandard and seldom appeared in writing until the 1820s. Gradually, it lost its stigma. By the mid-nineteenth century, the word was in use on both sides of the Atlantic, usually metaphorically to mean depreciate. Most of the other new verb coinages were also accepted in time, or like *happify* and *retrospect*, became obsolete.

Besides new words, colonial Americans invented colorful new expressions. Many were based on features of the country, or on settlement activities. These include *blaze a trail, back track, sit on the fence, make the fur fly, pull up stakes, clear out, stay put, bark up the wrong tree* (from dogs barking at treed raccoons), *play possum* (from that animal's instinct to play dead when in danger), *bury the hatchet*, and *make a stump speech*.

In many cases, the first known uses of these expressions were literal. For instance, burying war hatchets and other weapons as part of a peace pact was a tradition among some Native American nations, and the earliest mentions of this term refer to actual events. Samuel Sewall, a Puritan immigrant to the Massachusetts colony, wrote to his brother in 1680: "They [the English and the Mohawks] came to an agreemt and buried two Axes in the Ground."[39] *Bury the hatchet* was not used figuratively until the late eighteenth century.

Similarly, *back track* first meant a track leading backward or toward a starting point. "We lay still and kept scouts upon our back tracks to see if there would any pursue," wrote a Massachusetts colonist in a 1724 journal entry. Stump speeches were so-called because public speakers stood on stumps, which were plentiful in early settlements, to raise themselves above the level of their audience. "The harangues are called stump-speeches, from the practice of candidates mounting the stumps of trees, and there addressing themselves to the people," wrote one observer in 1822.[40] Again, these terms didn't become fully figurative until decades later, when the activities they described no longer occurred.

By the early nineteenth century, the basic elements of the American variety of English were all in place. These included pronunciation patterns that had grown distinct from those in England; a lively tradition of word creation and adoption that drew on the physical and cultural features of the United States, and included input from both Native American and immigrant languages; and colorful expressions and ways of talking that were likewise inspired by American surroundings.

Americans were also in the early stages of developing their own regional dialects. The United States has never been a place of only one English (or only the English language, as noted in the Introduction). Regional variation has always been part of the mix. Just as the United States is made up of different states, American English is a collection of different dialects, all equally legitimate and longstanding, even if not all are recognized as standard.

# 2

# Early Regional Dialects

## Americans with Accents

On June 1, 1721, the *American Weekly Mercury* of Philadelphia published the following notice: "Run away . . . a Servant Man, named William Newberry, aged about Twenty Years: He is a West-Country man, and talks like one."[1] Newberry, like thousands of others who arrived in North America during the eighteenth century, was an indentured servant. His master had paid his passage to the colonies and, in return, he had promised to work for free for between five and seven years. The harsh realities of indenture, which often included exhausting labor and physical abuse, inspired Newberry to strike out on his own before his contract was up. Now his former owner was tracking him down by advertising what he saw as an identifying feature, Newberry's "West-Country" accent (meaning the southwestern counties of England, including Cornwall and Devon).

Newberry was not alone in trying to escape. Ads appeared daily in newspapers all around the colonies, alerting the public to runaway servants. Many identified them primarily by the way they talked ("broad" here means with a noticeable regional accent):[2]

- Run away . . . a Servant Man named John Doren, a middle-siz'd Man, aged about 30 Years . . . he has the Brogue on his Tongue, being an Irishman. (*American Weekly Mercury*, September 19, 1734)
- Ran-away . . . an indented Servant called Archibald Kier, a Scotchman about twenty four Years old, . . . talks pretty broad Scotch. (*Boston Gazette*, January 2, 1738)

- Run away from the subscriber's schooner yesterday, an indented servant, named William Rickard . . . born in Cornwall, and speaks very broad English. (*Georgia Gazette*, March 15, 1764)
- Run away from the subscriber . . . a servant man named Thomas Wise, about 25 years old. . . . He says that he is a Yorkshireman born, and talks broad. (*Virginia Gazette*, March 24, 1768)

It wasn't only recent arrivals who displayed noticeable accents. The speech patterns of Americans living in different regions of the country also varied in typical ways. Noah Webster had some critical remarks to make about the dialectal peculiarities of fellow Americans. He complained about the "drawling, whining cant" of rural New Englanders, saying they pronounced their words "in a careless lazy manner, or the sound finds a passage thro the nose." Also, they omitted the aspiration in words beginning with *wh*, so *white* and *whip* (previously pronounced 'hwite' and 'hwip') became 'wite' and 'wip', and pronounced the *e* before *r* like *a*, "as *marcy* for mercy," in Webster's words.

Other regions also used what Webster considered idiosyncratic pronunciations. Speakers in Boston and Philadelphia often substituted *w* for *v*—'wessel' for *vessel*. Southerners tended to drop the *r* after vowels. In the middle regions of the country, people pronounced the vowel in words like *off*, *soft*, *drop*, and *crop* with the 'ah' sound of *hot* ("*aff*, *saft*, *drap*, *crap*" according to Webster). They also gave *once* and *twice* a final *t* ('oncet' and 'twicet').[3]

Anne Royall, a popular travel writer of the early nineteenth century, also noted distinctive speech patterns in different parts of the country. Like Webster, she identified a "whining tone" in New England speech, and she too noticed that Southerners omitted the *r* sound after a vowel, as in "*want* for *warrant*" and "*wocked* for *worked*." While visiting what is now West Virginia, she recorded that residents pronounced *blaze* as 'bleeze', *chairs* as 'cheers', *handkerchief* as 'hankorchy', and *one* as 'waun'. They also dropped the final consonants on some words, so *end*, for instance, was said 'en'.[4]

Observers were aware of regional vocabulary, although examples tend to be idiosyncratic and in some cases were probably less local than the hearer supposed. Royall noted the southern use of *road* for way, as in *any road*. Also, she wrote, "When they would say *pretence*, they say *lettinon* [letting on]. . . . It signifies a jest. . . . Polly is not mad. She is only lettinon."[5] She also recorded the nonstandard verbs that she heard in the South, such as *seed* (for saw) and *comed*.

John Witherspoon, president of Princeton University from 1768 until his death in 1794, recorded *improved* to mean made use of in some parts of New England, *chunks* for half-burned pieces of wood, and *tote* for carry in the South.[6] A more extensive early list appeared in the *Virginia Literary Museum and Journal of Belles Lettres, Arts, Sciences, &c*, published by the University of Virginia in 1829. Much of the list gives general "provincialisms" current in America, but it also lists words specific to a region. Among those recorded for New England are *considerable of* to mean very much so, *doom* for a tax, *notions* for small items for sale, *rugged* for robust, and *ugly* to mean ill-tempered. Southernisms include *corn blades* for the husks of corn, *disremember* for forget, *mush* as a name for a boiled cornmeal dish, *pine barrens* for pine forests, *season* for weather, and *whip* meaning to defeat someone.[7]

English visitors also noticed regional distinctions similar to those written about by Webster and Royall. Nicholas Cresswell, an Englishman who visited the colonies between 1774 and 1777, recognized the "whining cadence" of New Englanders, as did Thomas Anburey, a lieutenant in Burgoyne's army who spent time in New England as a prisoner of war. In his memoir, he recalled "the twang peculiar to the New Englanders."[8]

The English actress and writer Fanny Kemble, who married a Georgia plantation owner, wrote in her diary in 1832 of traveling by stagecoach with two young women who talked at the top of their voices in the "national nasal twang." Kemble discerned "strong peculiarities of enunciation" in "the southern, western, and eastern states." She wrote, "The Virginian and New England accents appear to me the most striking."[9]

Interestingly, other Englishmen found American English relatively lacking in regional variety. Many mention being surprised by the uniformity of speech among people of all classes. Traveling through the colonies in 1764 and 1765, the Scottish Lord Adam Gordon remarked on "the propriety of Language" spoken "by all ranks." Boston struck him as being very much like an English town. William Eddis, a visitor to Maryland around the same time, was likewise impressed by "the uniformity of language" in the colonies. He mused in a letter home, "In England, almost every county is distinguished by a peculiar dialect; . . . but in Maryland, and throughout adjacent provinces . . . a striking similarity of speech universally prevails."[10]

American speech may have seemed more uniform to English visitors than it did to Americans themselves because the visitors, generally from the upper classes, spent most of their time among educated urban Americans whose speech would show fewer distinctive local traits. Also, there was much greater dialect diversity in the British Isles, where English had had many more centuries to evolve. As Eddis remarked, nearly every county had its own "peculiar dialect."

Only a few of the more discerning commenters recognized that not only did American speech vary in different places, but also some of that variation matched regional features of British speech. One who did was Jonathan Boucher, an Anglican clergyman who traveled widely in America during the mid-eighteenth century. He agreed with the general view that Americans did not have much in the way of dialects, but what he did notice, he put down to the influence of their ancestral speech:[11]

> some scanty remains of the croaking, guttural idioms of the Dutch, still observable in New York; the Scotch-Irish [language] . . . in some of the back settlers of the Middle States; . . . the whining, canting drawl brought by some republican [anti-royalist], Oliverian and Puritan emigrants from the west of England.

He also noticed that archaic verbs like *holp* for *help* and *mought* for *might*, once found in England but long extinct, could still be heard in Virginia.

Boucher's instincts were right. The earliest colonists did not invent American regional speech from scratch. To a large extent, they brought it from home. The Virginian and New England accents noticed by Kemble, the whining cadence that Webster and others deplored, and other distinctive linguistic features of early America can be traced back, at least in part, to the local speech of seventeenth- and eighteenth-century British immigrants.

## Dialects from the Old Country

By the time the first English-speaking settlers reached North American shores, English had been evolving in the British Isles for several hundred years. During that time, the forces of language change had broken it into progressively smaller chunks—that is, dialects—each with its own unique set of pronunciations, vocabulary, and grammatical structures.

Although all English speakers shared a basic linguistic foundation, details of the language could vary not only from county to county, but also from village to village. There was little travel and even less permanent relocation during the Middle Ages. Most people spent their lives in the place where they were born. Under such isolated conditions, local dialects flourished.[12] That was true for all levels of society until the late eighteenth century, when the British upper classes started to adopt the London standard. The earliest colonists belonged to various social ranks, but if they came from the same area, they shared many of the same linguistic traits.

The historian David Hackett Fischer identified four major streams of English-speaking immigrants who arrived after the settlement of the Jamestown and Plymouth colonies, settling in different parts of British North America between the early seventeenth century and the eve of the Revolutionary War. Among other traditions, such as shared religion and shared ways of organizing their communities, each group hailed largely from a single dialect region. Their regional speech had a lasting impact on the places where they settled.[13]

Puritans were the first contingent to arrive in large numbers. Like the Plymouth colonists, they came in search of a place to practice their pared-down form of Anglicanism without interference from the English government. Between 1629 and 1640, around 21,000 Puritans arrived in the Massachusetts Bay Colony. They came mainly from East Anglia, an area of southeastern England that encompasses the counties of Norfolk, Suffolk, Essex, and Cambridgeshire.

By 1640, the political fortunes of the Puritans were on the rise, with Oliver Cromwell and the Puritan "Roundheads" about to seize control of Parliament. Puritan migration dwindled, and when the English Civil War started in 1642, some colonists returned home to fight for the Roundhead cause. As they departed, the next surge of immigrants arrived. These were the "Cavaliers," members of the landed classes loyal to Charles I. Between 1642 and 1675, approximately 40,000 Cavaliers and their servants settled in Virginia to escape living under Puritan rule. (The upper-class Cavaliers would have been greatly outnumbered by the servants they brought with them.) Their homes had been mainly in the south and west of England, within a short distance from London.

The Quakers were the next group to come ashore in search of religious freedom. Between 1675 and 1715, about 23,000 Quakers arrived in the Delaware Valley. They were a more mixed population than the Puritans, but the majority came from the North Midlands, a loosely defined region in the middle of England that included Derbyshire, Cheshire, Yorkshire, Nottinghamshire, and Lancashire. William Penn and the founders of Pennsylvania were part of this migration.

Finally, between 1717 and 1775, a steady stream of people immigrated to America from the border regions of Scotland and northern England, as well as northern Ireland. The northern Irish were "Ulster Scots," descendants of the Scots who had settled there a century earlier as part of James I's plan to establish a Protestant presence in Ireland. Migrants from these areas are usually known collectively as the Scots-Irish. (In earlier times, they were sometimes called Scotch-Irish, but in Great Britain, *scotch* generally refers to whiskey, not to people, so *Scots* is preferred.) The Scots-Irish came to America mainly to escape the political violence and dire poverty of their homelands. As relative latecomers, they found the Eastern Seaboard crowded and land scarce. Eventually, they moved into western Pennsylvania and gradually made their way into the Appalachians and the frontier areas of Tennessee and Kentucky.

The early American dialect picture is more complicated than Fischer's categories suggest.[14] Several factors make it hard to draw a straight line between the speech of any one American region and a specific ancestral birthplace. One problem is that even the most homogeneous settlements still included an admixture of people from other regions of England, or from other countries. Although the Puritans were mostly from East Anglia, a substantial minority came from other English counties. The middle colonies were even more mixed. Quakers came from everywhere, along with others attracted by the colony's reputation for tolerance. Thousands of Germans immigrated to Pennsylvania during the same years as the great Quaker migrations.

Another issue is that it's sometimes hard to determine whether certain word uses or pronunciations were truly confined to one region or were part of Early Modern English as a whole. Written records from the period have many gaps, so it's not always possible to track examples of a colonial usage back to their home territory. Usages usually associated with a single region sometimes turn out to be remnants of a speech pattern that once covered a broader area. One example is antiquated verb forms like *holp* and *mought*, which were heard among the Scots-Irish as late as the early twentieth century. Although they lasted longer in the Appalachians than in other places, and are sometimes claimed to be typical of the region, they weren't specific to the Scots-Irish. They are remnants of verb forms that once would have been common everywhere. As mentioned in the previous section, Jonathan Boucher noticed *holp* and *mought* in eighteenth-century Virginia.

Like modern Americans, early settlers had footloose tendencies. They didn't always stay in the first colonies where they settled. Many landed in urban centers of the Northeast such as Boston or Philadelphia, then eventually moved into the interior of the country, or they moved from one colony to another in search of work, available land, or a more congenial religious climate. Over time, as populations became more mixed and speakers from different areas mingled, their dialectal features would have leveled out and obscured their original differences.

With these caveats in mind, it's possible to trace many strands of the speech patterns that the earliest colonists brought with them. Some have persisted into modern times, still visible amid the built-up layers of language change. Linguist Hans Kurath, one of the first to explore this issue, thought that some deviations from standard American English could only be explained if they grew out of earlier British speech. In 1928, he wrote, "To my mind, most of the dialectal differences existing at present between New England, the South, and the North-and-West . . . have their bases . . . partly in the strongly dialectal speech which the earlier settlers of these regions brought with them."[15] This lasting influence is sometimes called "the founder effect." The founder effect means that the features of the English varieties spoken by the first permanent colonists determined to some extent the speech patterns of later generations.[16]

The following sections take an in-depth look at the linguistic development connected with each British settlement wave. Examining early speech patterns can give us a sense of how and why later regional dialects developed, revealing the complexities of language change and retention in each place, and long-term traces of the founder effect. Although individual British dialects were not the direct ancestors of modern American dialects, they were the foundation on which a new variety of English was built.

## The Puritans: A City upon a Hill

In 1629, five ships set sail for America under the auspices of the Massachusetts Bay Company. The Company was formed by a group of investors sympathetic to the Puritan cause, who hoped to make a profit by opening trade with the Indians while providing Puritan dissidents with a place to practice their religion in peace. These ships were the first of what became known as the Great Migration. Puritan immigrants arrived regularly in Massachusetts Bay over the next thirteen years, all lit by a single purpose—to create a godly colony organized according to the tenets of the Puritan faith.

The future governor of the colony, John Winthrop, famously expressed this vision in a sermon that he preached while crossing the ocean in 1630 in the second fleet of Puritan ships. Referring to a passage from Jesus's Sermon on the Mount, he told his fellow colonists, "For we must consider that we shall be as a city upon a hill. The eyes of all people are upon us." If they failed in their purpose, "we shall be made a story and a by-word throughout the world."[17] The metaphor "city upon a hill" to allude to America as a noble example later became part of the American vernacular.

The Puritans were the most uniform of the major settlement streams. As previously noted, the majority came from the southeastern counties of England. They typically traveled in families, which meant that they were older on average than settlers in other colonies, who often arrived as young single people looking for work (or as indentured servants). It also meant that there were more women than usual in the group. The Puritan colonists were also more prosperous on the whole. Most came from the middling classes. They were yeoman farmers, artisans, and tradesmen. A few were aristocrats. Only a small number were either common laborers or servants.

One reason the population was more uniform than elsewhere is that the leaders of the migration were particular about who should be allowed to come to the colony. They preferred men of substance who could pay their own way. Once settled in Massachusetts, the Puritan leadership also winnowed out dissenters or those who didn't fit in. These were banished back home or to other colonies. Life in the new settlement was carefully structured, with little mingling between Puritans and others.

When the main wave of Puritans began arriving in Massachusetts Bay, the Pilgrims had already been settled at Plymouth for nine years. They came from various areas of England—Governor William Bradford was a Yorkshire man—and they had lived for more than a decade in the Netherlands before sailing for North America, so their speech patterns weren't the same as those of the later arrivals. However, they were soon engulfed by the flood of new immigrants and so didn't have as much linguistic influence as they otherwise would have.

Because the Puritans emphasized Bible reading, literacy was high. By one estimate two-thirds of Massachusetts men were able to sign their own names, an impressively large number for the time.[18] The leaders were educated men. Winthrop, for example, had attended Cambridge. The Puritans kept local records from the beginning of settlement, so examples of early New England speech, complete with individualized spelling, are more plentiful than for other regions.

Certain features of Early Modern English, such as those found in the records of the Salem witchcraft trials, lingered in New England longer than in other areas. One example is the 'marcy' for *mercy* pronunciation, which according to Noah Webster, was still a common regionalism in the late eighteenth century. Webster also recorded that *creature*, *pasture*, *nature*, and similar words were still pronounced 'creater', 'paster', and 'nater' in New England.[19] Another typical early New England sound that was still part of the regional speech in Webster's day was dropping the *h* sound (the puff of air) in the pronunciation of *wh*, so *whale* sounded like 'wale' rather than 'hwale'. They also had "lagging" pronunciations for certain words, for example, *deaf* was pronounced 'deef' and *deceit* sounded like 'desate'.

Early New Englanders used distinctive verb forms. Replacing a past participle with simple past was common, as in *he had spoke, we would have took*. They might also use present-tense verb forms to express the past tense, omitting the *s* ending that signifies third-person singular, such as *He come here yesterday*. Another carryover from England was invariant *be* in sentences like *Where you be going?* This use would later become a stereotypical feature of the regional speech. New Englanders also said *you was*, as in this example from the witchcraft trials: "Was you angry with them yourself?"[20] Again, these usages were still common in New England in the late eighteenth century, or at least more common than in other parts of the country, and in some cases, such as invariant *be*, lasted into later centuries.

Archaic plurals, formed by adding *en* rather than *s* to nouns, lasted longer as well. Some are still current in modern English—*oxen, children, brethren*—but others have since gone obsolete—*housen, cheesen, shoon* (shoes), *kine* (cows). These once common forms began to fade by the end of the eighteenth century, but they could be heard in western New England for some time after that. John Russell Bartlett listed *housen* in his 1848 *Dictionary of Americanisms,* saying, "This old form is still used by the illiterate in the interior of New England. . . . It is provincial in various parts of England." He also included the term *housen-stuff* to mean household furniture.[21]

New Englanders tended to preserve old vocabulary as well, perhaps because of their conservative Puritan culture or greater social uniformity. Bartlett's dictionary lists a number of New Englandisms that were also found in dialects of eastern England, according to dialect dictionaries of the nineteenth century. These include *bettermost, brash* for brittle wood, *cow-lease* for a leased pasture, *dubersome* meaning doubtful, *freshet* for a gush of water due to rain or snowmelt, *meeting-house* for a place of worship, *reckon* to mean believe, and *swale* for a patch of low land. New Englanders also said 'hain't' for *have not* and 'wan't' for *wasn't*.

Written records such as diaries yield some of the earliest examples of American usages, including *sick* for ill, *bug* for any insect, *barbecue* to name a gathering, and *fix* to mean "do anything." *To hay, to oat* (a horse) and *to truck* (convey by truck, meaning a two-wheeled cart) are early New England verb inventions. There are also early examples of usages that disappeared in England, but stayed current in America. Two are *to hill corn* (plant it in hills), which was obsolete in England by the sixteenth century, but heard in New England for at least another hundred years, and *captivate* meaning to capture, not recorded in England after the mid-seventeenth century, but in use in New England until sometime in the nineteenth century.

Perhaps the most direct linguistic connection between Puritan New England and East Anglia is one that doesn't show up in written records. That is the "Yankee twang" or "drawling, whining cant" noticed by so many British and American observers. In England, this same intonation pattern has been called "the Norfolk whine," and is reportedly still heard in remote corners of East Anglia.[22] The sound has been described as both a drawl and a twang, but its main identifying trait seems to be its nasal quality.

One late-nineteenth-century observer was convinced that New England speech grew out of the dialect of his native county of Essex (in East Anglia), based on their common "twang" alone. In 1898, he wrote, "In my own parish of Colne Engaine I heard it on all sides of me. One man says to another, 'where are you a-gooin together?' 'I'm gooin to Colne,' was his sing-song reply."[23] The linguist Maximilian Schele de Vere, writing around the same time, agreed. He wrote, "They [the Massachusetts colonists] brought not only their words, . . . but also a sound of the voice and a mode of utterance which have been faithfully preserved, and are now spoken of as 'the New England drawl.'"[24]

Many of these New England dialectal features, while still evident well into the nineteenth century, were considered part of informal rural speech. Webster critiqued several pronunciations as uneducated or "low," for instance, 'desate' and 'deef'. He also deprecated the habit of saying words like *cow* and *vow* with a gliding vowel ('ki-yow', 'vi-yow'), and the occasional pronunciation of *v* as *w* ('wessel'), both holdovers from earlier times. However, he accepted the 'creater' pronunciation, although it was moving toward its modern sound in other places. He also accepted *you was*, which he considered more logical than *you were*, although it was beginning to be thought of as nonstandard.

Early Massachusetts settlers carried their speech patterns with them as they spilled into the surrounding territories. By the end of the seventeenth century, speakers of the New England dialect were established in Connecticut, Rhode Island, New Hampshire, and Maine. By the early nineteenth century, their archaic usages were stereotyped as the typical "Yankee" or "Down East" dialect (both originally nicknames for New England residents), and their speech was put into the mouths of colorful yokel characters in humorous writing.

One example is Major Jack Downing, a character created by Maine newspaperman Seba Smith in 1830. Major Downing's signature appeared under letters to the editor actually written by Smith. Downing was meant to personify an unsophisticated rural New Englander observing the machinations of government with bemusement. As such, he spoke in the country dialect of the region. The following excerpts from Jack Downing's letters feature several pronunciations and word uses (bold) that can also be found in New England records from the seventeenth century:[25]

- Ax handles here **don't** fetch **nothing**.
- If the tenant isn't out, an officer goes and puts him into the street, neck and heels, with his wife and children and all his **housen-stuff**.
- Oh **marcy** on us, said she.
- In the arternoon, that **legislater** they call the **Sinnet** got stuck.
- He **come** in at last.

## The Cavaliers: The Old Dominion

While the Puritans came to America to break away from the restrictions of the old country, the second major stream of immigrants wanted to re-create the old country in their new location. "If New England may be called a Receptacle of Dissenters, . . . Virginia may be justly esteemed the happy Retreat of true Britons," wrote Hugh Jones, an Anglican clergyman who taught at the College of William and Mary in the 1720s.[26] The colonists who fled to Virginia during the 1640s to escape the Civil War were members of the aristocracy and landed gentry or their households. The leaders were committed Royalists who had fought on the side of King Charles I and were still loyal to the Crown after Charles's defeat and execution in 1649. Most came from London and its environs, as well as elsewhere in southern and southwestern England.

Although the Cavaliers couldn't tolerate life under Cromwell's Commonwealth, they considered England their true home. The first seal of the Virginia Company of London (the investors who backed the colony) emphasized that commitment. It bore the motto "En dat Virginia quintam," which translates as "Behold, Virginia gives the fifth," proclaiming Virginia's status as the fifth dominion of Great Britain. (The others were England and Wales together, Ireland, Scotland, and France.) Virginia's nickname, "Old Dominion," most likely grew out of the Company's motto.[27]

Besides avoiding life under the Puritans, an added inducement to settle in Virginia was the chance to acquire a large grant of land. English estates were bequeathed intact to the oldest son of the family, leaving younger sons landless. The Virginia Company took advantage of this pent-up demand. The original aims of the Jamestown settlement had been to search for gold and other minerals, and to establish profitable trade relations with the Indians. By 1618, the colonists had failed in both goals. Jamestown was in a run-down state and struggling to survive. To encourage more settlers, the Company instituted a "headright" policy. They awarded fifty acres of land for each passage paid for. Those who could afford to pay for the passage of a dozen or more servants as well as themselves instantly became owners of large plantations.

At around the same time, Virginians discovered the potential of tobacco as a cash crop and began investing in tobacco production for overseas export. The prospect of owning a profitable tobacco plantation continued to draw younger sons to the colony, even after the monarchy was restored in 1660. Once settled, they had money and leisure to re-create the kind of aristocratic society they had left back in England.

Because the Cavaliers still felt tied to the old country, they kept in closer touch with it than settlers in other regions. Many chose to send their sons to school in England, where they were exposed to the speech of the British upper classes, and no doubt picked up on new trends such as the loss of r after vowels, and brought them back to America.

The situation was different for the servants and laborers who made up the great majority of new arrivals during the rush of Cavalier settlement. By one estimate, 75 percent of the approximately 40,000 people who arrived during those years were indentured servants.[28] Most were illiterate. Unlike New Englanders, Bible reading was not part of their culture. Isolated on rural plantations, they would not have mixed much with speakers from other regions or social classes. They would have preserved their original speech patterns and passed them down to the next generation.

As in New England, there were already established settlers in Jamestown when the main contingent of Cavaliers began arriving. The original Jamestown colonists of 1607 came from various places, and may not have spoken the same way as the new arrivals. Again, however, they were swamped by the much larger number of later immigrants, so their speech traits didn't have much lasting influence on the colony, aside from the words they coined or borrowed from Algonquian.

Written records from seventeenth-century Virginia are not nearly as plentiful or as useful for identifying folk speech as those from New England. Since most people were illiterate, communal efforts equivalent to the transcripts of the Salem witch trials don't exist. The Virginia land-owning class was educated in England, so their writing is standardized, with few localisms or idiosyncratic spellings. However, we can still tease out some features of early Virginia speech.

Virginia, and later the southern colonies generally, were major areas of colonial lag. For the reasons just cited, speakers preserved numerous features of seventeenth-century English longer than in other regions, with the result that some pronunciations that were widespread throughout the earliest North American settlements are now considered typical of the South. One description of early-twentieth-century western Virginia speech identifies several sounds that could also be heard in seventeenth-century England and among the first colonists. These include pronouncing short *e* as short *i* ('kittle' for *kettle*, 'git' for *get*); "intrusive" *r* after unstressed final syllables ('potater' for *potato*, 'widder' for *widow*); 'bile' for *boil*; dropping of a final consonant ('pos' for *post*); and loss of the *r* before *s* ('bust', 'hoss', 'cuss').[29] These pronunciations can ultimately be traced back to British English. Other Southernisms attributable to the south of England are rhyming *head* with *laid*, pronouncing words like *tune* and *due* with a gliding *y* sound ('tyune', 'dyue'), and 'd' for *th* in words like *the*.[30]

Another old British usage that is still current in Appalachian speech is the prefix *a-* attached to certain present participles, such as *a-blowing, a-crying, a-hunting*. (The *a-* is likely the remains of a preposition, *at* or *on*.)[31] Two early American examples come from the 1675 town records of Hempstead, New York: "Junnins [Jennings] said he was agoing to cut wood for Mr. Jackson" and later, "Junnins was there asmokin of it."[32] Much later, such verbs were also part of George Washington's Virginia dialect. On February 24, 1768, he wrote in his diary, "Went aducking between breakfast and dinner and killed 2 mallards."[33]

Similarly, the southern expression *like to* (sometimes transcribed *liketa*), meaning almost or virtually, as in *I like to died laughing* or *He fell off his horse and like to broke his neck*, grew out of earlier British English. The phrase *be like to* appears as early as the fifteenth century, and is found in both northern and southern England, as well as Ireland and Scotland. A story published in 1592 includes the line, "In Temes streete a brewers carte was lyke to have runne over me."[34]

In the southern colonies, the *be* disappeared and *like to* turned into a regular adverb.

A number of southern regional words can be traced back to the speech of southern England. Examples include *bray* for a horse's neigh, *carry* meaning to give someone transport, *chitterlings* for hog intestines, *disremember* for forget, *favor* for resemble, *lightning bug* for a firefly, and *mantelpiece* for mantel. A word list from the southern English county of Sussex features *atwixt, bide, bimebye* (by and by), *flapjack, holp, innards, moonshine, passel, skillet,* and *traipse,* all words recorded in early Virginia as well.[35]

One hallmark of modern southern speech seems to be a late development. Evidence is limited for the appearance of the so-called southern drawl, a tendency to lengthen vowel sounds so one syllable becomes two ('see-it' for *sit*), but the consensus is that it arose sometime in the mid- to late nineteenth century. Although the intonation pattern of the southwest of England can also be described as a drawl, it's difficult to make a direct connection between the two. Unlike the Yankee twang, the southern drawl isn't mentioned in early descriptions of colonial speech. If it existed, it wasn't distinctive enough at that time to be noticeable. (Chapter 5 explores the southern drawl in more detail.)[36]

The loss of *r* after a vowel and at the end of a word was noticeable in the early nineteenth century. Anne Royall, one of the first writers to comment on Virginia speech, described the *r*-lessness of her Virginia landlady in an 1830 memoir of traveling throughout the South: "I am obliged to retain the *r* in hear, fire, etc. or not be understood; but she *sounded* it not in speaking, nor does any of her sort. *For* they sound like *fow* . . . and *nor* like *now*."[37] As Royall's landlady was not a member of the upper classes, it seems clear that the dropped *r* was part of the general southern speech pattern by that time.

Royall gives another sample of Virginia speech of the period by quoting a young man's story about a hunting trip:[38]

> You know da is heap of baw (bear) on de Kenhawa . . . Kenhawa mighty far—so we walk . . . last we come to da Kenhawa . . . well, I goes out into da woods—I hear noise—I look up a tree, and see baw!

Besides the loss of *r*, the storyteller used 'd' for *th* and present-tense verbs for past tense, all archaic usages. He also used *mighty* to mean a lot, a colloquialism noticed earlier by Philip Vickers Fithian, a tutor in a Virginia household in 1774, who wrote, "I piddled at my Exegesis, but (as they say here in Virginia), I did a mighty little."[39]

Very few records from the period mention or describe the speech of Africans, who formed a second significant population stream into Virginia both before and during the years of Cavalier settlement. Most that do offer information about African speech suggest that Africans born into enslavement in America spoke approximately the same English as uneducated White Americans. Hugh Jones noted as much in his 1774 report on Virginia, saying, "they that are born there talk good English, and affect our Language, Habits, and Customs." Later, he reiterates, "the Planters and even the Native Negroes generally talk good English without Idiom or Tone."[40]

On the other hand, one English visitor criticized Southerners for letting their children play with the children of slaves, "which insensibly causes them to imbibe their Manner and broken Speech." Another visitor had difficulty understanding Black Virginians and speculated that they spoke "a mixed dialect between the Guinea and English."[41] No doubt, command of the language varied depending on the speaker's circumstances. Perceived differences could also reflect the linguistic judgments of the observers. The "broken speech" referred to in the first quotation might not have differed noticeably from the nonstandard speech of White speakers.

As with ads for runaway indentured servants, ads for runaway slaves often mention their language skills. Unsurprisingly, these show that enslaved Africans' proficiency with the language depended on how long they had been in the country:

- Ran way from the Subscriber . . . two new Negroe Men imported from Gambia, . . . They understand no English. (*Virginia Gazette*, October 17–24, 1745)
- Now in the public Gaol of this City, a new Negroe Man Slave, who answers to the Name of Thomas. . . . He cannot speak English or tell the Name of his Master. (*Virginia Gazette*, January 10, 1752)
- A Negro Manservant, about 25 Years of Age, speaks pretty good English, hath been in the Country about three Years. (*Boston Weekly News-letter*, May 30–June 6, 1728)
- Run away from the subscriber, a Negroe Man named Jasper, . . . talks good English. (*Georgia Gazette*, August 4, 1763)[42]

The dialect often referred to as African American English, spoken by some, although not all, African Americans, almost certainly developed later. As Chapter 6 will explain, linguists have proposed various theories about the origins of the dialect and the extent to which it's based on either African languages or early English.[43] Whatever its roots, it appears not to have existed in the early colonies.

## The Quakers: Brotherly Love

When William Penn founded the capital of his new colony of Pennsylvania in 1682, he named it Philadelphia, from the Greek words *phileo* and *adelphós*, loosely translating as brotherly love. Penn was an aristocrat and a convert to the Society of Friends, or Quakers. When King Charles II granted him a substantial tract of American land as payment for a debt owed to Penn's father, he decided to make it a place of refuge and tolerance, not only for Quakers, who were being jailed by the thousands for refusing to pay tithes to the Church of England, but also for other religious minorities.

Penn considered the colony a "holy experiment," where all ethnicities and religions would live together in harmony. He treated the native Lenape (Delaware) tribes with unusual consideration for the time, paying them for the land granted by Charles and purchasing other parcels of land before reselling it cheaply to colonists. Most of those who arrived in the colony were artisans, small farmers, or merchants (the aristocratic Penn was an exception), and property was distributed equally, so there were no large plantations. Quakers didn't believe in making distinctions of class. Government was by elected assembly, and Pennsylvania was the first colony to outlaw slavery.

Partly because of Penn's embrace of all comers, the settlers to the Delaware Valley were the most heterogeneous of the four migrant streams. Quakers came from all over. Although many were from the Midlands of England, significant numbers were Celtic-language speakers from Wales and Ireland, or were from elsewhere in Europe. Reporting on the progress of the settlement to people back home, Penn wrote, "The People are a Collection of divers Nations in Europe: As French, Dutch, Germans, Sweeds, Danes, Finns, Scotch-Irish, and English; . . . But as they are of one kind, . . . so they live like People of one Count[r]y."[44]

The colony also attracted many people who weren't Quakers. Some relocated from New England looking for greater religious tolerance. Penn also actively recruited potential settlers. He traveled to Germany to encourage Moravians, Mennonites, and Amish to come to Pennsylvania. Thousands of them did, settling mainly in the western part of the territory. When the Quakers arrived, colonies of Dutch and Swedish traders were already settled in what is now Delaware (part of Pennsylvania until 1701), and they remained there after Penn took over the land. Within a couple of decades, the Quakers were a numerical minority of residents, although they continued to dominate the business and political life of the colony.

Because of this melding of regions and cultures, it's hard to isolate distinctively Midlands features in the speech of early Pennsylvanians. Midlands word lists from the nineteenth century include a number of words that later turned up in the Delaware Valley, although some of them may have had wider currency in England. These include *all out* to mean going to the limit, *apple-pie order, bamboozle, chock-full, crib* for a baby's bed, *egg on* to mean encourage, *elbow grease* for hard work, *gab, guzzle, sick* for ill, *skimpy,* and *tiff.*[45]

Penn himself contributed a few words to the early American vocabulary. He was the first to write down the term *hotcakes* to describe a Native food that he was served at a Lenape feast. He wrote, "Their entertainment was a green Seat by a Spring, under some shady Trees, with hot Cakes of new Corn, both Wheat and Beans, which they make up in a square form . . . and bake them in the Ashes."[46] He also recorded the terms *black perch* and *swamp oak.*

One effect of Quakers on the American vocabulary was the preservation of *thou* and *thee*, the ancient forms of the second-person singular (for instance, *Thou art welcome here; I welcome thee*). Traditionally, *you* was the second-person plural form of the pronoun. Beginning sometime during the Middle English period, *you* also became the respectful way to address individuals of high rank (similar to royalty referring to themselves as *we* rather than *I*). Quakers didn't observe social distinctions, so they made a point of addressing everyone as *thou* and *thee*.

The use of *you* continued to spread, and by the late seventeenth century, *you* had largely replaced other forms of the second-person pronoun, regardless of the addressee's social status. *Thou* and *thee* were nearly obsolete. Quakers continued to use them, however, although they eventually adopted *thee* for both subjects and objects (*Thee shall not*). Perhaps for this reason, the forms appeared in American grammar textbooks well into the nineteenth century, long after they dropped out of common use.

The main effect of the Pennsylvania settlement was to set the initial boundaries for what would later become the American Midland dialect region, an area that expands outward from the Delaware Valley. The early-twentieth-century linguist George Philip Krapp referred to this speech as "General American." More so than southern or New England speech, it's a "composite type" of English that reflects a mixture of sources.[47]

# Scots-Irish: People of the Borderlands

An early biographer of Andrew Jackson, writing about Jackson's Scots-Irish ancestors, notes, "There is a smack of the North-Irish brogue still to be observed in the speech of their grandchildren and great-grandchildren." He adds, "General Jackson himself . . . occasionally betrayed his lineage by the slightest possible twang of Scotch-Irish pronunciation." As examples of typical Scots-Irish usages, he gives *till* for the directional *to* (*He went till Charleston*) and *the like of* as a comparison (*There never was seen the like of him for mischief*).[48]

Jackson's family was part of the last great pre-Revolutionary migration from the British Isles to America, and they fit the pattern of this group in other ways besides speech. Jackson's father led a party of migrants from northern Ireland in 1765, one of two main sources of immigrants, along with the Scottish border area. Like most in this immigrant stream, they were Presbyterians and spoke English rather than a Celtic language. They likely entered the country through the port of Philadelphia, as did nearly everyone else.

Jackson's family was unusual in one way. His father had owned his own farm in Ireland and was not as desperately poor as most Scots-Irish immigrants. Many had been tenant farmers who came to America after being evicted from their land. On the whole, the Scots-Irish were poorer and less educated than previous migrant streams, although the group did include some skilled professionals. Even the poorest were proud individualists who didn't fit easily into established Pennsylvania society. Earlier arrivals in the Delaware Valley considered them a disruptive nuisance and competitors for increasingly scarce land. The Quaker leadership soon made it clear that they were expected to move on.

Jackson's family settled in the Carolina upcountry of the Appalachians. Other Scots-Irish immigrants only got as far as western Pennsylvania, while still others moved down the Blue Ridge as far as Georgia, and eventually into the frontier territory of Kentucky and Tennessee. They squatted on whatever land was open, living for the most part in tight family groups on small, isolated farms. Fleeing from the violence of the Scottish border region, they found themselves in another border region, where they often clashed violently with Cherokees, Shawnees, and other Native tribes whose territory they impinged on.

The Scots-Irish settlers had an outsize impact on American speech. The dialect of the old Kentucky-Tennessee frontier looms larger in the folk imagination than that of any other region. Like the Virginia colonists, the backcountry settlers preserved some archaisms that were once common in more than one region of England, such as irregular verbs like *comed* and *hain't*, old pronunciations such as 'sartin' for *certain*, 'creater' for *creature*, and 'deef' for *deaf*, and old forms like *a-hunting*. Other features of their speech were part of the essentially Scottish English that they brought with them.

By the eighteenth century, literate people wrote fairly standardized English, so there aren't many spelling variations of the kind to be found in earlier colonial records. However, people from other places noticed and commented on the spoken speech of the region. Notices of runaway servants mention that the culprit speaks "the Scotch-Irish dialect" or that his speech reveals him to be "a native of the north of Ireland."[49] Several early chroniclers singled out the backcountry accent discussed earlier. Anne Royall's description of West Virginians who say 'bleeze', 'cheer', and 'hankorchy', and use *road* for way, and Noah Webster's remarks on the pronunciation of *off, soft, drop*, and *crop* as "*aff, saft, drap, crap*" in the "middle states" are two examples. Jonathan Boucher also identified "the Scotch-Irish [language] . . . in some of the back settlers."

Part of what made Scots-Irish speech so easily recognizable was the grammatical forms. The linguist Michael Montgomery identified seven Appalachian usages that are also still current in Ulster speech, making it likely that they were part of the language that Scots-Irish immigrants brought with them. These are the combination of *all* with a question word (*Who all is coming?*); *need* followed by a past participle (*That shirt needs washed*); *wait on* for wait for; the expressions *want in* and *want out*; *till* for the time before the hour (*quarter till three*); *whenever* to mean when or as soon as (*Whenever my grandma died, we all went home for the funeral*); and *all the* to mean only (*That's all the daughter she has*). Most of these features have since spread into other areas of the South, and some have spread into the Midland region later settled by descendants of the Scots-Irish. (We'll come back to several of these structures in Chapter 5.)[50]

Another grammatical structure that's found in Scotland and northern England, as well as in the South, is the multiple modal, two (or occasionally three) modal auxiliaries (*can, could, shall, should, will, would, must, might,* and *may*) coming together where standard English would have only one (a feature of Early Modern English, as noted in Chapter 1). Typical combinations include *might could, might would, may would, should ought,* and *used to could.* While no direct written evidence connects this usage with eighteenth-century Scots-Irish settlers, they are the most probable source. Versions of double modals occurred in seventeenth-century Ulster speech, and are still heard in dialects of north British and Scottish speech, although typical combinations can differ. For instance, *will can* is possible in Scotland, but not in the American South. It's not unexpected, however, for a particular usage in two widely separated dialects to evolve in different ways.[51]

A number of vocabulary words from the borderlands were transplanted to the backcountry. These include *airish* for chilly, *biddable* for obedient, *brickle* for brittle, *chancy* to mean doubtful or risky, *fireboard* for a mantel, *ill* to mean bad tempered, *nicker* for the noise a horse makes, *poke* for a paper bag, and *I swan* as a swearing expression. *Bonny-clabber* to mean curdled sour milk also came from Ulster, but the term is found elsewhere in England and probably was used by seventeenth-century colonists in other regions. A western Pennsylvania variant, *cruddled milk,* apparently has a Scots-Irish origin. Other terms specific to western Pennsylvania are *drooth* for drought and *hap* for a quilt. *Hap* can also be used in a figurative sense to mean comfort or luck, as in *good hap* (probably from the same very old root as *happy*).

Although *cabin* for a crudely built house is not an exclusively Scots-Irish word, the earliest uses of *log cabin* come from their settlements and they probably helped popularize the term. *Piece* meaning a short distance (*down the road a piece*) is another likely contribution, as is *anymore* to mean these days, as in *We used to ride the bus, but anymore we just take a taxi.* This use is called "positive *anymore*," since unlike most statements that include *anymore* (such as *Don't do that anymore*), the sentences where it occurs don't have a negating word.

Because of the isolation of Scots-Irish settlements and because the residents preserved some older forms of British English speech, a myth grew up in the late nineteenth century that the denizens of these regions spoke Elizabethan English (although it should be noted that by the time settlers started arriving in the backcountry, the first Queen Elizabeth had been dead for well over a century). A major proponent of this idea was Berea College president William Goodell Frost, who explored the characteristics of "Appalachian America" in an 1899 *Atlantic* article.

Among other cultural survivals, such as rude log cabins lacking in "conveniences," the use of spinning wheels, and the existence of blood feuds, he noted "startling survivals of Saxon speech." Usages that he recorded include "strong past tenses, 'holp' for helped, 'drug' for dragged, and the like," *pack* for carry, *hain't* for hasn't, and *feisty* for lively. Questions he heard included, "What brung ye up this air way off branch?" and "How old be ye?"[52]

As romantic as this notion sounds, it doesn't hold up under closer examination.[53] Some antiquated verb forms found in Appalachian English are also found in Shakespeare, but typically, they were widespread in colonial English. Irregular verbs like *spake* and *holp* were recorded in grammar books into the early nineteenth century. These words may have held on longer in the backcountry, but they were not limited to Scots-Irish settlers. Other words, like *pack* and *feisty*, appear to be Americanisms. Language does not stay static, even in isolated Appalachian hamlets. While the Scots-Irish preserved some forms, their dialect was as subject to language change as the speech of other regions.

By the nineteenth century, settlers on the old frontier were known for a picturesque way of talking that might have been based on their ancestral dialect, but was distinctly American. John Russell Bartlett recorded a pronunciation in his 1848 dictionary that would become a defining trait of backcountry speech: "The chief peculiarity in the pronunciation of the Southern and Western people is the giving of a broader sound than is proper to certain vowels; as *whar* for *where, thar* for *there,* bar for *bear.*"[54] "Broad" pronunciation became a shorthand way of identifying colorful backwoods characters, along with outlandish word creations and earthy metaphors.

This colorful way of talking is on full display in the humorous tales of frontiersman Davy Crockett, riverboat man Mike Fink, and other hardy pioneer characters that were popular during the mid-nineteenth century. Crockett and his friends favored elaborate words (some handed down from rural Britain) like *blustiferous* (blustery), *conbobberation* (commotion), *flummox* (overcome), *hornswoggle* (fool or embarrass), *lickspittle* (a groveler), and *rapscallion* (a rascal). They also peppered their speech with down-home expressions like *kick the bucket* (die), *knee-high to a frog* (a youngster, that is, very short), *see how the cat jumps* (see what develops), *too high for picking cotton* (drunk), and *root hog or die* (work hard or fail).

Extravagant boasts known as tall talk were also part of their repertoire. This typical example comes from a fictionalized account of Davy Crockett's adventures. When challenged by a drunken stranger at an inn, he introduces himself this way:[55]

> I'm that same David Crockett, fresh from the backwoods, half-horse, half-alligator, a little touched with the snapping turtle; can wade the Mississippi, leap the Ohio, ride upon a streak of lightning, and slip without a scratch down a honey locust; can whip my weight in wild cats—and if any gentleman pleases for a ten-dollar bill, he may throw in a panther.

The following quotations from humorous works of the nineteenth century are based on mountain speech, but exaggerate its characteristics. They feature archaic verbs, old-fashioned pronunciations, and outlandish vocabulary:[56]

- Why **sartin**, Mr. O'Neal, your compliments are **mighty** plenty.
- He was a **a-going** through **right slick**.
- I **div** down in a **slantidicular** direction.
- Hang me up for **bar** meat **ef** I don't push off without 'em.

Tales of Davy Crockett and other Appalachian characters helped to familiarize Americans in other places with the features of Scots-Irish speech, and made these traits a high-profile part of the American vernacular. Eventually, as settlement expanded westward, they would become clichés of western American speech.

These early dialectal features formed the foundation for later American English. Later chapters will show how the shape of the language kept changing as layers of word adoption, pronunciation shifts, and grammatical trends built up. However, the basic underlying structure would never completely disappear.

# 3

# Building the Vocabulary

## Creating Americanisms

The vocabulary has always been the fastest-growing and fastest-changing part of American English. The process of word creation and adoption that started with the first English colonists has continued ever since. The American lexicon continuously reshapes itself. New terms are invented, existing words are adapted to new uses, and words from other languages are welcomed into English. Words also exit the vocabulary when their day is over. As once-new inventions, common objects, and typical social behaviors become obsolete, the words that described them also drop out of use. The contours of American life are traceable through the shifting American vocabulary.

New words usually come into being for practical purposes, such as naming new inventions and discoveries, but word play and spontaneous creativity are also factors. That's especially true for slang, explored in more detail in Chapter 7, which can spring up seemingly overnight, gain quick popularity, then suddenly fade. For example, the mid-nineteenth century saw a fad for humorous word concoctions like *skedaddle* (leave in a hurry), *bumfuzzle* (perplex), and *discombobulate* (throw into confusion). These additions to the language were entertaining, but hardly necessary. Most have disappeared, although one or two are still familiar. Other words started out as jokes or puns, then gradually became standard terms. For example, *hot dog* was originally a joking reference to one rumored ingredient of sausages. *Okay*, arguably one of America's most successful word inventions, first appeared as a joke abbreviation in nineteenth-century newspapers (more about that below under "Founding the Republic").

Words also go obsolete for both predictable and unpredictable reasons. *Kinetoscope* is no longer a familiar word because the thing that it named (an early version of a moving picture, viewed through a peephole) no longer exists. On the other hand, certain usages will simply be popular for a while and then die out with no obvious cause. In nineteenth-century America, *clever* was a common way of describing any attractive, well-made item (*a clever boat*), but by the end of the century, the word reverted to its traditional meaning of skilled or intelligent. The early American word *netop* (friend) lost its appeal as a casual greeting and people quit saying it.

Words are hardly ever invented from scratch. By far the most common way to create a new term is by combining existing words or pieces of words. Dozens of such combinations entered the vocabulary in the decades after the arrival of the first colonists (*bottomland, pine barren, catfish, garter snake*). Another typical word-coining technique is attaching prefixes and suffixes. Early Americans used *-ate* and *-ize* to form verbs like *eventuate, legislate, deputize*, and *revolutionize*. During the 1950s, a fad arose for adding *-ville* to various nouns and adjectives to suggest places with those traits, such as *squaresville, nowheresville, bluesville, weirdsville*, and *endsville*. The suffix *-speak* is added to words as a negative description of certain ways of talking, for example, *doublespeak, business-speak, news-speak*, and *computer-speak*.

Shifts in meaning are another common way to expand the vocabulary. These include applying a word to a different object (*creek* for a freshwater stream, *buffalo* for a bison), broadening the meaning (*bug* for any insect, *fix* for "do anything"), or narrowing the meaning (*corn* specifically for maize). Other ways to create words include blending (*guesstimate* from *guess* and *estimate, snowpocalypse* from *snow* and *apocalypse*), shortening (*condo* from *condominium*), and back-formation, which forms a new root from an existing word (for instance, creating *-burger* from an original *hamburg + er*; see the "A Changing Nation" section that follows for more details). All these techniques and others have been used many times to add to the American word store.[1]

Besides words and phrases invented in America, there are the dozens of differences between what Americans call things and what the English call them. Examples include *elevator/lift, sidewalk/pavement, apartment/flat, cookie/biscuit, store/shop, construction/works, pullover/jumper*, and many others. These are not exactly Americanisms in the same way as newly created words or meaning shifts. In most cases, they are simply the result of making different choices between two terms that already existed in English. However, they also contribute to the distinctiveness of American English.[2]

Not every word that's introduced becomes part of the permanent vocabulary. For example, Lewis and Clark recorded a number of Native American words in their diaries, but only a few, like *camas*, made it into the mainstream. Words invented for a specific moment often fail to take permanent hold. As the turn of the millennium approached in 1999, concerns grew that computers' date storage systems would be unable to handle the year 2000, causing a universal crash. The Y2K problem, as it was called, led to several word inventions. These included *millennium bug*, *event horizon*, and *fix-on-failure*. However, as soon as January 1, 2000, came and went without disaster, they dropped out of use and are now barely remembered.

Linguist Allan Metcalf has identified five factors that contribute to words being widely adopted.[3] The first is frequency of use. A word or phrase must attain a certain level of prominence, either because it refers to a popular topic, or because many people (not just specialists) have a use for it. Once the first colonists started saying *corn* to refer to maize, it's not surprising that the changed meaning stuck. Corn was central to survival, so it would have been a frequent topic of conversation.

The second factor is unobtrusiveness. If a word fits into the language easily, it's more likely to catch on. That's why successful new words are so often made from existing words, and why words taken from another language are often recast to sound more like English. Diversity of uses also counts. A new use like *bee*, which can be modified to create *husking bee*, *quilting bee*, *raising bee*, and other terms for common activities, is more likely to gain wide currency than a specialized term like *sphygmometer*, the name for a nineteenth-century instrument for measuring the pulse.

*Bee* also illustrates the fourth factor, generation of new forms. Another example is *back* to mean rural or undeveloped, which gave the language *back country*, *back settlements*, *backwoods*, and *backwoodsman*. Finally, there is endurance of concept. When an item disappears or a fad dies, the accompanying words usually disappear as well. *Bee* has survived in the term *spelling bee* because that particular kind of bee still takes place regularly. In contrast, nearly all nineteenth-century nonsense words are obsolete now.

Americanisms tend to come from the same major sources over time. Striking and unfamiliar objects in the natural world inspired the first new words and word borrowings, as did contact with unfamiliar societies. Colonial settlement and western expansion to the Pacific coast were the source of dozens, if not hundreds, of new words. Immigrants have also continued to contribute words. Founding a new government required a host of new terms, and the politics of every era have added colorful language to the vocabulary. Public events, new technologies, and cultural innovations are also reliable conduits for new terminology.

## Founding the Republic

When Americans adopted the U.S. Constitution in 1789, turning the thirteen former colonies into the United States, a whole new structure of government came into being, and along with it, new uses for some old words. *Constitution*, for example, had been around since the fourteenth century with the possible meaning of the principles governing some religious or civil body. The delegates who gathered in Philadelphia in 1787 to hammer out a set of organizational rules for the new country adopted that meaning when they wrote in the preamble "this Constitution for the United States of America." *Senate* is a similar term. Although senates had existed as legislative bodies since Roman times, the default meaning of *senate* in America is the upper house of the U.S. Congress. *Federal*, another old word, originally described a religious compact or covenant, but beginning in 1783 it was used to refer to the national government of the country.

Another word that gained a specialized meaning in the early days of the republic is *impeachment*. The broad meaning of the verb *impeach* is to accuse someone or call their character or actions into question. In eighteenth-century England, a narrower meaning referred to charges of treason or other crimes against the state that were brought by the House of Commons and tried by the House of Lords. The authors of the Constitution adopted this meaning in Article 2, section 4, which states, "The President, Vice President, and all civil Officers of the United States, shall be removed from Office on Impeachment for, and Conviction of, Treason, Bribery, or other high Crimes and Misdemeanors." *Impeachment* is now rarely used in any other context.

*Lobby* arose in the 1830s. Lobbying first occurred in the lobbies of state capitol buildings. As one British visitor trenchantly described it, "Agents . . . are employed by public companies and private individuals, who have bills before the legislature. . . . These persons attend the lobby of the House daily, talk with members . . . invite them to dinner and suppers, . . . [and] usually succeed in corrupting a sufficient number of the members to effect their purpose."[4]

*Omnibus bill, pocket veto, fence-sitter, gag rule, lame duck*, and *spoils system* also came into use during the early decades of the nineteenth century. *Gag rule* originally referred to a rule forbidding debate on the issue of slavery, then expanded to cover a ban on any topic. Before *lame duck* meant elected officials who were voted out, it referred to losers on the stock market who couldn't meet their debts. *Spoil* or *spoils* generally refers to the plunder of war, as in the phrase "To the victor belong the spoils." In the early nineteenth century, it gained the extended meaning of spoils of office, when the practice of rewarding the party faithful with government jobs became common. The words *bunk* and *debunk* derive from an early-nineteenth-century representative from Buncome County, North Carolina. Criticized for giving a long-winded, pointless speech, he replied that he was talking to the folks in Buncombe. Respelled *bunkum* and then shortened to *bunk*, the word quickly became a synonym for nonsense.

*Filibuster* also appeared around this time. The word comes from the Dutch *vrijbuiter* (free-booter), meaning a pirate. The first filibusters were people—American adventurers who traveled to South American countries during the 1850s and 1860s to help carry out revolutions. The word acquired its legislative meaning around that time, along with the verb *to filibuster*, presumably as a way of comparing obstructive legislators with pirates. By the 1890s, *filibuster* referred to the act rather than the person.

*Gerrymander* is an unusual example of a word that started as a joke, but quickly entered the standard vocabulary. It's a play on the name of Elbridge Gerry, governor of Massachusetts in 1812 when the legislature redrew voting districts. His party (the now-extinct Democratic-Republicans) dominated, so they were able to creatively design the map to add to their number of safe seats. One result was a district with a strange, elongated S shape. It inspired artist Elkanah Tisdale to create a political cartoon by sketching in the wings, feet, and head of a mythical salamander. Since Gerry was held responsible for the new map, the creature was dubbed a Gerry-mander.[5]

The word quickly gained currency because newspapers immediately adopted it. Days after Tisdale made his drawing, it appeared in the *Boston Gazette* under the title "Gerry-mander," and then in other Massachusetts papers. The verb *to gerrymander* appeared soon after. By April 8, 1813, the *Gazette* could declare, "The term Gerrymander is now used throughout the U. S."

Governor Gerry said his name with a hard *g* (like *Gary*), so *gerrymander* would have been pronounced that way at first. Eventually, it lost its capital letter and started to be spelled as a single word, obscuring its origin. The *g* then became soft, bringing it into line with other *ge* words in English (e.g., *gentle, gem, gerbil, gesture*). These changes no doubt helped the word fit into the mainstream vocabulary.

Although political factions existed from the first days of the republic, the modern two-party system didn't arise until the 1830s. The first two major parties were the Democrats and the Whigs. The Democrats were the "people's party," and their standard-bearer was Andrew Jackson. The Whigs were more conservative. Their first successful candidate was William Henry Harrison.

America's current political parties settled into place in the 1850s. The Whig Party split over the issue of slavery, with pro-slavery Whigs joining the southern Democrats and those against slavery founding the Republican Party. Abraham Lincoln was the first Republican to win the presidency. Various minor parties also arose during and after that time, but typically did not play a major part in national elections. One short-lived 1850s party that gave its name to the larger vocabulary was the anti-immigrant Know-Nothings. Early voting-related terms include *ticket* for the slate of candidates, plus the voting terms *straight ticket* and *split ticket*, as well as *platform, plank*, and *primary*.

The first president to run a full-throated public campaign was Andrew Jackson, elected for the first time in 1828. His slogan "Jackson for president—go the whole hog" contributed a lasting expression to the language. It was probably an allusion to the common rural practice of killing a hog and salting it down to provide meat for the winter. Purchasing a whole hog rather than just a half or quarter was an expensive commitment. Going the whole hog for Jackson demonstrated his followers' enthusiasm and devotion.

Another nineteenth-century political slogan that found a permanent place in the vocabulary is *keep the ball rolling*. It comes from the 1840 presidential run of William Henry Harrison. Harrison, like Jackson, was a high-energy campaigner. One feature of his campaign was a slogan-plastered parade ball several feet high that party stalwarts rolled from town to town. As they walked, they encouraged spectators to "keep the ball rolling for Harrison." The Harrison campaign didn't invent the expression—it already meant to keep some activity (like conversation) moving along—but they helped ensure that it gained a lasting spot in the language.

*Okay* (or *OK*) owes its life to the campaign of Harrison's opponent in the presidential race, Martin van Buren. *Okay*, first spelled *o.k.*, originated as one of a number of joke abbreviations that first appeared in the *Boston Evening Post* in 1838 and were later copied by other papers. The letters stood for *oll korrect*, a comic misspelling of *all correct*. Similar abbreviations included *o.w.* for *oll wright* (all right) and *k.y.* for *know yuse* (no use).

After a few years, the joke got old, and most of the abbreviations dropped out of circulation. *O.k.* would no doubt have disappeared along with the others, but it was saved by a coincidence. Van Buren's nickname was Old Kinderhook, a reference to his hometown of Kinderhook, New York. His campaign seized on the matching abbreviation and created slogans like "Old Kinderhook is O.K." By the end of the campaign, *o.k.* (or *O.K.*) was familiar to a broad swath of Americans. It soon lost its periods and was spelled *OK* or *okay*, making it look more like a typical word and allowing it to slip unobtrusively into the lexicon.[6]

By the 1860s, *okay* was common across the United States and had begun to infiltrate British English. In a sure sign that it was evolving into a regular word, it started to be used as a noun (*give the okay*), a verb (*okay this purchase*), and an adjective (*an okay concert*, an expansion of meaning to indicate that a thing is acceptable if not great). In the twentieth century, it gained the forms *A-OK*, *okey-dokey*, and *K*. In modern times, *okay* is not only ubiquitous in English, it has also entered a number of other languages around the world.[7]

The years leading up to and surrounding the Civil War saw the creation of several terms related to slavery, including *slave power* (meaning the South), *slave state*, and *slave driver*. The phrase *peculiar institution* to refer to slavery came into use in the early nineteenth century.

*Emancipation,* an established word that meant to set free, gained a specialized meaning with the Emancipation Proclamation of September 22, 1862, freeing enslaved African Americans in the Confederate states.

During the Civil War, the federal government issued paper money for the first time, owing to a shortage of silver and gold. These one-dollar bills printed with green ink on the back were called *greenback dollars.* Greenbacks stopped being produced after the war, but the word *greenback* stayed around as slang for later versions of paper dollars.

*Deadline* started out with the literal meaning of a line that couldn't be crossed without the risk of being shot. A historian writing about the Andersonville Prison in Georgia shortly after the Civil War described "the 'dead-line'" 17 feet from the inner stockade, "over which no man could pass and live."[8] By the 1880s, the word had started to mean a figurative boundary and then a time limit.

After the war, the language added *Reconstruction,* another word with a broad meaning that narrowed to describe the postwar South. Northerners who went south to profit from Reconstruction projects were called *carpetbaggers.* The name came from the carpet bags they carried, soft-sided traveling bags made of carpet. The term *ballot-box stuffing* also came into use after the war. It started out with the literal meaning of cramming paper ballots into wooden ballot boxes. In some cases, the boxes had false bottoms that were stuffed with spurious ballots ahead of time and "discovered" during the counting process.

# Heading West

In 1775, trapper and explorer Daniel Boone led a party of a few dozen people over the Wilderness Road through the Appalachian Mountains into Kentucky. They were the first Anglo-Americans to settle west of the established colonies. Millions more would follow. Between the Revolution and the end of the nineteenth century, Americans continually pushed westward as the United States acquired more territory in North America.

Territorial gains started shortly after the Revolution. The Treaty of Paris, which ended the war, gave all British territory east of the Mississippi to the new American government. The Louisiana Purchase stretched American-controlled territory to the Rockies, followed by the 1821 acquisition of Florida from Spain. In 1846, the

United States gained another large parcel of land when, after decades of dispute, Great Britain agreed that Americans owned the Oregon Territory between the 42nd and 49th parallels. Those boundaries encompassed present-day Oregon, Washington, Idaho, and parts of Montana and Wyoming. In 1848, the United States reached approximately its current continental borders. Following the Mexican-American War, the Mexican government gave up its claim to Texas and ceded the regions that are now New Mexico, Arizona, Nevada, Utah, and California.[9]

Initially, land west of the Mississippi River was considered "Indian Territory," and for decades after the Revolution, nearly all settlement remained east of that boundary. However, as the population exploded during the first half of the nineteenth century, Americans began moving deeper into the continent in search of cheaper and emptier land. Gradually, Native nations were forced to sign treaties ceding most of their lands, and were relocated to reservations. The government then offered the land for sale or threw it open for settlement. The 1862 Homestead Act gave settlers up to 160 acres if they agreed to develop them. After the Civil War, millions of hopeful farmers, ranchers, and town developers swarmed into the plains. The 1848 Gold Rush and subsequent discoveries of silver and gold also drew prospectors west, along with those who catered for them.

Settlement activities contributed dozens of new words and expressions to American English. Most of them were well-known around the country within a short time, thanks to the books and newspaper stories that captured the color and romance of the region for readers back East. One of the older words is *pioneer*, based on an old word for military men who went ahead of the main troop. The boundary between settled and unsettled areas was called the frontier, a word that usually means the border between two countries. Its new specialized meaning gave rise to *frontiersman, frontierswoman, frontier post, frontier law*, and *frontier customs*. By the post–Civil War period, *frontier* meant more than a boundary line. It conjured up the idea of the "Wild West," a raucous, untamed territory.

The belief that White Americans were meant to inhabit all the land between the coasts was termed *manifest destiny*. The first to use the phrase was journalist John L. O'Sullivan. In a *New York Morning News* article for December 27, 1845, he wrote that the Oregon Territory, then under British control, should be part of the United States "by right of our manifest destiny to possess and overspread the continent which Providence has given us."

Settlers arrived at their destination in covered wagons, often as part of a wagon train. Both terms were common by the mid-eighteenth century. Much of the territory the pioneers passed through was designated *rolling country* or *rolling prairie*. Another word that gained a prairie-specific meaning is *sod*, used for previously uncultivated, usually grass-covered, soil. Pioneers lived in sod houses and planted an initial sod-crop like corn directly into the uncleared ground. Farmers who impinged on cattle regions were stigmatized by the ranchers as sodbusters. *Brush*, another word connected to the land, is an American shortening of *brushwood* (cuttings and branches). Related terms include *brush heap* and *brush fire*.

As the plains opened up to settlement, cattle ranching grew into a big business. The term *cowboy* to describe the men who worked these vast holdings came into use around the middle of the nineteenth century. Related terms include *bunkhouse, chuck wagon, cattle drive, cattle boss, range* meaning the land where herds roamed, *tenderfoot* for a new arrival to the West, and *ride herd*. Stetsons, the broad-brimmed, high-crowned hats favored by cowboys, owe their name to their maker, John Stetson. *Maverick*, which at first meant an unbranded yearling, comes from the name of Samuel Augustus Maverick, a Texas rancher who didn't bother to brand his cattle. The word's figurative meaning of a rugged individualist emerged by the late nineteenth century.

In 1848, shortly before California became American territory, gold was discovered in a riverbed at John Sutter's sawmill near the town of Coloma. The news triggered a rush of prospectors to the West Coast. Men came from all over the country and even overseas, hoping to strike it rich. They were called the *Forty-Niners*, since that's when most of them arrived. Several words and expressions came out of the Gold Rush.

Mining for gold by sifting through the sand of a riverbed was called *placer mining*, based on an old Spanish word for a shoal. *Sluice, rocker,* and *long tom* all named types of trough used to separate gold from dirt. The most common piece of equipment was a shallow pan. The process of scooping up a panful of riverbed and shaking it until the soil separated from the gold was called *panning for gold* or *panning out*. *Pan out* as a metaphor for a plan that turns out successfully was familiar by the 1870s. Other terms were *hit pay dirt* (soil with plenty of gold in it), *bonanza* (from a Spanish word for prosperity), and *claim jumper* (someone who seized another man's mining claim).

Many of the western words and phrases that came into the language in the latter decades of the nineteenth century suggest the rowdy lifestyle of the Forty-Niners and others who went West to "make their pile." A sample includes *sucker*, *yahoo* (country bumpkin), *no account* (worthless), and two words for jail, both from Spanish—*hoosegow*, from *juzgado* meaning tribunal, and *calaboose*, from *calabozo* meaning dungeon. Slang suggesting violence includes *sidewinder* (a punch from the side), *draw a bead* (aim a rifle), *rub out* (kill), and *be a goner*. Westerners also died with their boots on and cashed in their chips.

Revolvers, shotguns, and other weapons proliferated on the frontier. Besides the term *six-shooter* for a six-barreled revolver, several shooting-related expressions have since gained figurative meanings. These include *lock, stock, and barrel*, *get the drop on*, *shoot from the hip*, *draw a bead*, *be loaded for bear* (ready for anything), *flash in the pan* (a failed explosion of gunpowder), *take a pot-shot* (an unsportsmanlike shot), and *ride shotgun* (the position next to the stagecoach driver).

Americans in the West coined other imaginative expressions that reflected their surroundings and daily lives, for example, *eat crow*, *paddle your own canoe*, *be up the creek without a paddle*, *easy as falling off a log*, *head for the tall timber*, *chip off the old block*, and *fight fire with fire* (a way to handle prairie fires). *Go haywire* comes from the wire that was used to bundle hay and make repairs, from its tendency to tangle up. *Bite the dust*, often linked to the fate of western villains, meant fail or be defeated by the 1880s.

The Forty-Niners popularized the nickname *two bits* for a quarter. *Bit* was originally another name for a Spanish *real*, a coin worth 12½ cents. *Reales* were widely accepted as currency in the colonies and early republic because silver coins were in short supply. They were a familiar unit of money when the government started minting quarters in the early nineteenth century. Referring to quarters as bits was common in the South and West. "On the Pacific Coast," reported one early twentieth-centuryobserver, "the man who says a quarter, or twenty-five cents, is sized up for a tenderfoot. The Forty-niners and their descendants would say 'two bits.'"[10]

Words and phrases that came into the language from western poker games include *bluff*, *have an ace in the hole*, *bet one's bottom dollar*, *ante up*, *play one's cards close to the vest*, and *stand pat*. *Pass the buck* described a way of keeping track of whose turn it was by passing some item ("the buck") from player to player. The nature of the buck is not entirely clear. Some sources suggest that the word is short for *buckhorn knife*, but descriptions of the time indicate that any item passed around the table, such as a pocketknife or a pencil, was called a *buck*. The figurative meaning did not begin to appear until the early twentieth century.

Although American settlers tended to think of the trans-Mississippi West as a trackless wilderness, it was populated by both Native Americans and former Mexican citizens. The territories that Mexico ceded in 1848 held an estimated 75,000 to 100,000 Spanish-speaking Mexicans and approximately 100,000 Natives. At the end of the Civil War, the total Native population west of the Mississippi was at least 250,000.[11] The different tribal nations spoke hundreds of languages— Ojibwe, Cree, Cheyenne, Navajo, Apache, Dakota, Crow, Hopi, Yaqui, and many others. Nonetheless, only a handful of words came into English from these languages.

The later pioneers did not have the same daily contact with Native Americans as the Virginia and Massachusetts colonists. In the early decades of the nineteenth century, Europeans west of the Mississippi were mostly traders and trappers who communicated in a Native language or one of the pidgins used among the different tribes for trading, such as Mobilian, a Choctaw-Chickasaw pidgin, or the Chinook Jargon of the Pacific Northwest.[12] (A pidgin is a limited way of communicating that people adopt when they don't have a common native language. It combines words from the dominant language with words and grammar from the speakers' own languages.)[13] Settlers who moved into the region after the Civil War had few direct dealings with the Native population. Treaty negotiations between the tribes and the government relied largely on interpreters.

Native American words that were added to the vocabulary in the nineteenth century include *chipmunk* (Ojibwe), *tepee* (Dakota), *abalone* (the California language of Rumsen, through Spanish), and a few Chinook words—*cayuse* (pony), *potlatch* (a feast), and *muckamuck* (food). The nearly obsolete phrase *high mucketymuck* to mean someone important is likely a misinterpretation of *hiyu muckamuck*, meaning plenty to eat. Several southwestern words have also become familiar, at least regionally. These include *hogan* (a Navajo dwelling), *kiva* (a Hopi chamber for religious ceremonies), and *kachina* (a Hopi ancestral spirit). Americans adopted several terms that were more or less direct translations of phrases in Native languages, although they often took on changed meanings when used by English speakers. Some examples are *peace pipe*, *warpath*, *paleface*, and *fire water*.

Many more words came into American English from Spanish. Many Mexicans living in the ceded lands were ranchers, so several words relate to that way of life, including *ranch* itself, from the Spanish word for a primitive building. Other terms are *bronco* and *bronco buster*, *chaps*, *corral*, *lariat*, *lasso*, *rodeo*, *stampede* (from a Spanish word for uproar), *mustang*, and *pinto* (Spanish for mottled), both horses and beans. *Vigilante*, first used in the 1850s, is from the Spanish for vigilant. A number of words to describe the southwestern landscape, plants, and animals also come from Spanish. Some examples are *coyote*, *madrone*, *manzanita*, *saguaro*, *chapparal*, *canyon*, *arroyo*, and *sierra* (from the Spanish for a saw, describing the saw toothed appearance of mountains with high peaks). *Adobe* and *patio* are also Spanish words.

The French language made a small number of contributions to the vocabulary during this period. These words came from the New Orleans area, where most residents spoke a variety of French called Cajun French or Louisiana Regional French. Borrowings include *cache*, *bayou*, *levee*, *jambalaya*, *praline*, and *lagniappe* (something extra, as in a tip).

Expansion to the West Coast spurred calls for a transcontinental rail line. Work on this government-funded project started in 1863, with the Union Pacific Railroad laying track from Omaha west, and the Central Pacific Railroad working east from San Francisco. The two lines met in Utah in 1869. The completion of the transcontinental railroad led to a burst of new terminology, including *baggage room*, *baggage check*, and *baggage car*. *Baggage* is an Americanism for what the British call *luggage*. Other terms for passenger amenities were *dining car*, *smoking car*, and *sleeping car*. (*Car* at this time could refer to any kind of wheeled vehicle.) *Commute* and *commuter* appeared in the late nineteenth century.

*Depot* for a railway station was another Americanism (borrowed from French), as was *conductor* for the official who collects tickets. Trains carried freight as well as people, giving the language *freight train*, *boxcar*, *cattle car*, and *caboose* (originally a ship's galley, possibly from Dutch). A metal shield called a cattle guard or *cow-catcher* was fitted to the front of the train to sweep stray cattle off the tracks.

Railroads also contributed some figurative expressions, such as *to railroad*, *to sidetrack*, *whistle-stop*, and *jerkwater*. The last two terms both

evolved into slang terms for small towns. Whistle-stops were originally places where the train didn't stop unless a passenger requested
it by signaling with a whistle. *Jerkwater* comes from the need for
early steam-powered trains to halt periodically and take on water.
Eventually, water towers were built along the line for this purpose.
The driver positioned the train next to the tower and the engineer
jerked a chain to release the flow. Small settlements naturally grew up
around these water stops.

## A Changing Nation

As the West filled with settlers from the East Coast, the cities of the
East Coast absorbed millions of immigrants from overseas. Most
arrived between 1890 and 1924, when restrictive anti-immigrant laws
cut off the flow. Unlike earlier immigrants, who hailed mainly from
the British Isles and northern Europe, these later arrivals were largely
from southern and eastern Europe. They came fleeing poverty and
political upheaval. Nearly 25,000 Chinese men also immigrated to the
West in the late nineteenth century to work on railroad construction.[14] In many cases, their families followed them until barred by laws
excluding Chinese women, and then eventually all Chinese.

Most later immigrants did not have a big impact on American
English. Typically, their contributions were limited to food-related
words, and perhaps a few other cultural terms. Food words are frequent
candidates for borrowing since they usually name dishes or ingredients
that are new to the culture. For instance, Italian gave the language
*spaghetti* and other pasta names, plus *pasta* itself, *pizza*, *bruschetta*, *tutti
frutti*, and *zucchini*, among other words. Chinese contributed *chow mein*
and *yen* (originally a craving for opium). German added several food
words, including *pumpernickel*, *lager*, *bratwurst*, *frankfurter*, and *hamburger*,
plus *delicatessen*.

*Hamburger* has inspired many back-formations, or words formed
by resectioning the original word to create a new base. *Hamburger*
in German means coming from Hamburg, Germany (*Hamburg* + *er*),
but Americans separated the word into the recognizable *ham* and the
leftover *burger*. Any number of other burgers were then possible, for
example, *cheeseburger*, *chicken burger*, *fish burger*, *veggie burger*, and *buffalo
burger*, as well as the figurative *nothing burger*. German also gave English

the productive suffix *-fest*, as in *gabfest, songfest, swatfest, boozefest*, and similar words.

One language that made a larger than usual contribution is Yiddish, spoken by the millions of Jews from Russia and elsewhere in Eastern Europe who immigrated to escape religious persecution. Yiddish is based on German, but with elements of Hebrew. Like most other immigrant languages, Yiddish contributed food-related words like *kosher, nosh, bagel, lox, latke, knish, matzoh*, and others. It also produced a variety of other terms that have been assimilated into English. A sample includes *tush, schlep, glitz, maven, schmooze, chutzpah, schlock*, and *kvetch*. Yiddish sentence structure is also heard in phrases like *I should worry* and *Crazy she isn't*, and reduplications like *money schmoney*.

The late nineteenth and early twentieth centuries saw a plethora of new inventions that affected American consumers, from medical advances like penicillin and insulin to household appliances like vacuum cleaners and toasters. Besides the names of the new items themselves, some inventions brought a whole set of related terms. Telephones, for example, led to *switchboard, dial tone, busy signal, party line*, and *handset*, and to the activities *dial a number, pick up*, and *hang up*, many of which have lingered even though they're no longer relevant. For instance, telephones no longer feature handsets that need to be hung on a cradle to break the connection, but modern Americans still say *hang up*.

Radio and motion pictures brought entertainment to the masses, along with enduring words and phrases. Radio gave a new meaning to the word *broadcast*, and inspired other *-cast* words like *newscast* and *radiocast*. It also contributed the verbs *tune in* and *tune out*, which were used figuratively to mean be receptive (or not) by the 1920s. The element *ether* started to refer to the atmosphere through which radio waves were broadcast. *Commercial* for an advertisement broadcast during a radio program was in the language by the 1930s. Soap operas are so-named because these programs of domestic drama were sponsored by soap companies.

Movies also contributed a number of words that are now part of the mainstream vocabulary. *Movie*, short for *moving picture*, was first criticized as slang, but later became standard. Technical terms that most people understand include *studio, lot, extra, close-up, fade-out*, and *zoom*. The expression *cut to the chase* refers to the chase scene that traditional westerns typically featured. *Fan*, a shortening of *fanatic*, originally came from the baseball world. It was first used in the 1880s to describe fervent followers of the game. However, the word gained much wider use with movie stars.

No invention of the period had a greater impact on American life than the automobile. Although cars were being manufactured from the 1880s, the first car that was affordable for the middle class was automaker Henry Ford's Model-T, first produced in 1908. Model-Ts opened the door to American car culture. *Automobile*, a French term meaning something like self-propelled, may have been adopted because the French led in developing the technology.[15] It replaced older terms like *horseless carriage* and the preferred British English *motor car*. Gradually, *car* without a modifier (such as *railway* or *street*) narrowed to mean an automobile, then it replaced *automobile* as the usual term.

Car-related terms naturally included many words for the different parts—*headlight, ignition, dashboard, windshield, fender*. Car parts also gave the language the expression *hitting on all cylinders*. Driving led to a host of traffic terms as well, such as *traffic light, stop sign, blacktop, parking lot, parking meter*, and *double park*. *Motel*, a blend of *motor* and *hotel*, was invented to describe the lodgings that opened up to accommodate travelers. *Road hog, backseat driver, joy ride*, and *hitchhiker* also came from early car culture.

A different kind of nineteenth-century invention also had a pervasive impact on how Americans use language. In 1845, a New York bookseller named Alexander Cartwright organized the New York Knickerbocker Base Ball Club and helped formulate the first modern rules of the game. Similar versions of ball games existed in the British Isles, but features like the diamond-shaped playing field, foul lines, nine innings, and nine players to a team were American inventions. By the 1850s, dozens of clubs were dotted around the New York area. During the Civil War, soldiers from New York taught the game to young men from other places, helping spread it west and south. Soon baseball was being called "America's national game."

Virtually everything that happens on a baseball diamond can be used as a metaphor. Business and politics are particularly rife with sports terms. Examples include *see if they'll play ball* (make a deal), *step up to the plate* (take responsibility), *get a ballpark figure* (an estimate), *be in the ballpark* (more or less on target), *right off the bat* (immediately), *touch base* (make contact with), *play hardball* (the kind of ball used by professional men's teams, rather than the larger softball used by women's teams and people who play for fun), *throw a curve ball* (introduce an unwelcome surprise), *strike out* (fail), and *hit it out of the park* (have a big success).

Baseball terms are so deeply entrenched in American English that they are used casually as part of the public discourse. Two examples are routinely referring to laws aimed at putting habitual offenders in jail for life after three felonies as *three strikes laws*, and Supreme Court Chief Justice John Roberts's comparison of his job to that of an umpire calling balls and strikes.

Far-reaching social and political upheavals during the early decades of the twentieth century also had a powerful impact on the vocabulary. The Eighteenth Amendment, passed in 1920, banned the sale of alcoholic beverages nationwide. The era that followed is commonly called Prohibition, a sharp narrowing in meaning for this word. Prohibition lasted until the Eighteenth Amendment was repealed in 1933. It led to a booming illegal alcohol industry, along with new words and expressions. Much Prohibition language was slang that never had wide currency and didn't outlive its time. However, some words became part of the permanent lexicon. *Hooch* first appeared in the late nineteenth century, but gained popularity in the Roaring Twenties. It was short for *hoochinoo*, named for the liquor traditionally distilled by the Hoochinoo tribe of Alaska Natives. *Bootlegger*, a late-nineteenth-century word that first referred to traders who stashed flasks of illicit whisky in their boots, also became widespread.

*Scofflaw*, someone who flouts the law, is a deliberate invention that came about as the result of a contest sponsored by Delcevare King of the Anti-Saloon League of Boston to name and shame "lawless drinkers." Two people independently arrived at the word, possibly by analogy with *outlaw*. Newspapers publicized the contest and its outcome, introducing the word to the general public. Once its origins were forgotten, the word began to be applied more broadly. Usually, it implies a minor violation, such as speeding, rather than a major crime.[16]

Gangster terminology also came to the attention of more Americans as organized crime rings took over liquor production and distribution. *Gangster*, *mobster*, and *racketeer* are all Americanisms that appeared or were popularized around this time. *Fall guy* and *stool pigeon* also became much more common, although both were first heard in the nineteenth century. Fighting against the gangsters were the G-men, an abbreviation of *Government men*, meaning the FBI. G-men were also called *gang busters. Go like gangbusters* and similar phrases have been around since the early 1940s.

The Wall Street Crash of 1929 ushered in the Great Depression, which also brought some new word inventions to American English. The cascading economic disaster threw millions out of work and made *bread line* and *soup kitchen* familiar terms, although both existed earlier. *Hobo* and *panhandle*, Americanisms first heard in the late nineteenth century, are more associated now with the Depression. *Shanty* to mean a hovel had been in the language since at least the 1820s, borrowed from French explorers, but *shantytown* became more familiar during the 1930s. *Dust Bowl* also came into use around this period.

National politics in the first half of the twentieth century was dominated by two Roosevelts. Theodore, president from 1900 to 1909, had a knack for colorful word creations. *Bully pulpit* derives from Roosevelt's expressed opinion that the presidency provided him with "such a bully pulpit" for speaking out on any subject that he couldn't resist it. *Bully* at the time meant first rate or excellent, for example, in the phrase *bully for you*, now mostly used sarcastically. Roosevelt's other contributions include *lunatic fringe, loose cannon, malefactors of great wealth, pinko,* and *muckraker.*

Franklin D. Roosevelt, in office between 1932 and 1944, was not a word coiner like his distant relative, but he created *New Deal* (much better known than TR's *Square Deal*) and *fireside chat.* Another word first associated with the New Deal is *boondoggle.* This word's exact origins are mysterious. It appeared in a *New York Times* article of April 4, 1935, describing various skills being taught to the unemployed. One was the making of "boon doggles," which were small items made of leather, such as lanyards. According to the teacher, *boon doggle* was an old pioneer term meaning a gadget. However, the word hasn't been found in any earlier sources. Whatever its origin, skeptics gave it the broader meaning of a waste of time and money.[17]

Wars always generate their own word lists. Most are technical words or slang that never escapes a small, specialized circle. Americans didn't enter World War I until 1917, approximately one year before its end. Most words and phrases from the period that are known to Americans were also used in England, for instance, *foxhole, shell shock, battle front,* and *over the top.* The phrase *the war to end all wars* is often attributed to President Woodrow Wilson, but probably originated with a 1914 collection of articles by H. G. Wells titled *The War That Will End War.*

World War II inspired a number of words that are still common. These include *boot camp*; *G.I.*, likely short for *government-issue*, but soon taking on the extra meaning of enlisted man; *radar*, an acronym for *radio detection and ranging*; and *D-day*, with *D* simply standing for *day*. *Shooting war* referred to the American entry into combat, as opposed to previous measures like sanctions and blockades. *Dry run*, a dry creek or arroyo in the West, gained the meaning of a rehearsal, usually for an attack. Americans learned the word *kamikaze*, the Japanese term for a powerful mystical wind, from kamikaze pilots. Eventually, it was applied to any reckless activity, including dangerous surfing stunts.

The expression *go for broke* was popularized by the 442nd Regimental Combat Team, made up of Americans of Japanese ancestry, who took the phrase as their motto. Most members of the regiment were from Hawaii, and *go for broke* is often attributed to Hawaiian Pidgin, an English-based creole.[18] (A creole is a pidgin that has developed a stable grammar and acquired native speakers, which describes Hawaiian Pidgin, in spite of its name.) The expression probably originated as a gambling term for betting all your money. The 1951 movie about the 442nd titled *Go for Broke!* introduced many Americans to the phrase.

A block buster was the British name for an aerial bomb powerful enough to bring down a city block, but after the war Americans adopted *blockbuster* with its current figurative use.

*Atomic bomb*, *A-bomb*, *ground zero*, *mushroom cloud*, and *megaton*, which popularized the prefix *mega-*, also entered the linguistic mainstream after the war. *Radioactive* had been in the language for a while, but became more prominent. As postwar America entered the Atomic Age, words like *nuclear weapon* (shortened to *nuke*), *fallout*, *fallout shelter*, and *fail-safe* came into the language.

## Modern Times

The Soviet Union had been an ally during World War II, but after the war, that changed. Americans started to worry about the spread of communism, and the United States entered a Cold War (meaning not a shooting war) with Russia. *Red*, usually capitalized, had the possible meaning of communist since the nineteenth century, but it now made a resurgence, as did *pink* and *pinko*. *Red* probably alluded to the color of bloody revolution. Pinks were less extreme, so less red. *Anti-communist* and *card-carrying communist*, meaning a member of the Communist Party, also gained traction (with *communist* sometimes capitalized). *Useful idiot* came into vogue as a term for Americans or citizens of other western countries who naively supported the Soviet Union. It has since broadened to mean anyone who can be manipulated by the other side. As the United States and the Soviet Union came to dominate postwar international politics, the terms *superpowers* and *sphere of influence* were added to the lexicon. *Free world* referred to non-communist countries starting in the 1940s.

Wisconsin Senator Joseph McCarthy gave his name to the aggressive government attempts to track down fellow travelers in the United States. Two words first associated with McCarthyism are *blacklist* and *witch hunt*. The label *McCarthyism* later took on the expanded meaning of any form of politically motivated persecution, and *witch hunt* acquired a similarly broad meaning.

The United States also engaged in two hot wars during the mid-twentieth century. These were technically known as police actions because war was not formally declared. Only a handful of words from either conflict entered the mainstream vocabulary. *Boondocks*, from a Tagalog (Philippine) word for mountain, was known in the 1940s, but became more familiar during the Korean War. Other Korean War words include *brainwashing* to describe the coercive methods that North Korea practiced on prisoners of war and *domino theory* to explain the spread of communism. Words from the fighting in Vietnam that gained broad familiarity back home include *fire fight, counterinsurgency, friendly fire, fragging* (an attack on an officer by his own men, possibly with a fragmentation grenade), and *grunt* (a low-ranking soldier). *DMZ* for *demilitarized zone* was used in both wars.

The Vietnam War triggered an antiwar movement. Words that entered the mainstream vocabulary as a result include *hawk* and *dove* to describe those in favor of or against military action, and *chicken hawk* for someone who supported the war but didn't serve in the military. *Draft* for military conscription was an old word, but with the war, terms like *draft card, draft evasion,* and *draft dodger* became much more common. Those against the war and in favor of cultural change generally were sometimes described as the counterculture. *The Establishment* had been a name for those in power since the 1920s, but now *anti-establishment* became a popular term. Richard Nixon popularized *Silent Majority* to mean Americans who supported or didn't actively protest the war. In a televised speech on November 3, 1969, he addressed his listeners as "the great, silent majority of my fellow Americans."[19]

The civil rights movement predated the Vietnam antiwar movement by more than a decade. One tactic of the civil rights movement that antiwar protestors later borrowed was the sit-in. The first sit-in to draw national attention took place on February 1, 1960, when four Black college students in Greensboro, North Carolina, sat down at a Woolworth's lunch counter and refused to leave until they were served. Other sit-ins soon followed across the South.

*Sit-in* had occasionally been used before to describe sit-down strikes, when factory workers downed tools but stayed at their workstations. However, the civil rights sit-ins not only popularized the word, but inspired a number of other *-ins*. The earliest uses all refer to African American protests against segregation and include *swim-in* (at a segregated beach), *study-in* (at segregated schools), *kneel-in* (at White churches), and *shop-in* (a boycott of segregated stores). Later, antiwar protestors staged sit-ins in administrative offices of universities. They also held teach-ins, extracurricular classes where lecturers spoke about the war. Eventually, the suffix *-in* was attached to activities that didn't relate to protest, such as *love-in* and *be-in*.[20]

The civil rights movement contributed other terms to the language as well. In the 1940s, *civil rights* started referring specifically to the push for African American rights. (In the later twentieth century, *civil rights* expanded to apply to other disenfranchised groups, as in *women's rights*, *gay rights*, and *disability rights*.) *Desegregation* was first introduced in the 1950s and *tokenism* in the 1960s. *Freedom marcher* and *freedom rider* also appeared in the early 1960s. *Black* began to replace *Negro* during the same decade, for instance, in the phrase *Black power*, most often associated with activist Stokely Carmichael.

Besides *Silent Majority*, President Nixon made another significant donation to the American word store, although this one was inadvertent. On June 17, 1972, five men connected to Nixon's re-election campaign broke into the Democratic Party headquarters in Washington, D.C., located in the Watergate complex's office building. The ensuing uproar became known as the Watergate scandal. Since then, nearly every large and small scandal that makes the news is labeled with the suffix *-gate*. Examples are far too numerous to list, and the incidents that inspired them are now mostly forgotten. Some of the more notorious include *Climategate* (involving climate scientists), *Koreagate* (involving South Korean influence peddling), *Emailgate* (involving presidential candidate Hillary Clinton's email server), and *Bridgegate* (involving traffic lane closures ordered to punish New Jersey Governor Chris Christie's opponents).

The pace of life sped up in the late twentieth century. One cause was the Interstate Highway System, begun in 1956. Synonyms for this type of controlled access road without tolls are *freeway* (more common in the West), *expressway*, and *superhighway*. Along with interstates came such terms as *bypass*, *ring road*, *beltway*, *interchange*, and *exit ramp*. *Gas guzzler* was first heard in the 1920s, but became more familiar with the growing popularity of long-distance car travel. *Speed limit*'s earlier meaning as the fastest speed a car was capable of shifted in the early twentieth century to the maximum legal speed.

Commercial air travel also surged in postwar America. Fighter planes were used in both world wars, but civilian plane travel was uncommon before the 1950s. *Runway*, an Americanism that originally could refer to an animal track, a sloping ramp, or a projecting stage platform, acquired the added meaning of the surface where planes take off and land. The popularity of commercial air travel also resulted in the use of *coach* for the main seating area of a plane (probably derived from its earlier meaning of the economy class on trains).

Airlines introduced jets to their fleets in the 1950s, making it possible for the well-heeled to get places faster than ever. Igor Cassini, a journalist who wrote a syndicated gossip column from 1943 to 1965 under the name Cholly Knickerbocker, invented the term *jet set*. Cassini explained in an interview, "I used 'jet set' because it seemed appropriate in the age of the jet plane. . . . Jet setters are the people who fly away for weekends. They are the avant-garde, the pace-setters."[21]

Another way that life sped up was through the computer revolution. Like airplanes, computers were used for military purposes before they became available to the public, beginning with World War II. After the war, computer designers started to work on making the machines more practical, partly by making them much smaller and less expensive to build. By the 1970s, computers began appearing in business offices and on college campuses. By the 1980s, personal computers were commonplace; by the 1990s, they were essential. The World Wide Web, which made the Internet browsable, was introduced in 1989. Each of these seismic shifts in computing brought a new wave of words and phrases. Many were strictly technical terms or are outdated now, like *keypunch operator* and *floppy disk* (though the floppy disk remains visually in the "save" icon). Others entered the mainstream conversation.

The earliest computer-related terms often started as technical jargon and then moved into the general vocabulary. Some, like *word processor* and *personal computer* (PC), became more familiar as computers entered more offices, and then homes. *Bug* and *debug*, Americanisms that already referred to removing flaws from a system, extended their meanings to cover computers. *Multitasking* appeared in the 1960s to describe a computer that performed several processes concurrently. By the 1980s, Americans used it to describe people who take care of more than one chore at a time. Early computing also brought a collection of *cyber-* words, including *cybernetics*, *cyberspace*, *cybercafe*, *cybercrime*, and *cyberespionage*. *Shareware* meaning software available for free came into use during the 1980s.

The word *hacker* has a long history in English. Its many uses include people who hack the ground with a hoe and unskillful golfers who hack with their clubs. *Computer hacker* started out with the positive meaning of an expert programmer. By the 1980s, it had gained its now default negative sense of someone who breaks into a computer system without authorization. The meaning of *geek* has an unusual trajectory. The word started out as slang for a carnival sideshow performer with a bizarre act, for instance, biting off the heads of chickens. It gained its computer-related sense in the 1980s and, as with *hacker*, was at first a positive term for someone with computer skills (and still can be, depending on the circumstances).

Widespread use of the Internet led to a number of *electronic* or *e-*terms, such as *e-mail*, *e-ticket*, *e-commerce*, *e-vite*, and *e-card*. The existence of e-mail (now usually spelled *email*) created the new category of snail mail. The verb *to google* (to look something up using the Google search engine) came about during the 1990s. Surfing the Internet was so popular by the early 1990s that the American Dialect Society voted *information superhighway* the word of the year in 1993. *Spam*, from the brand name for a type of canned meat, first meant inappropriate postings, such as advertising, then shifted to unwanted email, or more recently unwanted cell phone calls and texts.

Social media and cell phones brought yet another round of technology-related words. *Friend* and *unfriend* as verbs, *text* as a verb, *scroll*, and *swipe* all acquired meanings related to the new technology. *Troll*, which used to mean a fairy-tale creature that lived underground, became a nickname for an online harasser. *Emoji* comes from a Japanese word for digital icons. Americans were using it by the late 1990s. *Emoticon*, which appeared in the late 1980s, is probably a blend of *emotion* and *icon*, and unrelated to *emoji*. The use of initials such as *imho* and *lol* in texting is reminiscent of the nineteenth-century fad of joke initials that gave us the word *okay*. Besides word creation, the Internet has had a pervasive influence on American language use in other ways. We'll explore those in Chapter 7.

# How Many Words?

It's impossible to say exactly how many American words are part of the English language. One problem is that the number depends on how words are counted. For instance, are *email* the noun and *email* the verb one word or two? Another issue is what counts as an American word. The first Americanisms to be noticed were words and usages that the English considered exotic or disapproved of. These included Native American words that weren't fully assimilated, like *wampum* and words like *eventuate* that were created through normal processes of English-language word-making, but struck the English (and some Americans) as perverse.

Princeton president John Witherspoon coined the term *Americanism* in 1781 in a series of articles written for the *Pennsylvania Journal* newspaper.[22] Witherspoon defined the term as "ways of speaking peculiar to this country." By 1781, dozens of words that had originated in America were part of the English vocabulary, but Witherspoon listed only a handful of examples. He concentrated on usages that seemed strange to him or that deviated from British English. For instance, he mentioned using *notify* for inform (in England, it meant announce or bring to the notice of), and *spell* to mean a period of time, as in a spell of sickness.

Throughout the nineteenth century, many Americanisms were classified as nonstandard or slangy. John Pickering, a language scholar and former diplomat, published the first substantial collection of Americanisms in 1816. Titled *A Vocabulary, or Collection of Words and Phrases Which Have Been Supposed to Be Peculiar to the United States of America*, it gathered over 500 words from various sources. Although Pickering listed some Americanisms just because he thought they might need explaining (e.g., *salt lick*), he concentrated on words and usages that he considered problematic, such as Jefferson's creation, *belittle*. Pickering's stated goal was "the preservation of the *English language* in its purity throughout the United States," or in other words, identifying words that he believed Americans shouldn't use. He didn't include American words like *raccoon*, which were widely understood and obviously necessary.[23]

John Russell Bartlett's 1848 *Dictionary of Americanisms* took a different tack. Bartlett recorded all the "familiar and the vulgar [i.e., colloquial] or slang language" that he could find, focusing on terms not found in standard dictionaries, not to warn against it, but with the aim of preserving it before it fell out of use.[24] He focused on colloquial language (*fork over*), slang (*bumfuzzle*), and regionalisms (New England *housen*). However, he also omitted more "standard," less colorful terms like *editorial* (meaning opinion piece), *grand jury*, and the verb *to patent*, three Americanisms found in Webster's 1828 dictionary.

Bartlett didn't limit his listing to words coined in America. He also chose words from England that had gone obsolete there or were used in a different sense, and words from other languages that first came into English in America. In his view, these also constituted Americanisms. The first edition of Bartlett's dictionary featured approximately 2,500 words. By the time the fourth edition was published in 1877, the list had grown to more than 6,000 words. Many of the additions came from new technology, like the railroad and land expansion into the West and Southwest.

The twentieth century saw the first attempts to compile a comprehensive list of Americanisms. The *Dictionary of American English on Historical Principles*, edited by William Craigie and James Hulbert, appeared in four volumes between 1938 and 1944. The editors cast a wide net while collecting their words. They looked for not only "those features by which the English of the American colonies and the United States is distinguished from that of England," but also "every word denoting something which has a real connection with the development of the country and the history of its people."[25] This included words that weren't invented in America or weren't used only by Americans, for instance, *post office*.

In 1951, Mitford M. Mathews published *A Dictionary of Americanisms on Historical Principles*, based on much of the same material as Craigie and Hulbert's *Dictionary of American English*, but with a narrower definition of an Americanism. Mathews restricted his list to words and expressions that were either coined in America or acquired a changed or additional meaning there, or words from another language that entered American English before British English. This meant that the *Dictionary of Americanisms*, at about 14,000 main entries, was less than half the size of the 35,000-entry *Dictionary of American English*.[26]

The number of Americanisms rises sharply when all the regional variations heard around the country are taken into account. The editors of the six-volume *Dictionary of American Regional English*, the last volume of which appeared in 2013, restricted their entries to regional words and folk speech, yet included more than 60,000 main entries. Many of these were too narrowly provincial to be included in earlier American dictionaries.[27]

Although these dictionaries vary wildly in number of entries and define the term *Americanism* in different ways, we can still draw some general conclusions. It's safe to say that words and phrases either created in America or with a specifically American meaning or usage now number many thousands. These collections also make it clear that the American vocabulary encompasses more than a list of terms. Rather, it's a way of using and shaping the language to reflect the shifting needs of its speakers. When the various ways of creating words and phrases are taken together—new combinations, meaning changes, figurative expressions, words invented just for fun—they add up to a particularly American way of talking.

# 4

# American Grammar and Usage

## Shifting Sentences and Restructured Words

Change comes to the grammatical structures of a language as surely as to the vocabulary, but the process is slower and not as obvious. Many words are created consciously and for practical reasons, and new words and word uses are easy to recognize. Changes to the grammar of a language—that is, to the structure of its words and sentences—usually happen incrementally and almost always at an unconscious level, so they are harder to spot. The English were beginning to remark on American innovations to the vocabulary by the mid-eighteenth century, but grammatical changes were less of an issue. Changes were nonetheless happening, both in American and British English.

By the late eighteenth century, American English had clearly evolved away from the language of John Smith and William Bradford and sounded much closer to present-day American speech. Yet the following examples, all taken from American political figures, show that American sentences as late as the end of the nineteenth century could still sound "unmodern" in subtle ways. They are easy enough to interpret, but they would sound jarring coming from a twenty-first-century speaker.

The first sentence is taken from a letter written by George Washington in the mid-eighteenth century, and the second is from his 1760 Farewell Address.[1]

- The road . . . whence the provisions and stores chiefly come . . . hath already worn out the greatest part of the horses.
- It is easy to see that . . . much pains will be taken.

*Whence* and *hath* make the first sentence sound almost like something Smith or Bradford would have written. *Hath* is obsolete now and was fairly old-fashioned even in the eighteenth century. *Whence* is not entirely obsolete, but if used at all, it would appear with a preposition (*from whence*). *Much pains* also sounds wrong to modern ears. English speakers now would say *many pains*.

The following two sentences were spoken a century later by Abraham Lincoln during an 1860 speech delivered at Cooper Union in New York City. They still show lingering traces of grammatical features that were common in colonial days.[2]

- Their names need not now be repeated.
- You will destroy the government unless you be allowed to construe . . . the Constitution as you please.

Lincoln used the archaic *need not* instead of *do not need*, which would be more natural in spoken speech. *Not* always followed the verb in Early Modern English, but that usage was almost extinct by Lincoln's day. Lincoln's second sentence uses invariant *be*, another regular feature of Early Modern English, as described in Chapter 1. Invariant *be* usually expressed the subjunctive mood (signaling a state that might be contrary to fact), appearing in clauses introduced by *if*, *whether*, *unless*, *although*, and similar words to describe something that might or might not happen. This use was less common by the nineteenth century, but could still appear, especially in writing and prepared speeches.

Two final examples are lines from a speech delivered by William Jennings Bryan during the 1896 Democratic Convention where he was nominated to run for president.[3]

- We care not upon which issue you force the fight.
- You shall not crucify mankind upon a cross of gold.

Bryan used the same archaic placement of *not* after the verb as Lincoln used. He also said *you shall* instead of *you will*, a traditional rhetorical device that turned a simple statement (*you will not*) into insistence or a command (*you shall not!*). *Shall* was not much heard in the United States by the time of Bryan's speech, but it was more common than it is now. Most modern Americans never use it at all except in questions. Bryan also said *upon*, which now sounds stilted, and referred to *mankind*, which would probably be replaced today with something gender-neutral like *society* or *the American people*.

Bryan's phrasings were not part of ordinary conversational English even at the time, but they were suitable for an elevated style. His audience would have considered his word choices appropriate and unremarkable for a speech given on a solemn occasion. Listeners today would find Bryan's language startling, even coming from a campaign platform or pulpit. Linguistic trends have changed enough to make his style not just archaic, but obsolete.

Grammatical changes can affect the language in a variety of ways. For instance, when more than one option exists for how to construct words and sentences, one dominant pattern often becomes the default and then subsumes the others. Such a change doesn't happen all at once or without exceptions. Competing structures can exist side by side for a long time before the losers disappear. An example of such a situation is the verb ending *-eth* for third-person singular (*he doth*, *she spaketh*). This ending coexisted with the third-person *-s* ending for hundreds of years. Records of spoken speech from the seventeenth century show examples that include *-eth* and *-s* in a single sentence:[4]

- His wief **maketh** bone lace, and he himself **selles** Inke.
- A vagrant **sayeth** hee is a Broomeman and **dwelles** in kent.

Eventually, *-s* became the default for third-person singular agreement. Nonetheless, as Washington's use of *hath* indicates, the old form of subject-verb agreement was still a possibility more than a century after it started losing ground.

Another way that words can change grammatically is in how they are interpreted. Such a shift often brings an unusual pattern into line with one that's more typical. The change from Washington's *much pains* to the present-day *many pains* is an example. *Pains* is one of a group of nouns that evolved from Middle English with *-s* endings, but were singular in sense (like *scissors* and *trousers*). The others were *means*, *odds*, *amends*, *alms*, *gallows*, *riches*, *wages*, *victuals*, and *news*. In the eighteenth century, these words were still treated like singular nouns most of the time, as in these examples:[5]

- Was ever riches gotten by your golden mediocrities?
- He gave much alms.

- What is the odds?
- This honor to him, when dead, was but a necessary amends.

However, because these words end in -s, they were sometimes interpreted as plurals, as the following examples from the mid-eighteenth and early nineteenth centuries show:[6]

- Means to an end are only valued so far as the end is valued.
- The Odds, at starting, were on Brabram.
- These wages amount to two dollars per diem.

For a while, both possibilities were available, but as time went on, these plural-looking words became unambiguously plural. The only exceptions are *news* and sometimes *gallows*. The same process is at work today with words adopted from Latin and Greek, such as *data, criteria, antennae, phenomena,* and *fungi.* These are all plural words, but because they don't look or sound particularly plural to English speakers, they are often treated like singulars (*The data tells the story*; *This criteria is the most important*), or the plurals are regularizing (*funguses, antennas*).

*Whence,* along with *hence* and *thence,* is a similar example. These words have been around since at least the fourteenth century, and originally meant from which place, from this place, and from that place. Over time, the prepositional part of their meanings was lost and they began to be treated more like other locational words, such as *where, here,* and *there.* Now, on the rare occasions when they're used, they are nearly always preceded by the preposition *from.*

The way sentences are put together can also change. In Middle English (1100–1500), modal verbs like *can, will, shall, must,* and *might* behaved very much like typical verbs. They could appear as the only verb in a sentence, for example, *The holy man could* [knew] *much of scripture* and *I will* [want] *none of it.* At the same time, non-modal verbs acted more like modals do now. The verb and subject inverted in questions (*Knowest thou the answer?*), and *not* came after the main verb (*I know not the answer*).

This situation began to change sometime in the sixteenth century. Modals lost the properties of verbs and a new category of "auxiliaries" arose that included modals, as well as auxiliary uses of *have, do,* and *be.* Questions were formed by inverting the subject and auxiliary rather than the subject and verb, and *not* started appearing after the first auxiliary in a sentence instead of after the main verb. This change was still in progress during the early seventeenth century when John Smith wrote his books about adventuring in North America. As we can see from the following examples, he sometimes formed negative sentences and questions the old way, but at other times, he chose the new option of using auxiliaries:[7]

- They durst not.
- They admitted him not to the sight of their trials.
- What call you this?
- I will not cease revenge.
- What shall I eate?

Eventually, the modern way of forming questions and using *not* pushed out the earlier way. Traces remain in fixed sayings like *waste not, want not*, and in the verbs *need not* and *dare not*, which are still occasionally seen in formal writing. Americans generally prefer verb phrases like *be going to, have to*, and *ought to*, rather than modals like *will, must*, and *should*, in contrast to the English, who favor modals more often.

Although grammatical changes usually enter the language more stealthily than words, when speakers do notice evolving usages, they have an urge to resist them. Noah Webster, for example, complained in his 1789 book about words like *pains* and *means* being used more often as plurals, arguing that they had always been singular in the past (i.e., appearing with singular verbs).[8] This view of language imagines an idealized unchanging standard, usually based on the usages (or perceived usages) of the upper classes. The language is thought to have been purer or more logical in previous times. In reality, as we've seen, English, like all languages, is always evolving and has always encompassed a variety of ways of talking.

Grammar book writers throughout the eighteenth and nineteenth centuries also continued to keep obsolete usages alive based on the notion of an idealized permanent linguistic standard. They included *thee* and *thou* as pronouns and gave examples of verb forms like *thou dost* and *he doth*, and irregular pasts like *holp*, long after such forms had disappeared from spoken speech. As we'll see, their ongoing influence has been another force affecting the shape of American English and how people feel about its use.

# Growing Apart

British and American grammatical structures started growing apart during early colonial times, and they are still diverging in modern times. Frequently, these differences are the result of more than one possibility being available. Divergent uses of *shall* and *will* are an early example of American and British English speakers choosing different options. In the eighteenth century, the British use of *shall* and *will* varied from region to region.[9] The norm for the educated social elite in London and southern England was to use *shall* with first-person nouns and pronouns, and *will* with the second and third person. The Irish and the Scots, on the other hand, usually used *will* with all three persons including the first.

By the eighteenth century, Americans also favored *will* most of the time. This development is usually attributed to the influence of Irish or Scots-Irish immigrants who arrived in the late eighteenth century. If they didn't inspire the trend, they no doubt reinforced it. A notice of a runaway indentured servant that appeared in the *Pennsylvania Chronicle* for November 11, 1767, indicates that *I will* was considered a distinctively Irish trait: "A native Irish servant man . . . very seldom answers yes or no, but I will . . . or I will not." Webster also observed that "the Scots and Irish . . . generally use *will* for *shall* in the first person." He thought that New Englanders were more likely than other Americans to use *shall*, and explained it by the fact that their dialect originated in southern England. Later writers also noticed that *shall* use was more prevalent in New England, especially in Boston.[10]

The specialized rhetorical uses of *shall* and *will* were a complicating issue. As with other modals, the meanings of *shall* and *will* had changed as they evolved from main verbs to auxiliaries. *Shall* originally conveyed the idea of necessity or obligation, and *will* meant to want or intend. When *shall* and *will* started being used to express future tense, they also retained some of their older connotations. Because *shall* implied obligation or commitment, it was deemed to be impolite except with the first person. When used with the second or third person (for instance, the biblical commandment "Thou shalt not kill," or Bryan's "You shall not crucify mankind"), *shall* sounded more like a command. *Will*, when used with the first person, conveyed intention.

*I shall go on Friday* was simply a statement of future action, but *I will go* implied that the speaker was determined or promising to go. *Will* with the second or third person (*You will go, won't you?*) simply indicated future tense.

Since *shall* was seldom used in the United States, these distinctive uses wouldn't have been heard much in conversational American English, but "insistence *shall*" remained an option for formal writing or spoken rhetoric until at least the beginning of the twentieth century, as Bryan's "Cross of Gold" speech shows. In modern times, Americans have almost completely dropped *shall*. An exception is for invitations like *Shall we go?*, but even in this instance, many people would be more likely to say something like *Should we go* or *Do you want to go*.

The English have continued to use *shall* in traditional ways. Linguist John Algeo, who made a detailed study of differences between modern British and American usage, estimated that the English use *shall* approximately five times as often as Americans.[11] Besides using *shall* with *I* and *we* to express the future, British English speakers can still use it with the second and third person to imply determination (*We must learn lessons from it so it shall never happen again*). They also use the contraction *shan't* (shall not), which is never heard in American English.

American and British English speakers also have different preferences when it comes to the past tense of verbs. Past tenses offer a good example of a grammatical change that is still in flux after a millennium. In Old English, hundreds of so-called strong verbs formed their past tense by changing their root vowel (*sing/sang*, *break/broke*, *drive/drove*, and many others that are now obsolete). Old English also had "weak" verbs that formed their past tense by adding *-ed* to the end of the word. Over time, the weak ending became the default. Whenever new verbs came into the language, they always got a past tense that ended in *-ed*. (The past tense of *jive*, e.g., became *jived*, not *jove*.) Over time, many formerly strong verbs have shed their irregular forms in favor of *-ed*.

Some verbs that were irregular in the early republic are now regular. For example, *climb/clomb*, *drag/drug*, *abide/abode*, *help/holp*, *beseech/besought*, *thrive/throve*, *dare/durst*, and *work/wrought* were all in the process of switching over in the eighteenth century. Others haven't settled yet. Some examples of verbs with variable past tenses include *shine*, *dive*, *plead*, *prove*, *strive*, and *light*. In these cases, Americans have sometimes held with the older past tense or past participle, for instance, using *proven*, *pled*, *dove*, and *shone* more often, while the English prefer *proved, pleaded, dived,* and *shined.* In other cases, the opposite is true. The English are more likely to say *strove* and *lit,* but Americans favor *strived* and *lighted.*[12]

Other verbs show differences as well. British English speakers mark the past tense of certain verbs with a *t* sound (and *t* spelling), for example, *knelt, smelt, spilt, leapt, learnt,* and *dwelt.* Americans also say *do you have* more easily than *have you got.* The past participle for Americans when they do say *got* is *gotten,* but a British speaker would say *He hasn't got beyond the first stage.*

British English speakers also use questions at the end of statements (called tag questions) more often than Americans. Typical forms are *You can help, can't you?, James wouldn't do that, would he?,* and *You think so, do you?.* Americans also use all these forms, but British English speakers use rhetorical tag questions when they're not expecting an answer, for example, *Well, I was tempted, wasn't I?.* Americans rarely if ever use rhetorical tags. Recently, young people in England have adopted the general tag *innit,* used even when the subject of the sentence is not *it,* as in *The teachers are unfair here, innit?* This tag is not commonly heard in the United States.[13]

Dozens of small differences like these have accumulated over the centuries, adding up to two recognizably different dialects. *Whilst, amongst,* and *amidst* are common in British English, but sound artificial in America. British English speakers can fill in a missing verb phrase with *do* (e.g., *If you don't know the answer already, you should do*), which sounds strange in American English. The English prefer *which* in relative clauses, while Americans choose *that* (*the book which I read most recently* vs. *the book that I read most recently*). In the United States, English speakers use singular verbs with most collective nouns, so they say *The council is arguing over its next step* and *The company is planning a recall.* In England, such nouns are considered plural, so the English say *The council are arguing* and *The company are planning.* Although *different from* is correct in both places, most Americans say *different than* and their British counterparts say *different to.* All three forms have been around for a while.

Americans have also been using *real* instead of *very,* as in *real nice,* for a long time, as well as *some* to mean somewhat, as in *He was some better yesterday* (more common in certain areas, such as the South). As these are also heard in Scotland, Ireland, and northern England, they may be among the many linguistic features contributed by the Scots-Irish. These and many other slight but distinctive grammatical shifts give certain sentences an ineffably British or American feel.

British English may seem to be the more "traditional" version because it existed first, but both British and American English introduced innovations after the two dialects split. Americans innovated when they started using singular verbs with collective nouns, even while they also preserved older forms, such as certain past tenses, after these disappeared from British speech. English innovations include regularizing various past tenses, adding *do* after an auxiliary, and using the *innit* tag.

## Building on the Past

Certain structures and word usages that now seem quintessentially American have deep roots in earlier English. Instead of fading into obsolescence as they did in England, they became a naturalized part of American English, often being retained as regionalisms. Their meanings and uses, as well as who uses them, have also continued to change. In some cases, they've broken out of their traditional boundaries and are gaining popularity with new groups of speakers.

The various plural *you* forms in America have evolved and diversified over time and are still changing. Today, *y'all*, *you all* (with the stress on *you*), and *you'uns* are closely identified with American regional speech. *Y'all* is among the most prominent features of southern speech. *You'uns* is probably the best-known feature of Pittsburgh speech (where it is typically spelled *yinz*), and it is widely heard in the upper Ohio Valley and the southern Appalachian region.[14] These usages almost certainly came to the United States with the Scots-Irish. *Y'all* may have derived from *ye aw*, the Scottish version of *you all*. A 1737 letter written by a Scots-Irish immigrant contains an early written example: "I beg of ye aw to come [over] here." A likely derivation of *you'uns* is the Scottish *you* or *ye* plus *yins*, meaning ones. This form was also around in the early nineteenth century. In 1810, a young woman traveling through western Pennsylvania on her way to Ohio noted in her journal, "Youns is a word I have heard used several times, but what it means I don't know."[15]

No doubt part of the explanation for why these varieties of *you* took hold is that English had lost its ability to distinguish between singular and plural second-person pronouns. As noted in the discussion of Quakers in Chapter 2, *you* originally referred to more than one person. *Thou* and *thee* were the singular forms. During the fourteenth century, *you* started being used as a polite way to address people whose social rank the speaker respected, and gradually that trend spread. By the seventeenth century, *you* had almost completely replaced *thee* and *thou*. That left a gap in the grammar where a plural form had been before.

This gap is filled today partly by *y'all*, which is used all across the South as far west as Texas by people of every social background and educational level. Examples in print are scarce before the twentieth century. However, this sentence from an 1886 *New York Times* article describing "quaint" South Carolina speech indicates that it was a feature of southern English much earlier: "'You all,' or as it should be abbreviated, 'y'all,' is one of the most ridiculous of all the Southernisms I can call to mind."[16]

One much discussed issue is whether *y'all* can refer to a single individual. Most Southerners, when asked this question, will insist that it cannot. However, a 1993 survey of *y'all* users found that nearly one-third used it at least occasionally to address a single person, although it is still overwhelmingly treated like a plural.[17] Singular *y'all* seems to occur mainly in situations where the speaker is being friendly or informal, or establishing a bond. A frequently mentioned example is a restaurant server checking to see if a (single) customer wants anything (*Y'all doing okay here?*). This usage may be a change from earlier times.

In recent decades, *y'all* has begun to transcend its regional borders. In spite of the fact that "southern accents" are usually deprecated outside their home territory, *y'all* appears to be spreading. According to surveys done in the mid-1990s, *you all* and *y'all* are getting established in states that border the South (like Kansas) and in the Rocky Mountain area, and are occasionally heard in other areas outside the South as well. Among younger users, *y'all* is preferred over *you all*. One explanation for the increasing popularity of *y'all* might be its convenience as a single-syllable way to express the second-person plural. It may also have become more acceptable to younger speakers as a word that's heard in rap lyrics.[18] The expanded expression *all y'all* is also becoming more familiar outside the South.

Other plural *you* forms have also continued to change over time. In the Pittsburgh area, *you'uns* (*yinz*) has become more than a way to address a group. It can represent Pittsburgh itself, for example, in the words *Yinzer* (someone from Pittsburgh) and *Yinzburgh*. It can also be used as an adjective in phrases like *Yinz Play*, *YinzBlog*, and *YinzSports*. *You'uns* is also still used in the Appalachian region, although *y'all* competes with it there.

At the same time as *y'all* is expanding outside the South, *you guys*, yet another way to address a group, is making inroads in the region. Although the phrase *you guys* is fairly recent, the word *guy* has been around for a long time. It derives from Guy Fawkes, leader of the ill-fated 1605 "Gunpowder Plot" to blow up the English Parliament. In past times, Guy Fawkes Night (November 5) was celebrated by burning raggedly dressed effigies called guys. By the early nineteenth century, *guy* was slang for a strangely or shabbily dressed man, and by the mid-nineteenth century, Americans were using it as a casual way to refer to a male. By the early twentieth century, *good guys*, *bad guys*, and *tough guys* were all in use.

At first *you guys* referred to a group of males, but gradually the phrase lost its exclusively male meaning, especially when used for direct address. By the 1980s, it was starting to be applied to mixed groups or even groups composed entirely of females. *You guys* has now become a generalized second-person plural. In the last couple of decades, it has also become much more common in the South, where traditionally *y'all* was heavily preferred. It was initially limited to college students, but now appears to be gaining popularity with older speakers as well.[19]

Another grammatical feature from earlier times that may be expanding its range is multiple modals. Although multiple modals were fairly common in Middle and Early Modern English (see Chapter 1), most dialects today allow only one modal verb per sentence. However, multiple modals are still common across the South, as well as a few other areas outside the United States.[20] The most typical combinations in present-day American English are *might could* and *used to could* (*I might could do that for you*; *She used to could dance all night*), but others that are heard frequently include *might can*, *may can*, *might should*, *might would*, and *might ought to*. Multiple modals are another form found in Scotland and the north of England, suggesting an origin there.

In the United States, multiple modals are still essentially a Southernism, but they have occasionally been heard as far north as southern Pennsylvania and New Jersey, and as far west as Utah. Chicano English speakers use *used to could* and *might could*, and speakers of African American English outside the South also use multiple modals. (We'll explore Chicano English and African American English in more detail in Chapter 6.)

## The Changing Uses of Invariant *Be*

Another grammatical structure that has persisted through the centuries is untensed or invariant *be*, but it has undergone significant changes, both in who uses it and how it's used. Today, invariant *be* is associated almost exclusively with African American English, but it once had a broader distribution. In earlier English, the untensed form of *be* had two main purposes. Its most common use was in conditional (subjunctive) phrases, such as Lincoln's "unless you be allowed to construe . . . the Constitution as you please." This use of *be* was almost obsolete by the late eighteenth century and has virtually disappeared.

Earlier English *be* also appeared occasionally in straightforward indicative statements, almost always with third-person subjects instead of *are*, as in the example given in Chapter 1, "The younger provide for those that be aged." By the eighteenth century, this use of invariant *be* in America was confined to New England and the South. In those places, it was part of the folk speech, used mainly by people who lived in rural areas and did not have much formal education.[21]

During the nineteenth and early twentieth centuries, the folk use of *be* was considered a stereotypical feature of rustic New England speech. New Englanders paired it with all three persons, and with singular as well as plural subjects. Writing in 1789, Webster described it as a typical New Englandism, giving as examples *I be, we be, you be,* and *they be*. This novel use of *be* was usually but not always used in questions:[22]

- My water pipe was frozen and there I be!
- Be ye goin' to buy more cows?
- How be ye?

*Be* also featured in fictional portrayals of New Englanders, as in this line from a Harriet Beecher Stowe story: "'Be there ghosts?' said Sam." However, by the mid-twentieth century, this use of invariant *be* was on the wane in the region, and it's now obsolete.

Invariant *be* has also historically been characteristic of southern vernacular English. In the mid-1980s, linguists studying popular speech in several southern states surveyed the use of invariant *be* among Black and White speakers.[23] They found that both Black and White dialects included invariant *be*, most often used in ways similar to Early Modern English. That is, it almost always showed up as a replacement for *are*, and it usually referred to actions that occurred repeatedly or habitually. For instance:

- He sells his pigs when they be six to eight weeks old.
- In the wintertime . . . tha's where they be at.
- Some be fat, some small.
- They didn't be there in the kitchen.

Speakers occasionally also used *be* in other situations, for instance, with a first-person pronoun ("I just don't be worried about finding help") or for one-time actions ("She just be fussing").

These studies of folk speech uncovered differences between Black and White usage, indicating that *be* was moving in different directions for the two groups. Older people in both groups used invariant *be* the most, especially men over the age of sixty. However, Black speakers used it much more frequently than White speakers. Researchers also found that African Americans of all age groups used it at least occasionally, while younger White speakers did not use it at all. A form that had once been common to the two sets of speakers was still current in Black speech, although apparently less used by younger people, but was disappearing from White speech.

Invariant *be* has all but died out in southern White speech, except for one or two restricted locations. One is the Piedmont region of southeastern North Carolina and northeastern South Carolina, where some White speakers use *be* and, more frequently, *bes*. The context is usually habitual, but not always:[24]

- That baby bes crying all afternoon.
- This house bes a mess.

Another exception is the speech of the Lumbee tribe of North Carolina, discussed in Chapter 6. Lumbee speakers use *be* and *bes* in similar ways.

Invariant *be* has taken a different trajectory among Black speakers. It is a widespread feature of current African American English, standardly indicating a habitual action or permanent state of affairs.

It's used with first- and second-person subjects as well as third-person subjects. Although the most usual form is *be*, *bes* is also heard:[25]

- She be telling people she eight.
- I be looking for somewhere to waste time.
- I be in my office by 7:30.
- It be knives in here.
- Well, that's the way it bes.

The invariant *be* of current African American English is not necessarily a direct descendant of previous iterations of *be*. While it has some features in common with earlier versions, in other respects it is new. For instance, *be* appears to be used only for habitual or permanent states in African American English, which is not true historically or for the Piedmont or Lumbee dialects. Also, the preponderance of uses occurs with a progressive verb form (with an *-ing* ending). The shift to this usage as the heavily preferred one appears to have started a few decades ago with young speakers, and is a break from earlier varieties of African American speech.[26]

As mentioned in Chapter 2 (and discussed further in Chapter 6), it's unclear how much African American English owes to input from early varieties of Anglo-American English and how much comes from a possible early creole influenced by West African languages, which could also be a source of invariant *be*. This way of using *be* is a feature of many creoles.[27] In either case, it's clear that invariant *be* has evolved in numerous ways in American English, and that its uses have shifted considerably during the twentieth century.

Invariant *be* and the grammatical structures described in the previous section show both the persistence of some historical English forms and the inevitability of language change and variation. Traces of earlier British and American speech are still woven through the language after four centuries. At the same time, American English speakers have continued to reshape the language, adding new forms and shedding old ones, or putting them to new uses.

## Grammar by the Book

One reason why obsolescent forms like insistence *shall* lingered in American English is that they were enshrined in grammar books.

Understanding and using what is usually termed "standard English"—that is, the English used by well-off, socially influential people—were important to Americans in the early republic. Those at the bottom of the socioeconomic ladder saw the new country as a place of unprecedented opportunities for self-betterment, but they believed that to climb to the higher rungs, they needed to speak and write like the people above them. Americans also cared about language study because they believed that citizens in a participatory democracy should be well educated so they could understand complex social and political issues. Memorizing the contents of a grammar book was considered an essential first step toward reaching both those goals.

A traditional education of the sort mainly available to the sons of the upper classes emphasized the study of Latin and Greek. Studying classical languages was thought to be good mental training. The discipline of memorizing words and grammatical structures prepared students for more complex topics like philosophy, rhetoric, and the natural sciences. It was also thought to build character. For most Americans in the late eighteenth and nineteenth centuries, however, a classical education was not only out of reach, but also impractical. It was wasted on anyone not going on to higher education. Studying English grammar made much more sense. It was equally useful for mental training and character building, but had the perceived added advantage of teaching students how to speak and write eloquently in their own language.

Another advantage of grammar books is that they allowed people to learn on their own. Most towns of any size, especially in New England, had at least one school, but in rural areas and frontier territories schools were widely scattered. Many taught only the bare minimum of reading and writing skills, never advancing as far as grammar studies. In any case, families needed their children to work on their farms for part of the year, which didn't leave much time for school. Anyone who missed out on formal grammar studies for these or any other reasons could take their education into their own hands by getting a standard grammar book and working through it. Abraham Lincoln, who grew up in poverty on the Indiana frontier, famously began his own higher education by studying borrowed grammar books.[28]

By the turn of the nineteenth century, grammar textbooks were among the best-selling books in the country. Dozens of titles were in print, with new ones appearing every year. The most popular went through many editions and sold hundreds of thousands of copies. Since the total population of the United States during the first part of the century was under 10 million, these are impressive numbers. Books were an expensive luxury in those days, but most households owned a grammar book. They were prized possessions, along with the family Bible and perhaps one or two other morally uplifting volumes.[29]

The first grammar books were produced in England. A few were written in the seventeenth century, but they didn't become broadly popular in either England or the United States until the mid-eighteenth century.[30] Most were organized according to the same pattern. Typically, they started with the alphabet and sounds, then progressed to the study of words and spelling. Next came parts of speech and sentence grammar. A final section contained practice readings, usually on uplifting topics. The content was normally arranged in brief sections that students were meant to memorize and later recite to the teacher. Grammar books constituted a complete course of study in compact form. In a one-room schoolhouse that held children of all ages, the youngest could concentrate on learning to read from the first sections of the book, while older, more advanced students tackled the grammar proper.

The first grammar book to gain a wide readership in America was *A Short Introduction to English Grammar* by Anglican bishop Robert Lowth, first published in 1762. *A Short Introduction* first appeared in America in 1775 and went through multiple editions. At the height of the book's popularity at the turn of the nineteenth century, nearly every classroom in the land possessed at least one copy, and it sat on many private bookshelves as well. Harvard adopted it for classroom use in 1774 and used it until 1841.[31] Other colleges also assigned it to their students. Later grammar book writers borrowed from it freely, sometimes lifting large sections verbatim.

Many ideas that Americans have about what constitutes "correct" grammar come from Bishop Lowth's book, even though they may never have studied any grammar book themselves. Lowth was the first to state that two negatives "are equivalent to an affirmative" (i.e., make a positive).[32] He also claimed that *whose* should be used only with a human referent, although avoiding it sometimes resulted in an awkward phrase like *the question the solution to which I require*. He argued that when a pronoun appeared after a conjunction such as *than* or *as*, it should be treated like the subject of an understood sentence, so *You are not so tall as me* should be *You are not so tall as I (am)*. The verb *to be* should also be followed by a nominative (subject) pronoun, for instance, *I am he* because it logically referred back to the subject.

Most famously, Lowth suggested that prepositions should not be separated from their relative pronoun objects (*which* or *whom*) and left at the end of the sentence, as in "Horace is an author whom I am much delighted with." He admitted that "this idiom" prevailed in "common conversation," but thought that "the placing of the Preposition before the Relative is more graceful . . . and agrees much better with the solemn and elevated Style."[33] Later grammar writers simplified this rule into a ban on ending a sentence with a preposition.

Most of the usages that Lowth advised against were, in fact, a normal part of "common conversation" at the time in both England and the United States for all classes of speakers, and in many cases, they had been for centuries. That included using more than one negative for emphasis (*nor there are not none*) and using *whose* with other than human referents. Object pronouns like *me*, *her*, and *them* were also routine after the verb *to be*. Later grammarians added bans on other common usages as well, such as double comparatives (*most unkindest*) and "splitting" an infinitive by placing an adverb between *to* and the verb (e.g., *to fiercely argue*).

Lowth and grammarians who came after him were probably not deliberately trying to change normal usage. More likely, they were choosing between two options according to which one sounded more refined to them. Since one of their goals was to present a standardized version of English, they didn't allow for language variation. Their descriptions sometimes matched the reality of most American speech, but at other times ignored widespread usages. Eighteenth- and nineteenth-century grammarians also tended to believe that English grammar should pattern after Latin, which had been the language of scholarship and education until very recently, so Latin grammatical features like the use of nominative case after *to be* were claimed to be correct for English as well. This approach reinforced the idea of an unchanging linguistic standard that was superior to other varieties of speech (even if the reality was that nobody talked exactly like a grammar book), and convinced many Americans that their natural way of talking was defective.

As mentioned before, grammar books lagged behind the spoken language when it came to ongoing changes like regularizing past tenses, the preference for *will* over *shall*, and the abandonment of *thou* and *thee*. This meant that grammar books presented an outdated picture of the language and preserved archaic usages that otherwise might have faded sooner, such as those in Lincoln's and Bryan's speeches. On the other hand, grammar books also encouraged the demise of traditional usages like double negatives and double comparatives that were deemed socially less elegant. There's no way to know for sure how much the principles laid down in grammar books affected the way Americans actually used their language, but people striving to learn educated speech habits would certainly have paid attention to the rules, at least for writing and formal oratory.

Much of Lowth's usage advice is phrased as guidelines rather than absolute rules. For instance, he didn't say that prepositions should never end a sentence; he simply suggested that keeping them with their relative pronoun antecedent sounded better in the "solemn and elevated Style." These nuances were generally lost in the grammar books that came after him. Rules like "never end a sentence with a preposition" and "two negatives make a positive" took on the air of linguistic truths. Occasionally, a dissenting voice was heard. Noah Webster championed the use of sentences like *Who did he speak to?*, claiming the structure was acceptable "until some Latin student began to suspect it [of being] bad English."[34] Such views were in the minority among grammar specialists, however.

By far the most popular grammar book in America until the mid-nineteenth century was *English Grammar, Adapted to the Different Classes of Learners*, written by Lindley Murray, an American expatriate living in York, England. Murray, a Quaker, originally wrote his book in 1794 for the students of the local Quaker girls' school. Partly because he was not at first planning to publish it more widely, he took much of the content from Lowth rather than creating his own. Most of the grammar rules that appeared in Lowth were repeated in Murray's book, frequently word for word. He also added some discussion of usages that he saw as problematic, for instance, using *they* with a singular antecedent like *anyone* (*Anyone can come if they want to*), even when these were a normal part of English. He organized his book so it was easy to use, with plenty of examples and practice exercises.

Murray's *English Grammar* was so popular among the teachers who first used it that he decided to publish it for a larger audience. The first edition appeared in 1797, and it was an immediate success. It reached the United States in 1800 and quickly went into numerous American editions. By 1812, it had gone through at least forty editions, and by the middle of the century, when sales started to decline, over 1 million copies had been sold. Murray also produced separate workbooks and abridged editions, which also sold extremely well. Other publishers pirated their own editions, probably bringing the total sales of Murray's work to something over 2 million copies.[35]

In nineteenth-century America, the name of Murray was synonymous with correct speech. In her 1852 novel *Uncle Tom's Cabin*, Harriet Beecher Stowe described the slave trader Haley as a man whose conversation "was in free and easy defiance of Murray's grammar." A character in a comic sketch from around the same period warns a schoolmaster, "They tell me you have some newfangled notion on the subject of grammar; and I never will have *nothing* to do with *no* one that does not know Murray's Grammar." Lincoln once remarked that Murray's grammar was "the best schoolbook ever placed in the hands of a child."[36]

Because Murray relied heavily on Lowth, and because his books were so universally popular, Lowth's grammar rules remained part of a typical education for most schoolchildren for most of the nineteenth century. These books were also familiar to all adults who studied grammar on their own. They became part of the way that Americans think about language use and what constitutes correct speech. As we'll see in Chapter 8, the influence of early American grammar books is still being felt, even though schools today seldom use grammar texts as part of their curriculum. The dynamics of language change and linguistic variety affect the structure of American English as well as the words and the sounds, but they are often not as easily recognized, or as readily accepted, in this part of the language.

# 5

# The Spread of Regional Speech

## The Real Life of Language

What do you call a sudden, heavy rain? Do you have another word for pancakes? How about a name for a carbonated drink? What's your word for someone who worries or fusses a lot? If your answers to these questions are *gully washer*, *fritters*, *soft drink*, and *fuss-box*, chances are excellent that you are a lifelong resident of a southern state. People in other parts of the country have different favored words. A heavy storm might be called a goose-drownder in the Midwest, but more likely a cloudburst in California. The word for a carbonated drink in New England is *tonic*, in the northern tier states and the West it's commonly *pop*, and in the Northeast it's usually *soda*. People who worry a lot are known as fuss-budgets in the northern and western states, fuss-buttons in the Midwest, and fusspots in New England. They might be called worry warts almost anywhere in the country.

The questions noted here are four of the more than 1,600 that linguistic fieldworkers asked while collecting material for the *Dictionary of American Regional English* (DARE). Between 1965 and 1970, interviewers armed with questionnaires fanned out to over 1,000 communities around the country, seeking out residents who had lived in the same area since birth. Their aim was to record the everyday speech that people used when talking to family and friends, especially the colorful local words and phrases seldom heard in formal situations and rarely written down. Questions covered forty-one categories touching on many aspects of daily life. These ranged from the weather to household items to common foods, as well as more abstract topics like family relationships, religion, and emotional states. Researchers collected material from over 3,000 informants, noting not only words and phrases, but also pronunciations.[1]

The DARE questionnaire was the final stage of a project that originated many decades earlier. It began in the late nineteenth century, when language scholars started to think about preserving and studying American vernacular and regional speech, part of a wider scholarly trend toward exploring American folklore and traditional lifeways. In the early twentieth century, it progressed to the mapping of American dialect regions in a series of "linguistic atlases," and eventually to the organized collecting, categorizing, and recording of American regional speech.

The first step that led toward DARE was the 1889 founding of the American Dialect Society by a group of twenty-eight Harvard professors and other interested people. Their purpose was to investigate "the English dialects in America with regard to pronunciation, grammar, vocabulary, phraseology, and geographical distribution." They believed, in the words of one founding member, that "the real life of language is found only in the folk-dialects. These are not . . . corruptions of the standard language, but are the native and natural growths."[2]

This respect for "folk-dialects," that is, the vernacular speech of people in all parts of the country, was a sharp change from the attitude of earlier language scholars. Grammar book writers of the eighteenth and nineteenth centuries concentrated on preserving and promoting the prestige dialect. The Dialect Society's statement reflected the modern linguist's way of looking at language. It was a recognition that American English encompassed many varieties, each equally valid. The standardized language of formal writing was only one small part.

The Society's long-term goal was to compile a dictionary of American dialects. To get started, members began collecting folk speech and publishing their findings in the Society's journal, *Dialect Notes*. A sampling of typical articles from volume II (1900–1904) includes "The Pioneer Dialect of Southern Illinois," "The Term State-House," "Cape Cod Dialect," "The Dialect of Southeastern Missouri," and "The Language of the Oil Fields." Dialect collections frequently reflected the author's own speech or knowledge of a local dialect. For example, the list of words, expressions, and pronunciations in "Cape Cod Dialect" is based on the author's parents' speech.

Because lists often focused on the speech of older residents, they could reach back into the nineteenth century for language that might be even older. In many cases, they captured words and usages that were on the verge of extinction. For example, the author of the Cape Cod article reported that the "old folks" of his parents' generation still pronounced *er* as 'ar', so they said 'marcy', 'parfectly', 'consarn', 'narvous', and the like, just as the earliest colonists had. He also noted archaic grammatical forms like *I be*, *I h'aint* [ain't], and nonstandard verb forms like *knowed, catched, busted,* and *seed*. By the beginning of the twentieth century, these features were dying out. The Cape Cod list, like some others, is a mix of strictly local terms and others that were more widespread, but nonstandard. It includes *duff*, a flour pudding, and *catouse*, an uproar, two words specific to New England, but also *flustrated*, a colloquialism found in many parts of the country since the eighteenth century.[3]

While some Dialect Society members gathered material from informants or their own observations, others combed through print sources including regional novels, diaries, newspapers, pamphlets, geographical and botanical guides, local histories, and other material. These also yielded many nonstandard and regional terms, some of which were no longer heard very often. For instance, the 1838 "Down East" novel *The Clockmaker* by Thomas Chandler Haliburton provided such old-fashioned New England words as *didoes* (shenanigans), *meeching* (skulking), *galluses* (suspenders), and *wamble-cropped* (queasy). The 1834 *Narrative of the Life of David Crockett* yielded words and expressions from the southern backcountry like *brand-fire-new* (completely new), *mind* (to notice), *lick-log* (a notched log), and *root hog or die* (work hard or fail).

In 1929, while the Dialect Society was gathering regional and archaic words, the American Council of Learned Societies founded a parallel project called the Linguistic Atlas Project. Their idea was to create a series of maps that would delineate regional differences in word use. Linguistic Atlas researchers, headed by Hans Kurath, a linguistics professor at the University of Michigan, pioneered the word-collecting method later used for the DARE questionnaire. Starting with New England, they visited hundreds of communities, focusing on small, rural places and interviewing life-long residents. The *Linguistic Atlas of New England* appeared in 1941. Atlases of the eastern United States, the Middle and South Atlantic states, the Gulf states, the Upper

Midwest, and the Rocky Mountain regions followed over the next few decades.[4]

Regional mappings showed that in some cases, two words with similar meanings had distinct ranges with little or no overlap. For example, instances of the word *bucket* clustered thickly across central and southern Pennsylvania and into the South, but were rare in areas north of there. In contrast, *pail* was very common from northern Pennsylvania to New England, but rare in the South. Sometimes several words showed the same ranges. In the North, where *pail* was common, a dragonfly was known as a darning needle. In Pennsylvania and areas to the south, where *bucket* was the default, the term for a dragonfly was more likely to be *snake feeder* or *snake doctor*. The boundary lines separating these bundles of regionally distinctive terms, known as isoglosses, reveal the geographical ranges of different dialects (see Figure 5.1 for a map of American dialect regions).

By the mid-twentieth century, the American Dialect Society and the Linguistic Atlas Project together had collected a massive amount of material. It included over 230,000 quotations from around 1,300 print sources, and at least 30,000 words from lists in *Dialect Notes*, as well as

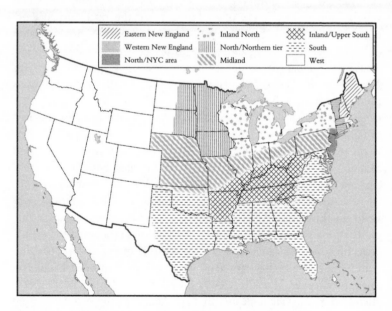

**Figure 5.1** Major Dialect Regions of the United States

the word mappings from the linguistic atlases.[5] However, there were still many gaps in the linguistic record. For the projected dictionary of regional speech to be truly comprehensive, a more organized approach was called for. In 1962, Frederick G. Cassidy was appointed editor of the proposed dictionary and began the work that eventually led to the DARE questionnaire.

In 1970, when the survey was complete, answers were classified and processed with the help of computers. At the same time, the previously collected material was also being organized and incorporated. The first volume of the *Dictionary of American Regional English, A–C*, appeared in 1985. Four more volumes completed the alphabet. In 2013, a supplemental volume was published containing maps and fieldwork data. Dictionary entries provide much more than definitions. They also indicate pronunciation, trace the word's origins if known, and include illustrative quotations reaching back as early as possible. These capsule word histories preserve many words and expressions that are not recorded anywhere else.

The *Dictionary of American Regional English* may now be found online (https://www.daredictionary.com), where new words and meanings are added regularly. Dialectologists have also continued collecting and analyzing Americans' distinctive speech patterns in other ways. During the 1990s, the Telsur Project (short for *telephone survey*), based at the University of Pennsylvania, conducted telephone interviews to study the pronunciation differences of urban areas across the country. One motivation for using the telephone was to be able to gather and organize material faster, so results would be less out of date. Telsur researchers also wanted to collect the speech of a more diverse population, including younger and more urban people and more women. DARE and the linguistic atlases relied heavily on older rural males.

As with previous surveys, interviewers concentrated on respondents who were native to the place. Unlike earlier surveys, Telsur focused on pronunciation rather than lexical items. They recorded regional pronunciation differences and also tracked sound patterns that seemed to be changing from former times. Their research has added to and updated what we know about regional varieties.[6]

More than 130 years of collecting and classifying American folk speech has uncovered some intriguing facts about American English. One is that many regional words have long histories, and in some cases were widely used in more than one region before shrinking their range. *Bucket* and *pail* were interchangeable options to the Puritans who settled in New England in the seventeenth century, but *bucket* was becoming less common in the region by the time of the Revolution. Some mainstream words and uses that go obsolete in most places last much longer in a more restricted locale. *Mind* to mean notice or remember is a centuries-old word. It was common all over England and America before it became mostly a Southernism, probably sometime in the nineteenth century.

Another important discovery is that in spite of listening to the same television programs and watching the same movies, Americans in the twentieth century were not starting to talk more alike, at least not when it came to casual speech. Many Americans still had regional accents. When the Telsur project started in 1992, nearly 40 percent of Americans were living in a different state from where they had been born. Telephone interviewers frequently had to make several calls before finding a native of the area. Nonetheless, the study was able to identify definite regional patterns of pronunciation differences.[7]

All the studies conducted over the twentieth century showed that residents of every region displayed characteristic speech traits that set them apart from the rest of the country. Although the borders of regional usage overlapped in many cases and were seldom sharp or exact, they clearly existed. The boundaries that separated pronunciations in the Telsur survey closely followed the boundaries that separated word uses in DARE and the linguistic atlases. What's more, the regions they delineated were essentially the same ones that had evolved during the eighteenth century—New England and the North, the Southeast, Pennsylvania and the Delaware Valley, and the Appalachian backcountry.[8]

## Regional Dialects Expand Their Territory

Early settlers tended to move more or less directly west of their original locations. Among the first to relocate in large numbers were New Englanders. Their colonial towns were already becoming crowded by the mid-eighteenth century. They began spreading into western New York and northeastern Ohio (known as the Western Reserve) in the 1770s, when the federal government offered tracts of land for sale there. They re-created their New England way of life in the new territory. Many were small farmers who grew wheat, planted orchards, or raised dairy cattle. Compact bustling towns soon dotted the region, populated by merchants, artisans, and professionals, and anchored by schools and churches. By 1800, about 100,000 settlers were established in western New York.[9]

The opening of the Erie Canal in 1825 brought an accelerated rush of settlement into the upper part of the state. The possibility of traveling and shipping goods by steamboat encouraged settlement along the canal route, and led to the founding of Buffalo, Syracuse, and Rochester. New Englanders also spilled into the Great Lakes areas of northern Michigan and Illinois, where Chicago and Detroit were developing into major commercial centers. They also settled parts of Wisconsin.

Eventually, the New Englanders were joined by successive waves of immigrants from other places. Newly arrived Irish and Germans came west from Boston and New York City during the first part of the nineteenth century. Italians and Scandinavians followed during the 1870s. Large numbers of Scandinavians also colonized the northern tier of the country as far as the Dakotas, along with later contingents of German immigrants. These groups all had an impact on the region's basically New England speech.

After the War of 1812, another wave of expansion took place across the lower South, fueled by a soaring demand for cotton, coupled with the 1793 invention of the cotton gin. The cotton gin simplified the processing of certain types of cotton and made large-scale cotton growing profitable. The lands along the Gulf and the Mississippi Valley were especially suitable for this purpose. As Native Americans were forced westward, planters from the coastal Southeast took their place. They also transported an estimated 1 million enslaved Africans to the region to fill the increased need for labor.[10] By the 1850s, the Cotton Belt extended across the lower South as far west as central Texas and as far north as southern Tennessee. Dialect features that originated in the Southeast now stretched over a much larger area.

Just as New Englanders replicated New England towns across the North, cotton growers in the lower South brought plantation society with them. The Cotton Belt was essentially rural, a land of sprawling, self-sufficient plantations whose owners preserved the aristocratic lifestyle of their Cavalier ancestors. Towns were widely scattered and less developed than in northern settlements, and schools were less common.

Although southeastern speech patterns dominated, other strands were woven in. The French in New Orleans and Mexicans in Texas, both long established by the time English speakers arrived, added another cultural and linguistic layer. German settlements in Texas also had some impact on local speech. Two islands of backcountry southern speech also arose in the region. Kentuckians and Tennesseans began crossing over the border into Alabama as their home territories grew more crowded, and settlers from the Georgia and South Carolina uplands started moving into the Florida Panhandle after 1821, when Spain ceded the territory to the United States. Before that time, the state was populated mainly by Seminoles and had become a refuge for escaped slaves.

A mix of people settled the Midland, drawn mainly from two earlier settlement streams, Pennsylvanians and the Scots-Irish. The pioneers who followed Daniel Boone into Kentucky and Tennessee came from western Virginia. They staked their claims without waiting for the government's blessing and settled onto small subsistence farms. The next wave came from Virginia and western North Carolina in the early nineteenth century, followed by migrants from the Delaware Valley and western Pennsylvania. As the region filled to capacity, some of these settlers moved again, pressing into southern Missouri and northern Arkansas. A small number pushed as far north as southern Indiana and Illinois.

A separate influx of settlers from Pennsylvania and Maryland traveled into the central parts of Ohio, Illinois, and Indiana along the National Road, which connected Cumberland, Maryland, with St. Louis. Some fanned out north and west from St. Louis into the midwestern plains or traveled down the Ohio River to Cincinnati. These Midland settlers brought a tradition of large-scale, diversified farming. They grew corn and other grains, and raised livestock, which they shipped east via the river. (Cincinnati, the center of this trade, was known as Porkopolis.) This region was soon solidly packed with settlements. By 1840, nearly a third of the U.S. population lived west of the Appalachians.[11]

The Midland population was more varied than that of either the North or the South. It included Quakers, Pennsylvania German sects such as Moravians and Amish, German and Irish Catholics, and

Scots-Irish from western Pennsylvania and the Appalachians. As a result, the speech patterns were more mixed. All groups contributed to the area's linguistic character. Small numbers of New Englanders also settled on the northern edge of the Midland region, and Southerners pushed over the southern boundary in some areas, in both cases further complicating the linguistic mix by introducing their own dialect features into the Midland border regions.

The connection between settlement patterns and dialects breaks down west of the Rockies. During the nineteenth century, all kinds of people streamed into the Far West from everywhere, in some cases, before their destinations were officially declared part of the United States. American fur trappers and traders roamed the Oregon Territory as early as the late eighteenth century. So many were from New England that many Native Americans in the area, including Chinooks and Salish tribes, referred to all White people as Bostons. However, the New Englanders were later outnumbered by settlers from the Midland, who started trickling into the Northwest in the 1830s, traveling over the Oregon Trail from Independence, Missouri, to Oregon's Willamette Valley. By 1845, some 5,000 settlers had made the trip by wagon train. After the Civil War, Scandinavians also immigrated to the area in large numbers.

Thousands of members of the Church of Jesus Christ of the Latter-Day Saints also made their way westward during this time. The Church was founded in upstate New York, but relocated to Kirtland, Ohio, in 1831. Eventually, its members migrated to Missouri, and then to Nauvoo, Illinois. They fled Nauvoo in 1844 when their founder, Joseph Smith, was murdered. Led by Brigham Young, they trekked to the Salt Lake Valley of Utah, where they settled in 1847, although it was still part of Mexico. The Mormon pioneers came from many places, not only New York and Ohio, but also other locations where missionaries had made converts. Many emigrated from England, Scandinavia, or Germany.

After the Civil War, yet more people thronged into the newly opened territories between the Rockies and the West Coast. These included former soldiers of both armies, formerly enslaved people, and many others in search of a new start. They came from all points east. The California Gold Rush, followed by the discovery of gold in Oregon in 1850 and of the Comstock silver lode in Nevada in 1859, drew thousands who were looking to get rich quick. Prospectors came from as far away as Europe. As noted earlier, nearly 25,000 Chinese men also arrived in the West to work for the railroads and other employers.[12]

The opening of the first transcontinental railroad in 1869, and the building of other railroads across the West, brought another huge surge of population. Not only was travel to the area now easier and cheaper, but even more important, shipping to the eastern part of the country had become much faster and more convenient. That made large-scale agriculture and cattle raising more profitable and encouraged the growth of expansive farms and ranches. These, in turn, drew workers from all parts of the country, as well as overseas. Agricultural laborers in California included people from the Philippines, China, and Mexico. Ranch hands came from Europe and Mexico. By 1870, San Francisco was a teeming multicultural hub holding nearly 150,000 people. Los Angeles was slower to grow, but by 1900 it had a population of around 102,000.[13]

In most places west of the Rockies, English speakers from all parts of the United States mingled, with no single linguistic home region dominant enough to have a defining influence. The language that had the most significant regional influence is Spanish. When Mexico ceded California and the Southwest, the area was home to around 100,000 Spanish speakers whose families had lived there for generations.[14] The Mexican language and culture remained well established even when Americans started arriving in greater numbers. Spanish is still widely spoken across the Southwest and in California, and it has had an obvious impact on the American vocabulary, as we saw in Chapter 3.

All the caveats that applied when discussing early regional dialects in Chapter 2 apply with even greater force when we look at the modern spread of dialects. The strands of linguistic variety are even more numerous and intertwined. Just as early regional dialects could not be traced directly back to specific spots in England, today's regional dialects cannot be explained wholly by nineteenth-century settlement patterns. Dialect boundaries can never be drawn with exactness. As the history described previously shows, settlement streams in America frequently overlapped or crossed. Many people upped stakes and moved to a different region more than once as their farms failed or later arrivals crowded them out. Many immigrants who came to the West spoke a language other than English. These factors contributed to dialects mingling and to some degree leveling out over time, although never completely.

Even the most linguistically coherent region has a large measure of variety. No two speakers talk exactly alike. Variables such as age, gender, social status, education, and ethnicity all make a difference. Some people may use some regionalisms, but not others, or not all the time. For example, they might avoid certain local words or constructions like *might could* or *needs washed*, even while retaining typical pronunciations, or they might "standardize" their speech in more formal situations, perhaps pronouncing more *r*'s than they would in casual conversation. Even people who live all their lives in the place where they were born may not have strong local dialect features.

Certain features usually associated with a particular region may occur in more than one part of the country. For example, *you'uns*, an identifying feature of Pittsburgh speech, is also heard in some parts of the South. Both Southerners and Northeasterners have historically dropped *r* before a vowel and shared other pronunciations as well. Sound changes that start in one part of the country may later spread to other regions. Dialect boundaries are identified based on bundles of features that the people inside them share, even if some of those features appear in other places.

Because language continually changes, new features have evolved in every region since these areas were settled. At the same time, once typical words and patterns have disappeared or become less common, or their range is contracting. Linguistic subregions have developed over time, with pronunciations, words, and grammatical structures that distinguish them from the rest of their dialect area. Changes can also span more than one region, although usually with pockets of exceptions. Certain cities, such as New York, Boston, and Charleston, have their own local speech patterns.

In spite of the porousness of linguistic borders and the ever-shifting nature of language, America's dialect map has stayed remarkably recognizable over time. Although every region has changed in various ways, each still displays a core of distinct dialectal traits. Some are newly sprung up or are still in progress, but others have long roots that connect present-day American English with its colonial past and settlement patterns. Keeping in mind that regional features are more tendencies than absolutes (some people may have all of them, others only a few), a review of the characteristic features of the different regions can reveal the evolution, as well as the current state, of English use around the country.

# New England and the North:
# Preserving and Innovating

New England is part of the North, yet distinct from it in several ways. English speakers have been settled in New England for about 400 years, so the area has had plenty of time to develop entrenched local features. It's by far the smallest linguistic region geographically (compare the West, which encompasses nearly every place west of the Mississippi), but it can be subdivided still further into eastern and western sub-regions. (It does have a relatively high population density compared with other regions.)[15] The exact boundaries vary, depending on which linguistic traits are taken into account, but a common division puts Maine, New Hampshire, most of Massachusetts, and Rhode Island in the east, with Vermont, western Massachusetts, and Connecticut in the west.

As might be expected given its long settlement history and traditionally rural character, eastern New England preserves some old linguistic traits. Eastern New Englanders make a three-way distinction for the vowels of *Mary*, *merry*, and *marry*, so *Mary* has a long vowel like the one in *bait* and sounds something 'may-ry', *merry* has a short vowel similar to the vowel in *bet*, and *marry* has a low front vowel like the one in most people's pronunciation of *bat*. As late as the mid-twentieth century, this distinction was widespread in the eastern part of the United States, but now it's confined to eastern New England and the areas around New York City and Philadelphia. (Many Southerners have a two-way distinction between *merry* and *marry*, but with *Mary* and *merry* pronounced alike. More generally, words spelled with *err* like *cherry* have the same vowel as in *bet*, while *arr* words like *carry* have the same vowel as in *bat*.)

Eastern New England English also differentiates between word pairs like *horse* and *hoarse*, *morning* and *mourning*, and *forty* and *fourteen*, pronouncing the second word of each pair with a longer vowel so it sounds like a long *o* or the word 'owe' (something like 'ho-arse', 'mo-arning', 'fo-arty'). This usage was once found in many places in the North and South, but today most Americans pronounce these pairs alike. (Some Southerners still make the distinction.)

Two iconic features of eastern New England pronunciation are popularly associated with a Boston accent, as heard, for example, in President John F. Kennedy's speeches or in the 1997 movie *Good Will Hunting*. However, they are common throughout the subregion. One is the preservation of the British pronunciation of the letter *a* as 'ah' that was introduced in the eighteenth century (see Chapter 1). In this pronunciation, the vowel in words like *glass*, *dance*, *path*, and *aunt* sounds like the one in *hot* [a] ('glahs', 'dahns', 'pahth', 'ahnt'). The other is the omission of the *r* sound between vowels and at the end of a word unless the next word starts with a vowel. For example, *park the car* sounds something like 'pahk the cah'. On the other hand, when a word ending in a vowel sound is followed by one starting with a vowel, New Englanders may insert an *r* where there isn't one, for instance, 'lore and order' or 'vaniller ice cream'.

Although *r*-lessness has been a defining trait of eastern New England, the *r* sound is starting to show up more often, especially outside the Boston area. Younger speakers say *r* more than older speakers, people with more education use more *r*'s, and people in professional positions use *r* more than blue-collar workers. This pattern suggests that saying your *r*'s has become linguistically prestigious. As we'll see in the discussion that follows, the *r* sound is becoming much more common in New York City and formerly *r*-less parts of the South as well, no doubt for the same reason.[16]

An unusual structure that's found primarily in eastern New England is the response *so don't I* as an affirmative, where most people would say *so do I*. According to one theory, positive *so don't I* and similar sentences are a response to an implied negative in the first speaker's utterance. For example, if someone says, "I play basketball," the implication is that the person they're talking to does not. To reject that implication, the hearer says, "Well, so don't I," meaning something like "Your suggestion that I don't play is wrong." The formula also works with other auxiliary verbs, always in response to a positive statement. Another example is *Sure, it's trendy, but so aren't plenty of other New York City clubs.*[17]

Western New England is more linguistically varied than the east, and most of its pronunciations and usages fall much more in line with the larger North region. For example, western New Englanders do not make a distinction between *Mary*, *merry*, and *marry*, or between *horse* and *hoarse*. The English-style *a* in *glass* and *aunt* is seldom heard. Western New Englanders also pronounce their *r*'s like the rest of the North.

New England has a number of distinguishing vocabulary words. A storm that blows up along the coast may be called a *nor'easter* or a *nor'wester*, depending on its direction. A stream is commonly called a *brook*, a sycamore tree is a *buttonwood*, and a mountain pass is a *notch*. New Englanders use *woodchuck* rather than *groundhog*, which is more common in other parts of the country. *Dooryard*, which once meant a garden patch around the front door, is now a place to park the car. Siding made of wooden slats is called *clapboard*. A traffic circle is a *rotary*. In Maine, *dight* means a little bit and any kind of poor behavior is called *foolishness*.

Two New England desserts are *apple slump* and *apple dowdy*. New Englanders and sometimes other Northerners also eat a kind of griddled corn cake called a *johnnycake*. A *quahog* is a clam found in the region. Besides tonic, Bostonians drink *frappes*, otherwise known as milkshakes. In Rhode Island, the word for a milkshake is *cabinet*. Sandwiches on long rolls are called *grinders*. *Hamburger* is often shortened to *hamburg*, and green onions are usually called *scallions* (a term also used in the South Atlantic states). Bostonians and southern New Englanders get their liquor from *packies*, short for *package stores*. Water fountains are *bubblers*. A common intensifier is *wicked*, as in *That's wicked good!*

The remainder of the North dialect region encompasses places that were first settled by waves of New Englanders. It takes in the northeastern corner of Pennsylvania and the New York City area. It also includes the Inland North, a subregion covering upstate New York and the states around the Great Lakes, including Michigan, Wisconsin, and northern parts of Illinois, Indiana, and Ohio. At its western edge, it stretches into Minnesota and Iowa.

In the early twentieth century, some linguists designated the English of the Inland North and upper Midwest "General American," partly as a way to distinguish it from the dialects of New England and the South. General American was considered the American English default. The linguist George Krapp, writing in 1925, described it as "a composite type, more or less an abstraction of generalized national habits." Krapp listed characteristic traits that included pronouncing *r*; pronouncing words like *glass*, *path*, and *aunt* with the vowel of *hat* rather than the vowel of *hot*; and a tendency to nasalize vowels.[18] (Nasalized vowels have long been associated with northern speech. Recall from Chapter 2 that several eighteenth-century observers commented on the region's "nasal twang.") According to this idea, features of the General American dialect were less noticeable than those found in New England or southern speech. If you spoke General American, no one would ask you where you were from.

The label "General" gave rise to the idea that the speech of these places is "neutral" in some way. Many people identify northern American English with the standardized speech of newscasters and similar figures and assume that speakers of this dialect "don't have an accent." In reality, the English of the North and upper Midwest includes a variety of identifiable linguistic features, just like every other region, and these are fully as distinctive as the sounds of New England and the South. Moreover, different parts of the North display different linguistic traits.[19]

One of the most distinctive pronunciation features in the region, especially in urban areas, is known as the Northern Cities Vowel Shift. Linguists first observed the Northern Cities Vowel Shift in the 1970s. Like the Great Vowel Shift described in the first chapter, the Northern Cities Shift is a chain shift. This means that a set of vowels underwent pronunciation changes, one or two vowels at a time, as part of a general pattern. The first vowel to be pronounced differently (with the tongue higher in the mouth) displaced the vowel that used to be pronounced in that space, nudging it into a new position. At the same time, it left a space open that another vowel could fill. Each shift in pronunciation triggered the next one. As a result, at the end of the shift, the words that these vowels appear in all sounded different than they had before, but they were still distinct from each other.[20]

In the Northern Cities Shift, the first vowel to move was probably the "short *a*" [ɑ] of words like *hot* and *cot*. The vowel in these words is typically pronounced low and back in the mouth, but people who have the shift push their tongue forward and make it tenser, so their pronunciation comes out sounding more like the way other dialects say *hat* and *cat*, with a low front vowel [æ]. For example, they might complain about the heat with a sentence that sounds to speakers of other dialects like *It's hat in here!*

This shift led naturally to the next one. The displaced vowel of words like *hat* and *cat* was pronounced farther up in the mouth, moving toward the high front vowel usually heard in words like *hit* and *kit* [ɪ]. As an extra twist, it gained a gliding *y* sound, so *hat* and *cat* sound something like 'he-yet' and 'ke-yet' ([eə] or [ɪə]) in this dialect. One frequently noted contrast is that the name *Ann*, when pronounced with the Northern Cities Shift, sounds almost like the common pronunciation of *Ian*.

Because the new pronunciation of words like *hat* and *cat* was so close to the usual pronunciation of words like *hit* and *kit*, the vowel of those words moved so they would continue to sound different from *hat* and *cat*. Their vowel sound shifted back and down toward the mid-front vowel of *bet* [ɛ], so a speaker might talk about 'hetting' the ball or packing a first-aid 'ket'. That move, in turn, pushed the pronunciation of *bet* closer to the way most people say *but*, with a midback vowel [ʌ] (*Don't but on it*).

Meanwhile, the original forward movement of the short *a* ([ɑ]) had left a space that the rounded midback vowel [ɔ] of words like *bought* and *boss* could slot into, so *bought* began to sound something like 'bot' (with [ɑ], the same vowel as in *hot*). (Not all speakers make a sound distinction between *bought* and 'bot', but most people in the North and East pronounce *bought* with a rounded 'aw' sound [ɔ] rather than a short *a* [ɑ]. See the discussion of word pairs like *cot* and *caught* that follows.) This development left room for the *but* vowel [ʌ] to move back and down and become rounded, so, in a final shift, *but* sounds more like other dialects' pronunciation of *bought* (with 'aw') (*I bot it, bought then returned it*).

Many people associate this pattern with the "flat" sounds of Chicago speech, but it occurs throughout the Inland North region. The pattern is most advanced in cities. The Northern Cities Shift was first recorded in Detroit, Chicago, Buffalo, Rochester, and Syracuse. It has also spread to other parts of Michigan, into Wisconsin, and into cities in the northern parts of Ohio and Illinois. The eastern edge of the Shift touches on the New England areas of southern Vermont, western Massachusetts, and northwestern Connecticut. The Northern Cities Shift has apparently stopped spreading and has even started to recede in some areas.[21]

Other parts of the Inland North have other distinctive pronunciations. Residents of the northern tier states (Minnesota, Wisconsin, northern Michigan, and North Dakota) have adopted the raised vowels of their Canadian neighbors, so the low back vowel sound heard in words like *bite* [aɪ] moves up toward the vowel heard in *boy* [ɔɪ] and the low back vowel sound of *bout* [ɑu] moves up toward the high back *boot* vowel [u]. *Bite* sounds more like 'boit' and *about* sounds more like 'aboot'. Northern tier English also shows some influence from the large number of Scandinavian immigrants. The *th* of words like *three* and *then* is pronounced like a *t* or *d* ('tree', 'den'). Lack of the gliding sound that most Americans make when pronouncing long vowels (vowels formed with a tense tongue) makes their vowels sound more clipped and European. For example, the *o* in *Minnesota* sounds more like 'oh' [o] than 'oh-uh' [oʊ]. The affirmative is sometimes said as 'yah'. The 1996 movie *Fargo* presents a version of the northern tier accent.

One pronunciation that distinguishes both the North and Southeast from other parts of the country is the way speakers in these places pronounce word pairs like *cot* and *caught*, *Don* and *dawn*, *stock* and *stalk*. Historically, most of the country pronounced such word pairs with two different vowels. The first word of each pair (*cot*) is said with a low back vowel like the one in *hot* [ɑ], while the vowel of the second (*caught*) is pronounced with rounded lips, like the sound of 'aw', (the back rounded vowel [ɔ] in some pronunciations of *bought*, described earlier). During the twentieth century, these two sounds merged for English speakers in many parts of the country, including the Midland and much of the West, so both words now rhyme with *hot*. This merger of sounds appears to be spreading, but most of New England, the North, and the South still maintain a distinction. Boston and north-eastern New England are exceptions. People in these areas, who pre-serve so many older linguistic features, have innovated by moving to adopt the merger.

The North also has a number of regional vocabulary words. As mentioned in Chapter 1, the Dutch in the Hudson Valley contributed several words that have since spread out of the area, such as *cruller* and *stoop*. Another example that's more restricted in range is *sawbuck* for a sawhorse. In upstate New York, the limited-access highway is called the *throughway* (or *thruway*), and the median strip is called the *mall*. In many other places in the North, the word for a limited-access highway is *parkway* or *expressway*. In Chicago, however, *parkway* has a different meaning. It refers to the grassy strip between the sidewalk and the street. Chicagoans call the walkway between two buildings a *gangway*.

A sandwich on a long roll is called a *submarine*, or sub, in the North, and a doughnut may be called a *sinker*. Upstate New Yorkers eat pot cheese rather than cottage cheese. *Brat* (rhymes with *hot*) is short for *bratwurst*, a kind of German pork sausage especially popular in the upper Midwest. Rhubarb is called *pie plant*, a nod to its most frequent use, a term that has also spread across much of the West. Northerners put frosting on their cake, not icing. Tap water comes out of a faucet, and publicly available water comes out of a drinking fountain. Meals may be cooked in a cast-iron frying pan called a *spider*, a term also heard in some parts of the Southeast.

Other Northernisms include *teeter-totter* for what other people call a see-saw, *kitty-corner* to mean diagonally, and *persnickety* for a fussy person. New Jerseyans visit the shore rather than the beach. A version of plural *you* heard mostly in northeastern Pennsylvania is *youse*. This form is found in print from the mid-nineteenth century. It can also turn up in New York City and elsewhere in the Northeast and North Midland. People in the Inland North, especially Minnesota and Wisconsin, use the phrases *come with* and *go with* without the noun or pronoun that other speakers would add. For example, someone might ask, "I'm going to the movies. Want to come with?" This usage is acceptable in some other parts of the country, but it's especially characteristic of the Inland North.

Perhaps the most recognizable subdialect of the North is the speech of New York City, heard in countless television shows and movies.[22] As in Boston, the most easily identified feature of New York City pronunciation is the lack of *r* after vowels and at the end of the word. However, the *r* sound is on the rise in New York, as it is elsewhere, although *r*-lessness is still very widespread. As noted in the discussion of Boston, a probable reason why *r*-ful speech is becoming more common is that *r* pronunciation is seen as prestigious or more "correct."

A survey conducted in the early 1960s by linguist William Labov, probably the first to examine this feature of New York speech, elicited *r* pronunciations from salesclerks in three New York City department stores by asking for some item located on the fourth floor. Broadly speaking, the more exclusive and expensive the store, the more often employees pronounced the *r* in those words, presumably influenced by the socioeconomic status of the majority of their customers.[23]

Besides socioeconomic class, the percentage of postvocalic and word-final *r*'s someone articulates depends on factors such as age and the situation. The middle and upper classes say their *r*'s more often, and young people use more *r*'s than older people. Young upper-class speakers use it consistently, accounting for most of the overall rise in use. Speakers who are middle-aged or older tend to use *r* more in formal situations when they are more conscious of their speech. New Yorkers also insert *r*'s between two vowel sounds in phrases like 'lore and order'. White speakers always say *r* between vowels, but Black speakers, who use *r* less often, sometimes do not.

New York City has other distinctive pronunciations as well. The vowel sound in words like *coffee* and *talk* is fronted so the words sound more like 'cawfee' and 'tawk'. Certain words that have the vowel of *bat* are pronounced with a gliding sound, so *bat* and *cab* sound something like 'be-yat' and 'ke-yab'. The pronunciation of *oi* as *er* and vice versa, as in 'erl' for *oil* and 'goil' for *girl*, was once a classic indicator of New York City speech, but has died out in recent years. (These pronunciations are also part of old-fashioned New Orleans speech, but are now rare there as well.) In the past, the *th* in words like *three* was sometimes pronounced like *t*, making *thirty-third* sound like 'toity-toid', but that pronunciation is also extinct or nearly so these days.

Besides pronunciations, New York City has its own set of vocabulary words. Yiddish is especially prevalent in New York. Although a number of Yiddish words have entered the general American vocabulary (see Chapter 3), some that are less familiar, such as *bupkis* (nothing) and *nebbish* (a nonentity), are more common in New York. The sandwiches known as subs and grinders elsewhere are called *heroes* in New York. New Yorkers drink *egg creams*, a mixture of chocolate syrup, soda water, and milk that contains neither egg nor cream, although it once did. Regular coffee means coffee with milk. Manhattan is known to residents and those in nearby areas as *the City*.

Where Bostonians say *wicked*, New Yorkers say *mad* (for instance, a mad good egg cream). Most of the country stands in line, but New Yorkers stand on line. Another grammatical structure specific to New York is the use of *would* plus a form of *be* in *if* clauses. Instead of *If I were king of the world* or *If I had been king*, a New Yorker might say, *If I would be king* or *If I would have been king*.

# The South: A Changing
# Linguistic Landscape

The South has the most immediately recognizable way of talking of any place in the country, with the possible exception of New York City. That isn't necessarily a plus, since strongly marked dialectal speech is often stigmatized. Many Southerners, however, embrace their dialect as a proud badge of regional identity. In recent decades, the southern dialect has evolved as the area's population grows more diverse. Some traditional hallmarks of southern speech are disappearing or becoming less common, while others are still going strong. As we saw in Chapter 4, at least one high-profile Southernism, *y'all*, seems to be expanding outside its original boundaries.[24]

The South has been settled by English speakers longer than any other part of the country, but the language of the region is based on that of the settlers who started arriving in the 1640s rather than the original Jamestown colonists. Even so, the South has had nearly as long as New England to develop its own way of talking. Like New Englanders, Southerners preserve some longtime usages, especially in rural areas. The familiar "southern accent," however, is a relatively recent innovation, incorporating several pronunciations that did not appear until the mid- or late nineteenth century.[25]

The South covers a substantial territory, sweeping from Virginia in the east to central Texas in the west, including the southeastern and Gulf Coast states. It also encompasses an "Inland" or "Upper" subregion that covers Kentucky, Tennessee, and Arkansas, as well as the western uplands of Virginia, the Carolinas, and Georgia, sometimes referred to as the Appalachian subregion. A few southern linguistic features can also be heard in the southernmost sections of Illinois, Iowa, and Indiana, and parts of Missouri.

In some ways, the South is more linguistically homogeneous than the North. The Gulf states were largely settled by descendants of the people who colonized the coastal South, so traditional speech patterns carried over from one place to the next. However, the language of the Inland South, while it shares certain traits with the coastal areas, is closer to the speech of the Midland in other ways. That's not unexpected, since the Scots-Irish made up the majority of early settlers in both places.

The South experienced tremendous demographic shifts over the twentieth century. The rise of industrialization in the decades leading up to World War II drew many rural Southerners into cities and towns to find work, turning the population much more urban and bringing together people from different parts of the South. In the latter part of the century, large numbers of Northerners relocated to the region, and cities like Atlanta became home to people with many different dialectal patterns. Because of these changes, some localized vernaculars have died out. Other characteristic southern features grew more widespread as speakers from different parts of the region mingled. One example is the merger of the vowels in *pin* and *pen* ([ɪ] and [ɛ]), so both words are pronounced with a high front vowel [ɪ] that matches most dialects' pronunciation of *pin*. The result of these recent adjustments is a more uniform dialect across the South, although, as always, with exceptions.

Most people identify southern speech through the pronunciation, in particular the sound known as the southern drawl. The drawling effect comes from breaking certain vowels into two syllables, so, for example, *bid* and *bad* sound something like 'bee-id' [biɪd] and 'bay-id' [bæɪd]. The drawl, like many pronunciations closely associated with southern speech, is a late-developing feature that appeared sometime in the mid-nineteenth century.[26]

The southern drawl is connected with a series of sound changes known as the Southern Vowel Shift. The triggering shift was the loss of the gliding sound that's typical in most dialects when pronouncing the vowel of words like *high* and *time*, which in most dialects starts with an 'ah' sound and ends with a short i sound [aɪ]. In the speech of people who have the Southern Shift, the vowel "unglides," so the second part of the sound is dropped. *High time* sounds more like 'hah tahm' (with [a:]). This change occurs before voiced consonants (articulated with vibration of the vocal cords) like *m, b, g,* and *z,* and also at the end of a word. Speakers in the Inland South may further expand the ungliding of the *high time* vowel to include consonants pronounced without voicing, such as *t, s,* and *k.* In this dialect, *nice white rice* sounds like 'nahs whaht rahs'.

The Southern Shift has further stages, although they are more geographically restricted. In the second stage, the front vowels in words like *bit* and *beat* seem almost to switch places. *Bit* starts off with the long vowel in *beat* and then moves toward the short vowel of *bit*, so it's pronounced something like 'bee-it' [biɪt], and *beat* starts off with the sound of *bit* and moves toward *beat*, so it's said something like 'bih-eet' [bɪit]. In the next stage of the shift, the same kind of swtich happens to the front vowels in words like *bait* and *bet*. *Bait* sounds more like 'beh-ate' [bɛet], and *bet* sounds more like 'bay-et' [beɛt].

The second stage of the Southern Shift covers most of the lower South as far west as central and north Texas. It is completely absent from the speech of southeastern cities like Charleston, Atlanta, Savannah, and Richmond, and anywhere in Florida. The final stage is limited to the Appalachian areas of Tennessee and most of Alabama. The southern drawl is on the decline everywhere, heard mainly among older speakers. The Southern Shift as a whole is not part of African American speech, although White and Black Southerners do share other pronunciations.[27]

Besides the Southern Vowel Shift, the southern dialect has a number of other distinctive sounds. Vowels that are typically pronounced in the back of the mouth shift forward, so the high back vowel of *boot* [u] sounds more like 'bewt' [iu], the midback vowel of *boat* [o] sounds like 'bay-oat' [eo], and the low back vowel of *bout* [ɑu] sounds closer to 'bay-out' [æu]. Some Southerners have lost the distinction between certain vowels before *l*, so pairs like *feel* and *fill* both sound like the way most people pronounce *fill*, and *sale* and *sell* both sound like *sell*. For some speakers, the vowel sound of *oil* lost its glide and sounds the same as *all*. The addition of a gliding sound to the *u* in words like *tune*, *duty*, and *Tuesday* to make them 'tyune', 'dyuty', and 'Tyuesday' was once a common pronunciation, but this feature is dying out.[28]

The lack of a distinction between *pin* and *pen* (so they may need to be differentiated as an ink pin or a safety pin) is widespread across the South and also spills over into the southern parts of Illinois, Indiana, and parts of Missouri and Kansas. Many Southerners continue to pronounce *wh* and *w* differently, so pairs like *whale* and *wail* and *whether* and *weather* are not homonyms, a distinction that most of the country lost some time ago. As noted earlier, some speakers, mostly in the Southeast, still say *horse* and *hoarse* differently (pronouncing *hoarse* more like 'ho-arse'). Southerners also differentiate between *cot* and *caught* and similar words, although the sounds are starting to merge in one or two places, such as west Texas. Another identifying pronunciation is 'greazy' for *greasy*.

With the exception of the Inland South, Southerners traditionally have not pronounced the *r* sound after vowels or at the end of a word. In recent times, however, r pronunciation has exploded around the region. In contrast to New York, r-fulness is not strongly correlated with social class or the formality of the situation. More educated speakers do tend to use more r's, but the main factor driving r pronunciation is age. Younger White speakers consistently use r in all positions. Among African Americans, its use is mixed, with r-lessness more common.

Besides historically pronouncing r, Appalachian speakers of the Inland South have some other widely recognized pronunciations that distinguish them from speakers elsewhere in the region. These include replacing a with y at the end of a word so *soda* becomes 'sody' and *extra* is 'extry', and replacing ow with er, so *window* sounds like 'winder' and *hollow* sounds like 'holler'. Among older speakers of the dialect, a short a before f, s, sh, and th may lengthen, so *grass* may sound more like *grace*.

Several grammatical features specific to the South also set the region's dialect apart. Multiple modals like *might could*, discussed in earlier chapters, are common throughout the South. *Fixin' to* meaning about to is still a robust feature, as is *liketa* (*I like to died*). Southerners combine *all the* with an adjective to mean as much as, for example, in *That's all the far they got* and *That's all the high I can jump*. Some Southerners also use *done* to describe a finished action, as in *She done left already*.

Another grammatical construction is the inversion of a negative auxiliary to make a positive statement, such as *Can't nobody beat us* to mean that nobody can beat us, and *Can't everybody go at once* to mean that everybody can't go at once. Negative inversion is becoming more familiar and accepted around the country, but is still stronger in the South than elsewhere. Negative inversion and the usages described in the previous paragraph are heard in the speech of both White and Black Southerners, as well as in African American English outside the South. However, one group may use a construction more or less often or in a slightly different way.

Southerners also use indirect object pronouns in ways that are different from the rest of the country. For example:[29]

- I got me a job.
- Here's you some candy.
- He's looking for us a place to live.

Outside the South, these sentences would be paraphrased something like *I got myself a job*, *Here's some candy for you*, and *He's looking for a place for us to live*. These three constructions are acceptable all over the South and into the southern edges of the Midland. They are most common in the Inland South.

The first type of example, *I got me a job*, appears to be catching on more broadly in popular culture. An Internet search for the phrases *I love me some*, *I got me some*, and *I need me some* turns up countless examples, including an entry for *I love me some* on the website *Urban Dictionary*. The popularity of this specific phrase was probably helped by the 1997 release of the Toni Braxton song "I Love Me Some Him." However, the other two phrases also got numerous hits.

A variety of vocabulary words are specific to all or part of the South. Like other regions, these include several food words. Southerners call green peppers *bell peppers*, put icing rather than frosting on cake, and eat butter beans rather than lima beans. *Corn dodgers* are a kind of baked or griddled cornmeal cake, and *hush puppies* are balls of deep-fried cornmeal batter. Other dishes, found mainly in South Carolina and the surrounding area, include *chicken bog*, a chicken and rice dish, and *hoppin' John*, a dish of rice and black-eyed peas traditionally eaten on New Year's Day for good luck. Food may be cooked in a skillet, the southern term for a frying pan, also heard in the Midland. Two sandwiches found in New Orleans are the *po'boy*, that area's version of a sandwich on a long bun, and the *muffuletta*, filled with cold cuts and a chopped olive salad. New Orleanians get their drinks in a *go-cup*.

Other terms heard mostly in the South are *puny* to mean unwell or weak, *catty-corner* for kitty-corner (also heard in other places), *polecat* for skunk, *sack* for bag, and *haunt* for a ghost (sometimes spelled and said *hant*). To carry someone means to provide transportation or escort someone, as in *Her mother carried her to school today*. To bless someone out is to give the person a scolding, what people in other places might describe as cussing out. *Cut off* means to turn off, as in *Please cut off the lights*, and *wait on* means wait for, as in *I'm not waiting on you much longer*.

A faucet is a *spigot* in the South, a porch may be called a *veranda*, and a wardrobe might be a *chifforobe* or an *armoire*, the latter especially in Mississippi and Alabama. The word *yonder*, archaic in most dialects, is used as a directional word suggesting a fair distance, for example, *He's over yonder*. In the Appalachians, a mountain pass is called a *gap*, and *poke* may be used for a bag. In Kentucky and Tennessee, a lot is *oodlins*.

A casual southern greeting is *hey* instead of the *hi* heard elsewhere. *Hey* is another Southernism that is catching on outside its home region.

The speech of Charleston, South Carolina, is an example of a unique vernacular that has gone largely obsolete since the late twentieth century. Although Charlestonians have many of the same Southernisms as the larger South, Charleston pronunciation once stood out for its distinctly identifiable vowels. The vowels heard in *bait* and *boat* were pronounced with a gliding sound, something like 'be-yate' and 'be-yote'. (Compare with the usual Southern Shift, where *bait* sounds more like 'beh-ate'.) So were vowels following the *k* or *g* sound, so *car* and *garden* sounded like 'ke-yah' and 'ge-yahden' (since the *r* was not pronounced). The raising of the vowel in *bout* was also common, resulting in a Canadian-like pronunciation closer to *boot*. The *a* in *tomato* was short like the vowel in *hot* (so 'tomahto'), and *ear* and *air* were both pronounced the way other dialects say *air* [ɛɪ]. Most of these Charlestonian sounds are dying out. Instead, Charleston is adopting pronunciations from other places. It is becoming more *r*-ful and, among younger speakers, the vowels of *cot* and *caught* are merging (as they are beginning to among younger speakers in other places).[30]

## The Midland: Converging Dialects

The Midland region is more vaguely defined than the North or the South, which is explainable by the mix of people who settled in the area. It centers on western Pennsylvania and spreads out from there, taking in the middle sections of Ohio, Indiana, and Illinois, as well as Kansas, Nebraska, and Missouri, and possibly northern Oklahoma. Some linguists have suggested that most or all of the Midland could be incorporated into either the North or the South.[31] The South Midland shares many linguistic traits with the South, especially in the pronunciation of its vowels, while the northern edge of the region has some features of the North. However, the Midland as a whole shares a bundle of features that don't exactly match those of any other region.

Dialectologist William Labov and his co-authors have suggested that the Midland might have a better claim to being called "General American" than the Inland North these days, as several of their pronunciations are the most common ones across the country.[32]

Midlanders have always pronounced their *r*'s, as nearly everyone in the United States does today. Midland speakers also generally pronounce word pairs like *cot* and *caught* and *Don* and *dawn* with the same short-*a* vowel [ɑ], a trend that is growing in many parts of the country. This pronunciation is strongest in western Pennsylvania, but is heard nearly everywhere in the region. There's some evidence that the merged pronunciation arrived in western Pennsylvania as early as the late eighteenth century, imported by the Scots-Irish who first settled there. Recall from Chapter 2 that Noah Webster remarked in 1789 on Midland residents' tendency to pronounce words like *off* and *soft* with an 'ah' sound (*aff* and *saft*) rather than an 'aw' sound. If his observation was accurate, they were probably also saying *caught* so it rhymed with *cot*.[33]

South Midlanders sometimes sound a little like Southerners. People in this subregion tend to push the back vowel of *bout* forward and drop the gliding sound in *time* so it sounds like 'tahm', two spillovers from the South dialect region. Also, in central Ohio, the vowels of pairs like *feel* and *fill* and *sale* and *sell* are moving closer together, another southern feature.

The linguistic traits that define the Midland more than any other are grammatical. Some are shared with other parts of the country, but no other region has the same combination of possible grammatical structures. These are yet another enduring linguistic inheritance from the Scots-Irish. As described in Chapter 2, these usages have all been in evidence since early settlement times, and may still be found in parts of Ireland, Scotland, and northern England today, suggesting that they were imports rather than American innovations.

One such construction is *need* or *want* followed by *in*, *out*, *on*, or *off*. Usually, the phrase is directional, but can sometimes be abstract:[34]

- The cat wants out.
- Stop the bus—this lady wants off.
- If you're organizing a betting pool, I want in.

Speakers from all social classes and age groups use this formula throughout western Pennsylvania and the Midwest. It is more common in casual speech than in formal situations.

Another Midland way to use *need* and *want* is to follow them directly with a past participle without the intervening *to be* that most dialects call for:[35]

- The cat wants fed.
- That car needs washed.

This usage is not as widespread as the *want in* type, being heavily concentrated in western Pennsylvania and the North Midland. It is also still found in Scotland and northern England. Although used by White speakers of all social classes, few if any Black speakers include it as part of their speech.

Another grammatical feature found in the Midland is "positive" *anymore*, so called because it's used without the negative verb that would accompany *anymore* in most dialects. For example, instead of saying, *That restaurant is so crowded, we don't go there anymore*, someone from the Midland might say, *Anymore, we avoid that place—it's too crowded*. The meaning is similar to that of *nowadays*, and it can usually be used in the same way. Scattered instances of positive *anymore* have been found in other parts of the country, but the feature is by far most common in the Midland region.

Just as the South has *all the far* and similar phrases, the Midland has *all the farther*, as in *That's all the farther we got yesterday* and *Is that all the higher you can jump?* The two variations are undoubtedly related. *All the* with a comparative adjective was once heard wherever the Scots-Irish settled, but it is now limited to the Midwest and Pennsylvania.

The Midland dialect also encompasses vocabulary, although some words are also heard in the Inland South. Midland speakers say *bucket* instead of *pail*, *fishing worm* for an earthworm, and *mud dauber* for a kind of wasp, a term also used in the West. In the North Midland, *grinnie* is the name for what most people call a chipmunk. *Scrapple* is a breakfast dish originating with the Pennsylvania Dutch. Scraps of pork are made into a mush with cornmeal or flour, then shaped into loaves, sliced, and fried. Salt pork may be called *side meat* and bacon called *fat meat*, a term also heard in the South. String beans are called green beans. Roller shades are called *blinds*.

Midland babies are pushed around in *baby buggies*, not baby carriages, and they are pushed along the pavement, not the sidewalk. A *little piece* means a short distance. The old Scottish word *fornent*, meaning opposite to or in front of, is still in use. *Brag on* means brag about, also occasionally heard in a few eastern places, and *turn in* means to get to work, as in *We turned in and cleaned the whole house*. A distinctively pronounced word is *wash*, which Midlanders say as 'warsh'. As noted in

Chapter 2, *whenever* may be used for *when* in a sentence like *Whenever my grandma died, we all went home for the funeral.* This use is called punctual *whenever* because it specifies a particular one-time event.

Certain Midland cities have their own ways of talking. In Philadelphia, accents can sound very similar to those of New York City, but with the *r* sound. Philadelphians also have some local pronunciations. The vowel of *right* tends to move back and get rounded, so *right* sounds something like 'roight'. The short *e* moves back before *r* and *l* so *very* sounds like 'vurry' and *fell* sounds like 'full'. The long front vowels heard in *bait* and *beat* shift backward before *g*, making *bagel* sound like 'beggle' and the name of the Philadelphia football team sound like the 'Iggles'. Words like *attitude* and *beautiful* may be pronounced 'attytude' and 'beautyful'.

Philadelphia's grammatical features are mixed. Philadelphians say *youse* like some other Northeastern speakers and *go with* like the Inland North. However, they align with the Midland in saying *want in* and using positive *anymore*. Babies in Philadelphia ride in a *baby coach*. Classic Philly sandwiches on long buns are *hoagies*, the local version of a sub, and *cheesesteaks*, a bun filled with sliced steak, melted cheese, and maybe grilled onions and peppers.

A slang word particular to the Philadelphia area is *jawn*, an all-purpose noun that can stand in for just about anything, as in *Pass me that jawn* or *What's all that jawn in your car?* or *I've got a lot of jawn to do for class.* This use originated from the word *joint* in the sense of a place (*This joint is rockin'*). In the late 1970s, hip-hoppers expanded the meaning of *joint* to cover a thing as well as a place. By the 1980s, the word had expanded again to its current uses and the broader Philadelphia public had adopted it.[36]

On the other side of the state, the language of Pittsburgh displays a collection of high-profile traits.[37] Much of Pittsburgh's pronunciation is in line with the rest of the Midlands. The sounds of *cot* and *caught* are completely merged, but unusually, they both sound more like *caught* (with an 'aw' [ɔ] sound). Before *l*, the long vowels of *pool* and *steel* are starting to relax, so the words sound closer to *pull* and *still* (and the football team is the *Stillers*). In common with the South Midland, *time* is pronounced 'tahm'. *Wash* is sometimes pronounced 'warsh', but this sound is becoming less common. The distinctive pronunciation of 'drooth' for *drought*, in place since early settlement times, is still around.

Pittsburghese also includes several vocabulary words, again largely traceable to the Scots-Irish. *Redd up* means to clean and tidy, a diamond is a town square. Another Scots-Irish word is *neb*, slang for nose, originally an animal snout. To neb is to pry or nose around. A neighbor who does so is nebby and might be told to neb out. To jag is to annoy or tease someone. A jagger is a small, pointed object and a jag off is an irritating, foolish, or otherwise problematic person. To jag someone off is to annoy, tease, disparage, or reject the person. Pittsburghers also use punctual *whenever*.

Other words specific to the area are *spicket* for a spigot and *gum band* for a rubber band. A hutch, which usually signifies a cupboard, means a chest of drawers in Pennsylvania. Two local foods are *chipped ham*, a term for thinly sliced ham that originally referred to a product sold by the food retailer Isaly's, and *city chicken*, cubed pork or veal that's been breaded, skewered, and grilled. Directions include *upstreet* and *downstreet*. A usage that probably comes from the Pennsylvania Dutch is *leave* where most people would say *let*, for example, in a sentence like *Just leave it be*. As discussed in Chapter 4, *yinz* for plural *you* is one of the best-known features of Pittsburgh speech.

At the western edge of the Midland is the city of St. Louis. It was long the jumping-off point for the Far West, so settlers from all parts of the country converged there. Many were just passing through. Of those who stayed, most settlers before the Civil War were from the South and South Midlands. Afterward, more new arrivals came from the Inland North. St. Louisans sound more like Northerners than do the people in the surrounding rural areas, but they have a mix of traits. They say 'warsh', *want in*, *bag* instead of *sack*, *bucket* instead of *pail*, and *string beans* for green beans. A local St. Louis pronunciation is saying words that are spelled with an *or* as though they were spelled with an *ar*, so *fork*, *storm*, and *born* sound like 'fark', 'starm', and 'barn'. St. Louisans make a distinction between the sounds in *horse* and *hoarse*, but *horse* is pronounced 'harse'. Although the *ar* for *or* pronunciation was once very common, it has become a negative stereotype since the 1990s and is now heard less often, especially among young people.

## The West: Still under Construction

Many Americans think of the vast expanse of land between the Rocky Mountains and the Pacific Coast as dialect-free territory. Because English speakers arrived in the region relatively recently, the kinds of widely recognized speech patterns that make the dialects of the East so distinctive haven't yet had time to evolve. In spite of that limitation, the West has its share of linguistic variety, with different subregions in the process of developing their own dialectal patterns. Some aspects of western speech are also spreading eastward. California is so culturally dominant that dialectal changes starting on the West Coast have a good chance of influencing the language habits of the rest of the country.

To some extent, the western dialect can be defined by what makes it different from other dialects. The merger between the vowels of *cot* and *caught* is nearly universal in the West, which distinguishes it from most of the North and Southeast. Westerners also uniformly pronounce words like *marry* and *carry* with the same vowel as *merry*, so their speech is different in that way from much of New England and the South. The West also has other typical pronunciations that are not heard in the East, or that are heard in different combinations.

Many people from Texas and Oklahoma settled in the Southwest, and some features of their southern pronunciations have lingered there. These include the pronunciation of the *bout* vowel more forward in the mouth (so it sounds like 'bay-out' [æu]), and pronouncing words like *time* and *ride* closer to 'tahm' and 'rahd'. This pronunciation also shows up in parts of the Pacific Northwest. The intermountain West has another feature that was probably imported from the South Midland. That's the pronunciation of the short vowel of *bet* so it sounds more like the long vowel of *bait* when it occurs before the sounds of 'sh' [ʃ] or 'zh'[ʒ]. In this dialect, *special* is pronounced something like 'spayshul' and *measure* sounds like 'mayzhure' (with an [e]) instead of [ɛ].[38]

Utahns have several distinctive pronunciations. One is dropping the *t* before a syllabic *n* or *m* sound, so *mountains* sounds like 'moun-ens' [mɑuʔənz]. This pronunciation is heard most commonly among young females. Utah speakers also pronounce the vowel before *l* in words like *steel* and *sale*, so they sound closer to *still* and *sell*. A Utah sound that used to be heard more often, especially in Salt Lake City, is the pronunciation of *or* like *ar*, so *cord* sounded like *card*, similar to the pattern heard in St. Louis. This pronunciation is now in decline.[39]

Beginning in the 1980s, California vowel sounds began shifting in a variety of ways. In the California Vowel Shift, the long back vowels in *boat* and *boot* are pronounced more forward in the mouth, so *totally cool* sounds something like 'tee-yotally kewl'. The short back vowel of *but* is also moving forward closer to the short front vowel of *bet*, and the short front vowels are lowering. These changes make *bit* sound more like other dialects' pronunciation of *bet* and *bet* more like most people's pronunciation of *bat*. *Put a little bit of money on a bet* might come out sounding to other speakers like *put a lettle bet of money on a bat*. An exception to the lowering trend comes when the high short vowel in *bit* occurs before *ng*. In this case, it raises and tenses up, so *thing* sounds like 'theen'. The vowel merry-go-round continues with the low front vowel of *bat* moving toward the back of the mouth, so *bat* sounds closer to 'bot' (*a baseball bot*), except when the sound comes before nasal consonants (*n* or *m*). In that case, it picks up a glide, so *band* sounds something like 'be-and'.[40]

Along with "uptalk," the rising intonation that turns statements into questions, this constellation of sound changes is stereotyped as the surfer dude/Valley girl accent, heard, for example, in the speech of Cher Horowitz in the 1996 movie *Clueless*. However, this speech pattern is very common among young White Californians generally, not just Valley girls, and is also typical of many young Chinese American speakers. Most African Americans and Chicano English speakers have not adopted it to any great degree. The California Shift is spreading to other western states as well, although in varying combinations (see Chapter 9 for more about this new trend). The uptalk intonation has gone national and is now heard in the speech of Americans everywhere, especially younger ones.

Another California feature that is gaining ground in other places is pronouncing the combination of *d* followed by *n* or *nt* as a full syllable ('den' or 'dent') even when the syllable would normally be unstressed. In typical American English, vowels in unstressed syllables are reduced to an 'uh' sound [ə], so the second syllable of words like *hidden* and *garden* is pronounced almost without a vowel—'hidn', 'gardn'. In the English of many younger California speakers, this reduced vowel is pronounced as spelled, so *hidden* is 'hid-den' and *garden* is 'gar-den'. Even when a vowel isn't present in the spelling, the syllable after *d* gets a full pronunciation, so *didn't* is said 'did-dent'. This pronunciation is now heard outside California as well.

Like the other dialect regions, western states have some identifiable vocabulary words. The term of choice for major highways is *freeway*. Flat-topped hills are called *buttes* in many parts of the upper West and *mesas* in the Southwest (from the Spanish word for table). A mountain valley is called a *park* in Colorado, and a *hole* in some other western states (for instance, Jackson Hole, Wyoming). Another word for a small, steep-sided valley is a *gulch*. Big cats known as cougars elsewhere are often called *mountain lions* in the West. Horses and cattle are held in a *corral* (again from Spanish), whereas in the East they might be kept in a paddock or pen. A herd is called by the Spanish word *parada* (from *parada de caballos* meaning relay of horses). Alfalfa is called *lucerne*. Birds that steal food, especially jays, are known as *camp robbers*.

Utah is the only state where *gentile* has the meaning of anyone who isn't Mormon, instead of its more usual meaning of anyone who isn't Jewish. Utahns also exclaim *For fun!* or *For cute!* when pleased with some object or activity.

California has some distinctive terms for plant life. Fritillaries are called *mission bells*, and St. John's wort is known as *Klamath weed* or *goldwire*. A name for jimson weed is *angel's trumpet*. Californians experience the *Santa Ana wind*, a hot, dusty wind blowing down from the Santa Ana Mountains. They also have *tule fogs*. Tule is a bulrush that grows in low-lying land along rivers where the fog builds up.

California also has other local vocabulary. A *looky-loo* is someone who shops around without buying, or by extension, a *rubbernecker*. Californians who want to get something done better *get off the dime*. This expression for getting a move-on can be heard in other places, too, but seems most prevalent in California. Northern California's catch-all intensifier word is *hella*, as in *That's hella good* or *She's hella crazy*. California foods include Hangtown fry and cioppino. *Hangtown fry* is an omelet with oysters and bacon, reputedly invented in the mining town of Placerville, once known as Hangtown. *Cioppino* is a fish and shellfish stew. In spite of its Italian name (from a Ligurian fish soup), cioppino was invented in nineteenth-century San Francisco as a way to make the most of the day's catch.

In the Pacific Northwest, people go to the coast rather than the beach or the shore. Any item that costs a lot is said to be *spendy*. The strip of grass between the sidewalk and the curb is known as the *parking strip*. A climate feature is the *Chinook wind*, a warm, dry wind out of the Southwest. The Pacific Northwest is the place for microbrews, beer crafted in local breweries, which might be served at a *no-host bar*, where people pay for their own drinks. In the East, such an arrangement is known as a *cash bar*.

This review of American regional dialects highlights the highly flexible and accommodating nature of language, including American English. While the country can be divided into distinct dialect territories, and the boundaries of those territories have remained fairly stable over time, the exact nature of the linguistic features that make each one different is constantly shifting. Over the past few centuries, pronunciations have changed, sometimes drastically, and words have gone in and out of fashion. Features that were once confined to a single region or a small section of one have spilled over their boundaries into other parts of the country. The particulars of the ways that people speak are affected not only by where they grew up, but also by their awareness of trends, their age, their education, the social groups they identify with, and much more. As we'll see in the next chapters, American usage continues to build on the past, but at the same time is always taking off in new directions.

# 6

# Ethnic Dialects

## Dialects without Borders

When twentieth-century linguists started systematically recording the speech patterns of Americans around the country, they noted language varieties that couldn't be defined solely in terms of geography. One early mention of such a case comes from dialectologists Raven and Virginia McDavid. Describing the results of field work from the 1940s, the McDavids remarked that Chicago-born African American students at the University of Illinois "have preserved many characteristic southern words that are unknown to white students of the same age and city." They also found something similar in Michigan, where young African Americans pronounced words like *law* and *dance* with vowel sounds more typical of the Upper South than their native state. This pronunciation was a departure from the speech of their parents' generation, which was broadly the same as that of White residents of Michigan.[1]

These young people had adopted a way of talking that identified more strongly with their ethnicity and cultural heritage than with their region. As we saw in Chapters 4 and 5, African American English shares several grammatical and pronunciation features with the vernacular of White Southerners, but unlike that dialect, it isn't geographically bound. A European American who says *She done left already* and pronounces *dance* something like 'day-ence' is almost guaranteed to hail from somewhere in the southern United States, but an African American with similar usages might just as easily be from Chicago or Detroit. While all dialects are about their users' identity and attitudes, regional dialects are generally pinned to their place of origin. Ethnic dialects (sometimes called socioethnic dialects or ethnolects) transcend that limitation. They are more about a shared history and background than a shared current location.

For example, geography is irrelevant for the distinctive sentence intonation used by many Native Americans. This alternating high and low pitch, sometimes described as "singsong," can often be heard at intertribal gatherings like powwows and in other casual settings. The speech of storyteller Thomas Builds-the-Fire in the 1998 movie *Smoke Signals* provides one well-known example.[2] This intonation pattern isn't based on a specific ancestral language. Those who use it may speak any one of a number of unrelated Native languages, or only English, and they might be members of a tribe anywhere in the country. In the words of an anonymous website commenter, "The rez [reservation] accent knows no borders."[3] Rather, it identifies its users as members of a larger community.

Chicano English, spoken by many Mexican Americans in California and the Southwest, is more geographically constrained, but it's another example of a dialect based on a shared background and ethnic identity. Speakers of Chicano English are descendants of Spanish speakers. Certain features of Chicano English, such as vowel sounds and sentence stress patterns, show Spanish-language influence, reflecting the region's history as a part of Mexico. However, Chicano English is a variety of American English, and those who use it are native English speakers who may or may not speak Spanish themselves.

Although ethnic dialects transcend geographical borders, they resemble regional dialects in other ways. Like regional speech varieties, they're not monolithic. Just as not all residents of the Midland or New England or California adopt the typical linguistic patterns of their area, not everyone in an ethnic speech community uses dialectal features to the same extent or even at all. Some people may adopt certain expressions or pronunciations, but not others. Older speakers, especially of the middle class, tend to have more standardized speech habits. One study of older Chicano English speakers showed that while they used some vowel sounds typical of that dialect, their grammatical structures were the same as those of other Californians. Some features of a dialect may be seldom used, even by those who speak it consistently.[4]

Speakers of ethnic dialects are also like everyone else in adopting different speech styles depending on the situation. Some people may use dialectal features only with family and close friends. For instance, Native American college students, talking about their "rez" accents, have made comments like "It comes out in casual settings," or "In an academic setting, I speak differently."[5]

Ethnolects evolve over time, as all language does, with changes often introduced by younger people. One example is the sound change that the McDavids noted among young African Americans in mid-twentieth-century Michigan. Another is a grammatical structure first recorded for African American English during the late 1980s. Adolescent speakers started to use *had* plus a verb in sentences where other English varieties usually call for a simple past: *I had got strep throat on the last day of school* instead of *I got strep throat on the last day of school*. When new, this usage was confined to younger speakers, but it's now become an established part of the dialect.[6]

Ethnic dialects also overlap with regional dialects, since their speakers live in different parts of the country. Linguist John McWhorter has written, "Without a doubt, Black English manifests itself in different subdialects nationwide." As one instance, he recalled a St. Louis woman whose speech combined some typical African American traits with St. Louis vowels, such as saying 'wheelchur' for *wheelchair*.[7] A recent look at the language of Twitter users showed regional variation in the expression *put up* to mean put away (*I'm putting up the groceries now*). Among White speakers, *put up* is restricted to the South, but for Black speakers it extends to the Midwest as well. The most likely explanation is that it was part of the speech of African Americans who migrated to the area from the South during the early twentieth century. Another study of "Black Twitter" focused on nonstandard spellings that reflect pronunciation. It revealed that spelling preferences vary by region, but the regional boundaries are not the same as those of the standard regional dialects. Rather, they reflect earlier African American settlement patterns. Similarly, a recent study of English spoken by the Reno-Sparks Indian Colony of Nevada shows that members are adopting some of the sounds of the California Vowel Shift while also developing pronunciations specific to their community.[8]

What sets ethnic dialects apart is the unique circumstances of their development. The three varieties of English discussed in this chapter—African American, Native American, and Chicano—arose when groups of people who spoke other languages were forced to learn English to survive. At the same time, they remained socially and physically isolated from the majority of American English speakers, a basic condition for language variation. All three of these dialects almost certainly came about sometime during the twentieth century, when they grew to be identified more with a group than a location.

Before the population shift known as the Great Migration in the decades after World War I, the large majority of African Americans lived in the South, mostly in rural areas. After the war, and continuing until after World War II, tens of thousands moved to cities in the Northeast and Midwest. Living largely apart from the White population, they were more likely to maintain their southern speech patterns. Over time, their speech also evolved new patterns, adding up to a distinct dialect.

By the late nineteenth century, most Native Americans had been forced onto reservations that were isolated from the surrounding communities. Although tribal leaders needed English to conduct business with the outside world, most people weren't exposed to local mainstream speech. Instead, they developed their own ways of using English, influenced to some degree by their original languages. The use of English was reinforced when the government began a program to train Native children in White ways by sending them away to boarding schools, often against their family's will—a practice that started in the late nineteenth century and continued well into the twentieth. In many cases, the children were from different reservations and would not have had a common language other than English. Even if they did, they still spoke English because they were punished for speaking anything else. Cross-regional features like the distinctive intonation pattern described earlier are fairly recent developments that probably came from the boarding school world.

Mexicans living in the territories handed over by the Mexican government in 1848 went abruptly from being citizens of a Spanish-speaking country to being part of the United States. In the years after the Mexican American War, English-speaking Americans poured into the region. The first generation of Mexican Americans would probably have learned some English, and their children would have learned it natively. However, substantial numbers of immigrants from Mexico continued to come into the territory as well. Spanish remained a familiar language, and Mexicans, both recently arrived and long established, continued to see themselves as a separate community.

Some of the features that distinguish ethnic dialects would have started out as language-learning strategies. For instance, it's common for language learners to use present-tense verbs even when other tenses are called for. A version of this usage is now an established part of several varieties of Native American English, which use present tense for background or habitual actions, as in *Before, we eat at home a lot, but now we don't*. Another strategy is to transfer features from the speaker's original language, such as pronunciation. That explains why Spanish-influenced vowel sounds are found in Chicano English. Likewise, Native American vowel sounds can vary based on the speakers' ancestral language, even if they don't use that language now. Ethnic dialects may also reduce clusters of consonants at the end of a word ('pos' for *post*), especially if the speakers' first languages (or ancestral languages) don't include such sounds. Consonant dropping happens in mainstream varieties of American English as well, but to a lesser degree.

Most of the time, features of learner's English disappear with the second generation of speakers, who acquire English as their first language. Occasionally, traces of earlier ways of talking become a permanent part of the dialect. That's more likely to happen when people are physically or socially separated from the broader linguistic community, especially when those features become marks of identity.

## African American English: A Melding of Sources

To what extent African American English differs from other varieties of American English, and where those differences came from, are questions that linguists have been exploring since the mid-twentieth century.[9] The McDavids' observations about the dialectal differences of students in Illinois and Michigan were among the earliest studies, and they raised several issues that were important for later researchers. These include how much, if any, African American English is derived from the "British provincial speech" of the earliest colonists, and how many of its features might represent "the persistence of something from African speech."[10]

These issues don't have straightforward answers because, as noted in Chapter 2, records of African American speech before the twentieth century are sparse. The earliest consist of travelers' descriptions, fictional dialogue, and indirect evidence from the advertisements for runaway slaves. Observers disagreed about what characterized African American speech, with some people claiming that it was more or less the same as lower-class Anglo-American speech and others describing it as practically a foreign language. Commenters were no doubt influenced at least partly by their prejudices. Some probably had a more accurate ear for language than others, which would also affect their conclusions.

The sounds and structures of current African American English don't point to any single obvious origin. Some can be traced back to earlier American Englishes, while others suggest a creole—that is, a language based on English but with input from West African languages. Still other features are apparently recent developments from the early twentieth century or later. Because there is not much direct evidence from previous stages of the dialect, linguists have had to piece together different kinds of information to try to track it back to its origins. Early American history and demographics offer valuable clues about the emergence and spread of African American English.[11]

The first known attempt to record the speech of recently arrived Africans comes from Puritan minister Cotton Mather writing in 1721. Mather, who was in favor of the controversial new practice of inoculating for smallpox, supported his case by indirectly quoting a group of recently arrived Africans who had experienced it in their former country. He wrote:

> In their Countrey *grandy-many* dy of the *Small-Pox*: But now they learn this way: People take juice of *Small-Pox;* and *Cutty-skin,* and Putt in a Drop; then by'nd by a little *Sicky Sicky* . . . and no body dy of it.[12]

Compounds like *grandy-many* and reduplicated words like *sicky sicky*, as well as using the phrase *by and by* to mark the future rather than a future-tense verb, suggest that the group may have spoken a pidgin, using English as the common vocabulary.

J. F. D. Smyth, who concluded during his travels in Virginia and the Carolinas that many Africans spoke "a mixed dialect between the

Guinea and the English" (see Chapter 2), also provided a sample of speech from the man who paddled the canoe on one of his river excursions: "You just leave me, me sit here, great fish jump up into de canoe, here he be." Since in the early eighteenth century many enslaved people had recently come from Africa, this speech might be evidence of the beginning stages of language learning. Features such as using present tense and invariant *be* could also be evidence of pidgin speech. However, the quotation could also be a caricature of what Smyth heard, or simply mishearing, which often happened. (These caveats must be kept in mind for all examples from untrained observers.)

Daniel Horsmanden, who wrote about the 1742 trial of New York slaves accused of insurrection, also provided a few snippets of pidgin-like speech, such as "His master live in tall house Broadway. Ben ride de fat horse." Horsmanden also recorded the word *Backarara* (more often spelled *buckra*), defining it as "white people." The word is thought to derive from the Nigerian language of Efik, so its use is evidence of the speaker incorporating words from his native or ancestral language.[13]

Literary representations of African American speech are few and unreliable before the twentieth century. These include *Uncle Tom's Cabin* and the "Uncle Remus" folktales of Joel Chandler Harris, which first appeared in the 1881 *Uncle Remus: His Songs and His Sayings*. The renderings of African American speech in these and similar works tend to be idiosyncratic, and in many cases indistinguishable from more general colloquial speech.

The language of Uncle Tom himself, for instance, is mostly free from dialect, while that of other characters includes a mix of colloquialisms. For example:

- Why, she makes pies—sartin she does; but what kinder crust? . . . Why, I shouldn't sleep a wink for a week, if I had a batch of pies like dem ar.
- I spect I grow'd. Don't think nobody never made me.

George Phillip Krapp characterized such talk as "New England literary dialect, slightly adapted to a Southern climate." *Sartin*, *kinder*, and *spect* (expect) to mean suppose, for instance, could easily have been heard in New England. Other nonstandard usages, such as multiple negatives, might be heard in any region.[14] Similarly, Harris's characters spoke a dialect that was a mix of colloquial styles:

- Brer Fox wanter hurt Brer Rabbit bad ez he kin, so he cotch
  'im by de behime legs en slung 'im right in de middle er de
  briar-patch. . . . Bimeby he hear somebody call 'im.[15]

While *bimeby* (by and by) might have been specific to African American
speech (see the prior Cotton Mather quotation), other words, such as
*cotch* and *'im*, are found more generally in vernacular speech.

Earlier twentieth-century linguists often suggested that there were
few significant differences between the speech of Black and White
Americans, partly to counter the idea that Black speech was inferior
in some way. Krapp, writing in the *American Mercury*, claimed, "The
Negro speaks English of the same kind, and class for class, of the same
degree, as the English of the most authentic descendants of the first
settlers at Jamestown and Plymouth." Dialectologist Hans Kurath, in
the introduction to his groundbreaking collection of regional words,
concurred. He wrote that a Black Southerner "by and large . . . speaks
the language of the white man of his locality or area and of his level
of education."[16]

Later in the century, linguists revised this approach. As Chapter 5
described, they turned their attention to regional and vernacular speech,
describing and analyzing each variety on its own terms. This new perspective, coupled with more in-depth research on the details of African
American speech, showed African American English to be a distinct
language variety with its own set of structural and pronunciation rules.

Starting in the mid-twentieth century, linguists have identified a core
group of traits characteristic of African American English, although
not all African Americans use them to the same degree, or at all. As
already noted, dialect use varies from speaker to speaker. Also, many
of the early studies concentrated on young people living in northern
cities, so the words and usages collected may not reflect the speech of
older generations.

The verb system includes several notable features:

- absence of the verb *to be* in certain present-tense sentences:[17]

  He tall. You out the game.

- the use of invariant *be* rather than its tensed forms for habitual
  actions:

  He be walking every day.

- stressed *been* (often written *BIN* in linguistics literature) to indicate remote past:

  She BIN running (for a while).

- *had* to indicate simple past:

  She had left yesterday.

- *Done* to mark a completed action (also possible in southern vernacular English):

  I done lost my wallet.

- absence of *s* on third-person singular verbs:

  He eat late.

Plurals and possessives may also lack an *s* (*three ton, Mary book*).

African American English also shares certain features with the vernacular English of Southerners of any ethnicity. These include negative verb inversion (*Can't nobody beat us*); using the expressions *fixing to* and *like to* (*liketa*); using multiple modals; using *was* for *were* (*We was just standing there*); and saying *y'all*. Absence of *s* on plurals like *three ton* is also heard occasionally. Still other features, like using *ain't* and regularizing irregular past tenses (*I knowed her when she was little*), are found in many vernacular varieties of English. Some of these usages occur more frequently or in different contexts in African American English.

African American English also has some distinctive pronunciations. These include:

- a shift from word final *th* to *f* or *v*: 'baf' for *bath*, 'smoov' for *smooth*
- *skr* for *str*: 'skreet' for *street*
- reduction of word-final multiple consonants: 'pos' for *post*, 'ban' for *band*
- "devoicing" of certain word-final consonants: 'pik' for *pig*, 'feet' for *feed*, 'cap' for *cab*
- pronouncing the vowel in *drink* and *sing* more like 'drank' and 'sang'
- loss of *r* and *l* after a vowel, including when the sound is between vowels: 'flo' for *floor*, 'hep' for *help*, 'may' for *marry*
- pronouncing *pin* and *pen* alike
- shifting the pronunciation of *-ing* to 'in'

As with the grammar, some of these pronunciations can also be found in mainstream southern English (Chapter 5), including saying *pin* for *pen*, dropping the *r* after vowels, and reducing clusters of consonants at the end of a word. Pronouncing *-ing* as 'in' also happens in casual English generally.

Based partly on the earliest samples of African American speech, a group of linguists in the 1960s proposed that African American English grew out of a creole that emerged during early contacts between Africans and English speakers. They pointed to features commonly found in creoles, as well as the presence of words from African languages. They also explored the possibility that this early speech variety was connected to the creoles that developed in British Caribbean colonies like Barbados and Jamaica, which show similar traits.

Current African American English includes several features typical of creoles, especially in the verb system. Omission of the verb *to be* in certain kinds of sentences, having a word that indicates the remote past (*BIN*), using a word to mark completed actions (*done*), and having a way to express habitual actions (invariant *be*), are all common in creole languages. While the modern dialect is clearly no longer a creole, these features could be remnants of an original creole that later "decreolized," that is, became more like English, when the speakers came into greater contact with the linguistic mainstream.[18]

Creole languages take pidgins to a second stage. While pidgins are temporary makeshifts, creoles are established languages with native speakers. They have regular patterns of pronunciation and grammar, just like other languages. Creoles spring up in situations where a large number of speakers of unrelated languages are thrown together and must try to communicate, but are too isolated from the dominant language to learn it as native speakers do.[19]

The demographic evidence for the growth of a creole is mixed. For most of the seventeenth century, Africans remained a small minority of the population and were treated more like indentured servants than slaves. The population density and isolation required for a creole to develop weren't there. Africans would have picked up the language of the speakers around them, just as indentured servants did if they didn't speak English.[20]

In northern states, African Americans never made up a very large percentage of the population (around 2 percent, on average, by some estimates).[21] However, during the late seventeenth century, the situation began to change in some parts of the South. The rise of tobacco plantations, combined with the increasing difficulty of attracting indentured servants to the colonies, led to the transportation of many more Africans, and their status changed from servants who could potentially purchase their freedom to slaves for life. In the early eighteenth century, this trend accelerated with the growth of the vast rice and indigo plantations of coastal South Carolina and Georgia. Besides Africans, many enslaved people from the West Indies, especially Barbados, were transported to these two colonies.

Africans remained a minority in Virginia, including on tobacco plantations, but they soon outnumbered Europeans in the coastal areas of South Carolina and Georgia. Here, conditions were more conducive to the emergence of a creole. By the mid- to late eighteenth century, as many as three-quarters of the people in the coastal counties of South Carolina and Georgia were either African or of African descent.[22] Often a single plantation held hundreds of enslaved people, with a White population that was very much smaller. Most slaves had little contact with White English speakers, either on or off the plantation. New arrivals would have learned the language from other slaves. Those from Barbados probably already spoke the creole of that island.

A creole does exist today in the region. A small number of African Americans who live on islands off the South Carolina and Georgia coasts speak Gullah, also called Geechee or Sea Island Creole. Gullah speakers are descendants of the people who lived on the coastal plantations, the most likely places for a creole to have developed. Gullah resembles Barbadian creole to some extent (as well as other West Indian creoles), which is predictable if large numbers of creole-speaking slaves were brought from Barbados. Creolists argue that Gullah represents the remnants of a much more widespread language that they believe existed until after the Civil War. While this language decreolized in other places, it lingered on the Sea Islands because residents had little contact with outsiders until recent decades.[23]

It's unlikely, however, that Gullah or a similar creole took hold outside the immediate area of the large coastal plantations. In other parts of the South, even in the uplands of South Carolina and Georgia, population patterns didn't support creole development. The majority of people living there were small farmers, mostly of Scots-Irish descent. Few of them owned slaves. Those who did typically held only one or two. These people would have lived alongside the rest of the household and most likely spoken the same way as the people around them.

The enslaved Africans who were transported to large plantations in the Inland South at the beginning of the nineteenth century came mainly from the Chesapeake area rather than South Carolina or Georgia. They probably weren't creole speakers when they arrived. Once there, they were less isolated than people on the coastal plantations and had more interactions with the poor White workers of the region, so were also not likely to have developed a creole later.

Since the 1980s, the discovery of new material from the nineteenth century, such as letters and interviews, has led linguists to consider more carefully the possible links between current African American English and the British American English of previous centuries. Records indicate that African American speech was closer to that of Anglo-Americans in earlier times, and began diverging in various ways at some point during the twentieth century. That's the opposite of what we'd expect if African American English started out as a creole and later decreolized. In that case, it should have moved closer to mainstream English, not further away.[24]

The main source of nineteenth-century African American speech is a collection of interviews often referred to as the WPA (Works Progress Administration) Slave Narratives. These consist of over 2,000 extended interviews with African Americans born before the Civil War. They were conducted during the 1930s as part of the Federal Writer's Project. As a linguistic record, the narratives have some shortcomings. The interviews were handwritten, and individual writers decided for themselves whether or not to attempt representations of dialectal pronunciations and grammar. Some did so, while others translated responses into more standardized English. (All the interviewers were White.) In still other cases, the original language was revised to make it less like other varieties when the handwritten records were published, presumably to conform to the compiler's idea of how the subjects should have talked. For instance, in one case *am* was substituted for other forms of *be*: "De rope am cut" for an original "De rope was cut." Still, the narratives give many useful examples of the forms of earlier African American English.[25]

Edgar W. Schneider's detailed 1989 study of the WPA narratives, *American Earlier Black English*, shows that certain features characteristic of modern African American English were much less prominent among people who learned to talk in the mid-nineteenth century, as most of the interview subjects would have. For instance, most past-tense verbs are in regular past-tense form ("My mammy did de cookin'. . . . Dey all thought a lot of her"). Where the past-tense form is missing, its omission can often be explained as dropping the final consonant (spelled *-ed*) of regular past-tense verbs when speaking. Likewise, third-person singular verbs are said with *s* much more often than not ("My young Missus Mis' Katy Ellis lives on Hillsboro Street"), and plural nouns retain their *s* nearly all the time. While there is some use of *done* plus a verb for past tense (which also occurs more generally in southern varieties of English), there are also many instances of standard usage of past tenses, such as "I've heard her say" and "after dey had left us."

The speech of those interviewed also exhibits some features in common with earlier British colloquial English and other nonstandard speech. These include archaic irregular verb forms like *cotch* and *brung*, the pronouns *hisself* and *we'uns*, *a-* before a verb (*a'runnin'*), and *ain't* for *is/am not*.

Records from the beginning of the colonial era show that some linguistic traits found in African American speech (and in some cases, southern folk speech) were also present in seventeenth-century lower-class British English. During the first half of the century (until the 1640s), the Court of Governors of London's Bridewell Prison transported many petty criminals and vagrants to Virginia, partly as a way to provide the struggling colony with workers. Testimony at the defendants' trials was often recorded verbatim. These samples of seventeenth-century speech contain several grammatical usages similar to those found in African American and other vernacular speech. These earlier British usages are not identical to present-day African American usage, nor are they definitely their source. However, they might have formed part of the input for an African American dialect.[26]

One usage is invariant *be*, sometimes used in place of *are* and often referring to habitual actions or ongoing situations:

- Manie tymes there **be** those that sitt at the Dore whist their wifes do make them cockoldes.
- He is abell to tell of all sortes of men & wemen that **be** lewde.

Third-person singular marking is also occasionally omitted:

- He sayeth the same ffrenchman is a bawde & a pander and **declare** many thinges of divers men & wemen.

Possessives appear in a few instances with no *'s* marking:

- . . . widow **Goldwell house** . . . **Goldwell wife** is a bawde.

There are also examples of three usages still found generally in the South: *fixing to, like to*, and multiple modals. The fact that some of the previously mentioned grammatical features also appear frequently in creoles (invariant *be*, for instance) suggests the possibility that the two varieties reinforced each other. Patterns would have a better chance of being retained if they occurred both in the native languages (or later, in the creole speech) of newly arrived Africans and in the speech of the poor White Virginians from whom they learned English.[27]

Studies that compare the vernacular English of older Black Southerners with that of older White Southerners also find a number of common grammatical usages and pronunciations. Common grammatical features include multiple negatives, *done* to mark a finished action, lack of third-person singular *s*, *was* for *were*, and *is* for *are*, as well as the use of invariant *be*, discussed in Chapter 4. Some shared pronunciations include loss of *r* after certain consonants ('thow' for *throw*), dropping *r* after a vowel, saying 'tahm' for *time*, and saying *oil* more like 'all'.

Some of these features are absent from the language of younger speakers of one or the other dialect. For instance, *r*-lessness is declining among younger White Southerners, but is still current in African American English. Invariant *be*, once heard in both White and Black southern speech, has now virtually disappeared from White speech but has become a defining trait of African American English. Other features have evolved independently in only one variety during the twentieth century. Two examples are the African American verb usages listed here, and the Northern Cities Vowel Shift described in Chapter 5, which is essentially a feature of Anglo-American speech.[28]

The social situation for African Americans since the Civil War can explain to some degree the ways that later African American English developed. After the break-up of the plantation system, former slaves were incorporated into the larger population, but the Jim Crow laws that came in with the end of Reconstruction in 1877 once again isolated African Americans. By statute, they resided, traveled, went to school, and conducted business separately from other Southerners.

Under these conditions, the two language varieties would normally have started evolving away from each other in the late nineteenth century. However, the growth of the sharecropper system on former cotton plantations was a mitigating factor. Between approximately the 1880s and 1930s, both Black and White tenant farmers worked in close proximity, which explains why older rural lower-class Southerners of all ethnicities share some features of colloquial speech.[29]

The situation changed again with the Great Migration, when African Americans who spoke essentially a southern dialect brought their language to the urban Northeast and Midwest. The usual processes of language change then took over. African Americans preserved some of their old usages while at the same time inventing new ones, or using existing speech patterns in new ways. Meanwhile, the language of their former home also evolved in new ways. The resulting speech was distinct from both that of the surrounding culture and the language of the place they left behind, although connected to it.

Taken together, the various pieces of evidence suggest that, while African American English grew mainly out of the English current in America when Africans arrived, it also has some longstanding creole features that distinguish it from other American dialects. This result is easily imaginable. The contact situation that would have encouraged a creole existed in limited times and places. However, Africans were more often in a situation where they would have learned English the way non-English-speaking settlers did—by listening to the British English speakers around them. Most of the time, these would be indentured servants, yeoman farmers or farmworkers, and other people who used British provincial speech.[30]

Linguistic influence also flows in the other direction. Chapter 1 listed African words that came into the language early, such as *hoodoo* and *okra*. Anglo-Americans in coastal South Carolina and Georgia have also adopted, or are at least familiar with, several words from Gullah. These include *buckra* (White person), *jinky board* (seesaw), *cooter* (turtle), *goober* (peanut), and *benne* (sesame seeds). The next chapter will talk about some of the slang terms that entered the vocabulary from the worlds of jazz and rap.

One study of a small regional newspaper during the 1990s yielded sixty-nine expressions that crossed over from African American English, including *boogie, dis, gangsta, homeboy, jones, righteous, trash talk, the hood, you're the man, be down with, what's up with that,* and similar expressions.[31] Many are related to jazz or rap, but not all of them. *Boogie* first emerged in 1929 with the meaning of partying or having a good time. *Be down with*, or well-informed, hip, and up to date, was jive talk in the 1940s, and has been mainstream since the 1990s. *Homeboy* was first used in the 1960s as a term for a close friend or member of the same gang, but has been strongly associated with hip-hop since the 1980s. *The hood* was also first used in the late 1960s, but was popularized by the 1991 J. Singleton film *Boyz n the Hood.*

In her book *Black Talk*, linguist Geneva Smitherman notes that Black language is not the same as Black slang. The language of the African American community includes a fairly stable core vocabulary, spoken by all groups, that covers all aspects of African American life. "Crossover" words that are familiar to other American English users form only a small part of that. On the other hand, many words and expressions that originated in African American English, for example, *chill, don't go there, twenty-four seven*, and *throw down*, are widely used with seemingly no awareness of their origin. Since the beginning of the twentieth century, African American English has had a steady influence on the vocabulary as a whole, although speakers sometimes don't recognize the cultural source of the words.[32]

## Native American English: Building on Ancestral Speech

The kind and amount of English spoken by Native Americans before the late nineteenth century are even less documented than the language of African Americans. We know that the first colonists encountered at least a few Natives who knew some English, but we don't know what it sounded like. The Abenaki Samoset, whose contact with the Pilgrims is described in Chapter 1, was said by colonial governor William Bradford to have "broken English, which they [the Pilgrims] could well understand."[33] Bradford reported that Samoset's friend Tisquantum spoke better English than Samoset. Unlike Samoset, he had been to England, so had an opportunity to study the language over a long period. Tisquantum spent the last few years of his life with the Pilgrims, acting as an interpreter in their dealings with the local tribes, but Bradford doesn't report any of his speech directly.

A small number of other people, probably a few dozen, from various coastal regions made similar voyages to and from England, either voluntarily or, more often, as "exotic" captives to be shown to the Court. Typically, they learned English while there, often becoming interpreters for trading companies. English-speaking Natives would have remained a small minority during the seventeenth century, however, since most wouldn't have needed to use the language.

A certain number of Native Americans during the seventeenth and eighteenth centuries lived among the colonists, either voluntarily or under duress, and they naturally learned some English. During the early colonial era, British colonists enslaved many Indians who were captured during conflicts or acquired from tribes who had captured members of other tribes. By one estimate, from 30,000 to 50,000 Native people were enslaved between 1670 and 1715, mainly in Virginia and South Carolina, but also in some areas of the North.[34]

As settlers continued to encroach on their land, Native communities were less able to practice their traditional ways of life and so had to find other ways to sustain themselves. That led to more encounters with English speakers. Some chose to enter White-dominated trades. For instance, many Native American men living along the New England coast went to work on whaling ships and spent years at sea with their Anglo-American shipmates. Others engaged in the British fur trade. Natives, especially in New England, also entered indentured servitude during the early eighteenth century as a way of earning money. Ads for runaway Native American slaves and indentured servants almost invariably describe them as speaking "good English," presumably similar to that of the people around them.[35]

Occasional early examples of Native American pidgin speech appear in memoirs or works of fiction. Their reliability is questionable. As with examples of African speech, their accuracy depends on the ear and preconceptions of the writer. One or two of the following examples sound suspiciously like early examples of African English, while others are reminiscent of old movie portrayals of Indians:[36]

- They say, Englishman much foole—Lazie squaes! (Thomas Lechford, *Plaine Dealing; or, Newes from New England*, 1641)
- They will say Three sleeps me walk, or two three sleeps me do such a thing. (John Josselyn, *Account of Two Voyages*, 1674)
- You be de white man, you have soul; when we die we fling in water, big fish come carry us to an oder place. (William Rufus Chetwood, *The Voyages of Captain Richard Falconer*, 1720)

- White man want poison poor Indian. . . . Whiskey kill poor Peggy. (John Dunn Hunter, *Memoirs of a Captivity among the Indians of North America*, 1823)
- Sometimes I lookum side hill; sometimes I lookum locks [rocks]. (Henry David Thoreau, *The Maine Woods*, 1864)
- Heap good Indian, hunt buffalo and deer. (Fanny Kelley, *Narratives of My Captivity among the Sioux Indians*, 1871)

Nineteenth-century examples of Native American speeches are typically literary efforts meant to convey moving or inspirational sentiments to a White audience, and most were not originally spoken in English. One of the most famous is the 1877 surrender speech of Chief Joseph of the Nez Perce, which includes the poignant line, "From where the sun now stands, I will fight no more forever." Chief Joseph's statement was originally made in the Nez Perce language and translated into English as it was spoken. Later, the translation was revised and embellished by the writer Charles Erskine Scott Wood.

Chief Seattle of the Duwamish people is also credited with eloquent nineteenth-century prose. His most famous speech, made during a treaty signing in 1855, starts, "Yonder sky has wept tears of compassion on our fathers for centuries untold." However, Chief Seattle spoke in the Lushootseed language. His remarks were then translated into the Pacific Northwest trading language of Chinook Jargon before being rendered into English and later revised more than once. The most recent version, reworked by a screenwriter, appeared in the early 1970s to promote an environmental film produced by the Southern Baptist Radio and Television Commission.[37]

Possibly one reason why there is little information about earlier Native American English is that the majority of Natives spoke little or no English until late in the nineteenth century, in spite of the exceptions just described. Those who did speak English would have used it only as a second language and, in most cases, only intermittently. Unlike African Americans, most Native Americans did not at first have much reason to learn English. Tribal leaders would have handled negotiations with the colonists, and later with the American government. Even these meetings often involved interpreters.

Widespread adoption of English came about through the federal government's attempts to assimilate and "civilize" the Indians, especially through education. Sporadic efforts were made toward this goal as early as President Thomas Jefferson's administration. Jefferson encouraged Protestant missionaries to start schools among the eastern tribes, including Cherokees, Creeks, Delawares, and Choctaws. The mission schools concentrated on practical training in such trades as carpentry, blacksmithing, farming, and domestic arts. They also tried to imbue the children with the ways of Anglo-American culture, including the English language. A minority of students, including many who later became tribal leaders such as Cherokee chief John Ross, went on to further education and became fluent in English.

Fluent speakers nonetheless remained a minority until the late nineteenth century. Although Native Americans were forcibly relocated or crowded out of their homelands into foreign territory beginning in the eighteenth century, and nearly all were confined to reservations eventually, they moved as a tribe. They were thus able for the most part to keep speaking their ancestral languages.

Beginning in the 1870s, the government made a more concentrated effort to Americanize the Native population. One aspect of this plan was to take children off reservations and send them to co-educational boarding schools. The first school, the Carlisle Indian Industrial School of Carlisle, Pennsylvania, opened in 1879. By the end of the century, two dozen more had opened. The main aim of the boarding schools was expressed by Carlisle's founder, Richard Henry Pratt, whose motto was "Kill the Indian and save the man."[38]

New arrivals at the schools were issued uniforms, western-style haircuts, and English names, and started on a strict regimen of classroom study mixed with vocational training and manual labor. Teachers and administrators made concerted efforts to stamp out all traces of Native cultural practices. An important part of the assimilation process was an insistence on speaking English exclusively. Students were forbidden to speak their tribal languages and anyone caught doing so was severely punished. Except for a minority who lived close enough to their families' homes to travel there easily, boarding school students did not return home for visits between terms, so would rarely have had an opportunity to speak their first language. This led to more limited use of ancestral languages among younger generations and, eventually, fewer speakers.

One linguistic effect of boarding school attendance in the twentieth century can be seen in a 1962 study of the slang current at Haskell Institute in Lawrence, Kansas. Students that year came from eighty different tribes. Many spoke their tribal languages, but everyone spoke English, as they were required to do. They thus developed a common slang vocabulary based on English. Some Haskell slang was the same as that used by students generally at the time, such as *cram* to mean study, *fake out*, *goof off*, and *no sweat*. Students also invented numerous terms that were particular to their situation. These included slang for vocational programs, such as *ink dauber* for printer; *buffalo meat* and *dog meat* for good or bad beef served in the cafeteria; and *starring around* for showing off. Although these terms were no doubt as fleeting as most slang, they show how common ways of using English could have taken hold at boarding schools and later been transferred to multiple reservations as those students eventually returned home.[39]

The government's assault on Native languages inevitably took a toll. At the time of first European contact, North America was home to between 300 and 400 languages. The most recent census lists 152 Indigenous American languages. Most have no more than a few hundred speakers. The Navajo language has by far the most speakers, with nearly 167,000. Other languages with substantial numbers of speakers include the Alaska Native language of Yupik with nearly 20,000, the Dakota languages with nearly 18,000, and Apache with around 14,000. In most cases, these numbers are far lower than total population numbers for the tribes. The total number of people living on Navajo lands, for example, is around 330,000. Overall, only a small percentage of people who identify as Native Americans or Alaska Natives speak their ancestral language—fewer than 400,000 out of a total population of over 5 million.[40]

Nearly all Native American languages are losing speakers. Most people who speak an Indigenous language natively are middle aged or older. Some languages are down to only a few very old speakers, or only one. Although in recent decades a number of tribes have started language revival programs, the languages in many cases are not spoken regularly at home, so young people never become fluent speakers. More limited use of ancestral languages is part of the reason why Native Americans express their identity through distinctive English speech patterns. Some, like the intonation pattern described in the first section of this chapter, cross tribal boundaries. Others are specific to one group. One researcher of languages of the Southwest has remarked that "one can easily tell the Tribal identity of an individual by the way in which [he or she] spoke English."[41]

Different varieties of Native American English handle vowel sounds in distinctive ways, often as the result of influence from ancestral languages, whether or not these are still in use.[42] For example, Navajos may switch the vowel sounds in *his* and *he's*, and pronounce *yes* more like 'yis'. Isletan Pueblo English speakers (whose original language is Tiwa) make some vowels "tenser" than they are in mainstream English (more like long vowels), pronouncing *village* like 'veelage', *where* like 'whayre', and the vowel in *would* something like the vowel in 'wooed'.

Consonants can also vary from typical American English pronunciations. Several varieties of Native American English don't use the 'th' sounds of *thin* and *then*. Instead, these words become 'tin' and 'den'. Cheyenne English doesn't include the 'ng' sound in words like *singer*. To distinguish the word from *sinner*, speakers intensify the vowel so it sounds like 'seener'. Navajo English speakers might drop or reduce consonants at the end of a word.

Word stress, pitch, and intonation can also separate one variety from another, or from more mainstream varieties of American English. Possible differences include stressing words unexpectedly, or stressing multiple words in a sentence equally. Intonation has been described as "more level, with fewer pitch changes than in standard English," and without the typical American English rising pitch at the end of a question. These patterns contribute to non-Native perceptions that Natives speak in a monotone or singsong voice.[43]

Distinctive grammatical features also appear in many versions of Native American English. One feature mentioned earlier is the use of present-tense verbs for background or remote past, such as *In the old days, they don't let us go anywhere*, and *They all speak in Indian when we first started school*. As with the creole-like aspects of African American English verbs, this feature that's common to several tribes may be the result of language learners restructuring English as they acquired it, rather than influence from first languages. Other features include:

- omitting the *s* on plural nouns:
  There's two way of talking.
- adding plural to mass nouns:
  furnitures, homeworks
- preferring to form passive sentences with *got*:
  He got voted in. (also heard in other varieties of English, but less often)

- starting a sentence with the topic:

  They ride bikes is what they do.
  From the family is where we learn to be good.

Native American English also displays some features typical of vernacular American English. These include using multiple negatives (*We don't got no picks*) and changing word-final consonant clusters to single consonants ('contez' for *contest*).

The Lumbee tribe of Robeson County, North Carolina, provides an example of a Native American community developing its own way of talking without recourse to an ancestral language. The Lumbees are one of the largest tribes in the United States, but their situation is unusual. Congress recognized them in 1956 as having "Indian origins," but refused to give them the benefits that accrue to fully recognized tribes. One reason for this decision is that the Lumbees have not spoken a language other than English for several generations, and their original ancestral language or languages aren't known.

Archeological and historical evidence suggest that the Lumbees may be descended from a conglomerate of regional tribes that spoke different languages. These probably included languages from the Algonquian, Siouan, and Iroquoian families. In any case, Lumbees were apparently speaking English from an early time. According to one account, Scottish settlers arriving in the region around 1730 found "a large tribe of Indians, speaking English, tilling the soil, owning slaves, and practicing many of the arts of civilized life."[44]

Lumbee English shares a number of features with the adjacent southern dialect.[45] These include dropping some *r*'s after vowels (not as often as in African American speech, but more than in Anglo-American speech), attaching *a-* to verbs (*a-huntin'*, *a-fishin'*), and, specific to the nearby Outer Banks, pronouncing the vowel in words like *high* and *time* with an 'oi' sound like the vowel of *boy* [ɔɪ], so they sound like 'hoi toim'. They also sometimes drop the verb *to be* in sentences like *She good*, and use *weren't* for *wasn't* (*She weren't there*).

Lumbee speakers also have some distinct features of their own. One is how they use invariant *be* or *bes*.[46] Lumbee English gives the verb a broader range of uses than other vernaculars. For instance, Lumbees use invariant *be* to talk about one-time events as well as for habitual situations, as in *They be take their honeymoon there*. Lumbees also use *be* in sentences where speakers of other forms of English might use *have* or *has*:

- I told her don't get it cause Momma be got it.
- We be come here for nothing.
- If I'm got a dollar I'm got it.

They can also use it for an enduring state, as in *She bes my best friend.* Negative is expressed with *do*: *Liquor don't be as good.* Sometimes *be* becomes *bes* when the subject is third person: *It bes really crowded.* Occasionally, *bes* appears with other subjects, too: *I bes down there all the time.* The status of *bes* is changing in recent times. Younger speakers seem to use it mainly to express a habitual action, making it closer to African American English, rather than the more varied uses of older speakers.

Since invariant *be* and *bes* also occur in Anglo-American vernaculars of the Carolinas, they may be holdovers from the English of the first British settlers. Most Native American English varieties don't show remnants of earlier British English. The fact that Lumbee English does reflects its long history in the area. At the same time, it has evolved features that distinguish it from any other variety in the region and identify its speakers as members of a specific community.

As with African American English, Native American speech patterns reflect their speakers' common history. Native American English generally draws on the dominant language, but also shows evidence of strategies that people use when learning a new language. The dialectal differences from tribe to tribe also show influence from ancestral languages. Unlike African American English, Native versions of English haven't preserved traces of earlier British speech because Native American speakers of English didn't form the critical mass necessary for preserving and passing down linguistic traits until the late nineteenth century.

## Chicano English: A Spanish Heritage

In contrast to speakers of African American and Native American Englishes, all Chicano English speakers have the common ancestral language of Spanish. In California and the Southwest, where Chicano English is spoken, Mexican Americans make up a substantial part of the population. In California, for instance, nearly 40 percent of the population is Latino, including a large proportion of Mexicans.[47] Besides Mexicans whose families have lived in the area for generations, immigrants from Mexico and elsewhere in Latin America continue to migrate to regions along the Mexican border, which means that Spanish speakers continue to move into the area.

It's predictable under these conditions that Chicano English shows influence from Spanish. However, it also contains features that have apparently evolved without reference to Spanish. As noted in the first section, Chicano speakers are native speakers of English. While some speak Spanish also, others don't, and according to a study by linguist Manuel Godinez, Jr., bilingualism doesn't make a noticeable difference in how Chicano speakers use the language. Study participants who were bilingual in Spanish pronounced English vowels the same way as those who spoke only English, even though the pronunciations themselves may have originally been influenced by Spanish.[48]

Vowel pronunciations are one distinctive trait of Chicano English.[49] Vowels are often pronounced in the Spanish way without the English glide sound at the end, which makes them sound chopped off ('o' [o] rather than 'owuh' [oə]). Certain vowels have a "tense," unreduced sound that contrasts with the reduced unstressed vowels of mainstream English. In most dialects of American English, the vowels of unstressed syllables reduce to an 'uh' sound [ə], so, for example, *because* is pronounced something like 'buhcause' [bəkɔz]. However, in Chicano English, the word is said with a full vowel so it sounds more like 'beecause' [bikɔz]. This pronunciation happens most prominently with the long high vowels in *beat* [i] and *boot* [u]. *Look* may sound more like 'luke' [luk].

Many Chicano speakers also display a feature found in other California speech (part of the California Vowel Shift, as described in Chapter 5), raising and tensing of the short *i* vowel [ɪ] when it occurs before nasal sounds (*m* or *n*), especially in the *-ing* ending. Words like *something* and *anything* are pronounced 'sometheen' and 'anytheen'. This pronunciation is more prevalent and more distinct (with a tenser vowel) in Chicano English than in other California dialects, suggesting the possibility that Anglo-American Californians adopted it from Chicano speakers.[50]

This way of pronouncing -*ing* words was found to have social significance in a study of Chicana youth gangs by Norma Mendoza-Denton. Mendoza-Denton noticed that instances of tensing the short *i* varied according to which social group a speaker belonged to. Girls who were core members of either of two gangs, the Norteñas and Sureñas (Northerners and Southerners), had the highest rate of using long *i* in -*ing* words. A group of girls in the same school, referred to as the Jocks, who were not gang members and were more assimilated into the broader California culture, had the lowest rate of use.[51]

In other respects, the Norteñas and Sureñas were competitive and oppositional. They wore different styles of clothing, listened to different types of music, and sometimes fought each other. However, they were united in having a Latina-based identity (as opposed to the more assimilated Jocks). They were also more culturally unconventional than non-gang members. These factors suggest the possibility that use of tensed *i* was an expression of a specific type of Latina identity for these two groups (although a mostly unconscious one, as with language use in general).

Besides distinctive vowel sounds, Chicano English also uses some consonants differently. The 'th' of *thin* and *then* turn into *t* and *d*, and consonant clusters at the end of a word may be reduced or dropped ('lease' for *least*), two features also found in African American English and some Native American Englishes. Consonant cluster reduction is also found in vernacular speech generally.

Chicano English also shares some grammatical features with vernacular dialects, as well as with African American English. These include nonstandard past-tense verbs and multiple negatives:

- Everybody knew the Cowboys was gonna win again.
- It ain't okay.
- I haven't wrote in a long time.
- None of the girls don't like her.
- Things ain't gonna never change.

Many speakers also use invariant *be* and some use *had* instead of simple past verbs, usually associated with African American English:

- The news be showing it too much.
- Me and my mom be praying in Spanish.
- Before we had fought she had came up to see me.

Chicano English also has unique usages, for instance, using *would* in sentences that start with *if*, where a speaker of the standard variety would use *was* or *were*:

- If he'd be here right now, he'd make me laugh.
- If I would have been a gangster, I would have been throwing signs up.

This usage is also heard in New York City. It may show Spanish influence, as that language has a similar way of expressing such verbs. Another typical usage, which seems not to be related to either Spanish or other English dialects, is the use of *could* to express competence, as in *I learned that people who are left handed could draw better than people who are right-handed.*

Perhaps the most distinctive feature of Chicano English is its intonation pattern. According to one researcher, it's the only identifiable trait of Chicano English that some speakers adopt (or retain). Another linguist has written that he believes it's "the most distinctive, important, and characteristic feature" of the dialect. He goes on to remark that the intonation patterns of Chicano English speakers sometimes make speakers of other English dialects think they sound "wishy-washy" or as if they are asking a question when they should be making a statement.[52]

That's because in most varieties of American English, speakers use a rising intonation at the end of a sentence when they are asking a question, but a falling intonation for a statement. In Chicano English, rising intonation is used for emphasis rather than questioning. A rising-and-falling tone at the end of a sentence—the stereotypical "Mexican" accent of films and television—is simply declarative, although in most English dialects it would suggest uncertainty or introduce a qualifying remark (*He's okay? But...*). Both of these patterns are also common in Mexican Spanish. (Uptalk also gives a rising intonation to statements, but the overall intonation contours are different from Chicano English.)

In recent decades, communities of Mexican Americans (and other traditionally Spanish-speaking groups) have begun to settle in larger numbers in places outside California and the Southwest. Language use in these groups ranges from young people who were born in the United States and speak English natively, and who may or may not also be fluent in Spanish, to recent immigrants who mainly speak Spanish but are learning English. Their language patterns show influence from various sources, including Spanish, Chicano English, and the mainstream English of the region where they live.

A review of the English spoken in two small Mexican American communities in Illinois revealed a mix of features. These included some Chicano features, such as some types of consonant cluster reduction, the tensing of the vowel in -*ing*, and typical intonation patterns. Other Chicano features, such as the clipping of long vowels, were absent. While the speech of Mexican Americans differed from the other varieties spoken in the area, it also differed from the Chicano English of the Southwest.[53]

An examination of the English spoken in two North Carolina Latino communities, one in Raleigh and the other in a rural area, showed that some speakers were starting to unglide the vowel in *high time* (so it sounded like 'hah tahm' with [aː] instead of [ɑi]), a typical southern speech trait that's part of the Southern Vowel Shift. Some people also adopted high-profile Southernisms like *y'all* and *fixin' to*. The rate of adoption for these features was very variable, and depended at least partly on social factors. For instance, speakers who lived in Raleigh, which has a diverse population and less evidence of the Southern Vowel Shift, were less likely to pick up the unglided 'ah' sound than people who lived in a rural area. The degree to which people identified with the local culture also made a difference.[54]

Like the other ethnic dialects in this chapter, Chicano English encompasses the history and identity of its speakers. Traces of Spanish influence remain, along with contributions from other dialects of English. Using these features as input, Chicano speakers have evolved their own identifiable way of talking, both as communities and as individuals.

The three ethnolects featured in this chapter have relatively large numbers of speakers and are the most heavily studied, but are not by any means the only ones found in the United States. Other smaller, more localized dialects include two that were noted in Chapter 3 for their contributions to the American vocabulary. Hawaiian Pidgin, an English-based creole spoken by about half the population of the Hawaiian Islands, includes many words based on Hawaiian, as well as its own set of sounds and sentence structures.[55] Cajun English, spoken in southern Louisiana by descendants of French-speaking settlers to the area, has distinctive linguistic features that include pronunciations influenced by French. (*Cajun* derives from *Acadia*, an old name for Nova Scotia and the surrounding area.) These ethnolects are spoken by many fewer people, but along with other small, local speech communities, they add to the richness of American English.

Ethnic dialects, like regional dialects, build on the history of their speakers while also innovating in new directions. They are spoken in different ways, depending on the life histories and attitudes of their users. Some people adopt many or all of the typical features, and others perhaps only a few or even none. They may use these dialectal features in some situations, but not others. Like regional speech, ethnic dialects continue to be distinctly identifiable varieties, even in this age of increased national communication through television, movies, and online, and in spite of the fact that Americans are more mobile than ever. Like all language use, they continue to express their speakers' identities in complex ways.

# 7

# Language Innovation outside the Mainstream

## Words with an Edge

On January 6, 1737, the *Pennsylvania Gazette* published what may be the first collection of American slang to appear in print, "The Drinkers Dictionary." The dictionary consisted of 229 words and phrases synonymous with being drunk. The *Gazette*'s editor, Benjamin Franklin, thought the list would "surprize as well as divert the sober Reader." He commented, "Tho' every one may possibly recollect a Dozen at least of the expressions us'd on this Occasion, yet I think no one who has not much frequented Taverns would imagine the number of them so great as it really is."[1]

The terms collected range from the fairly obvious—*in liquor, cock-eyed, drunk as a wheelbarrow*—to the more opaque— *stiff as a ringbolt, burnt his shoulder, been to Jerico, he's Prince Eugene.* Some are cleverly allusive. For instance, *makes a Virginia fence* refers to fences constructed in a zig-zag pattern, known as Virginia fences. *Cherubimical* suggests being in an angelic state. *Too free with Sir John Strawberry* alludes to the color of wine. One or two words, like *nimptopsical*, are new coinages. Although most of the list is archaic, several words have survived. Besides *intoxicated*, which is now part of the standard vocabulary, these include *tipsy, stewed, soaked, fuddled, addled*, and *boozy*.

Franklin's collection illustrates some typical features of slang and other types of non-mainstream vocabulary. One, as Franklin points out, is that these words didn't come from the usual sources: "The Phrases in this Dictionary are not (like most of our Terms of Art) borrow'd from

Foreign Languages, neither are they collected from the Writings of the Learned in our own, but gather'd wholly from the modern Tavern-Conversation of Tiplers."

Franklin's list is typical in other ways, too. Slang often (although not always) deals with taboo subjects like drunkenness. One of its purposes is to provide an indirect, potentially facetious, way to talk about such topics. Another purpose, probably more important, is to separate those in the know from outsiders. Franklin assumed that his "sober Readers" would not know more than a dozen or so of the terms on the list, but those who "frequented Taverns" would be familiar with most of them. He also recognized that his collection probably only scraped the surface, saying, "I do not doubt but that there are many more [terms] in use." Knowledgeable use of the coded vocabulary signaled a common interest to fellow drinkers, as well as allowing them to disguise what they were talking about from disapproving outsiders.

Most slang is ephemeral, like nearly all the terms on Franklin's list (again, with exceptions, such as *tipsy* and *boozy*). That's partly because slang acts as a code language for closed groups. Most insider words never leak out to the general public. When they do, they lose their usefulness. Once slang enters the linguistic mainstream, it's no longer potent as an expression of group identity and needs to be replaced. By the time in-group language appears in a published list, usually compiled by a scholar, journalist, or other outsider, its primary users have already moved on to a fresher set of words.

The slang of young people is especially unstable and fast-changing because they avoid using the same trendy words that their parents used. Occasionally, a slang word or phrase will break its bonds and enter the permanent lexicon. When slang goes mainstream, it typically loses its edgy character. Words and expressions like *tipsy*, *phoney*, *loose cannon*, *hit the road*, and *hot* for sexy or popular are familiar across social and age groups, more colloquial speech than slang. Sometimes former slang words lose that label entirely and are simply treated like ordinary words. *Lame duck*, *gerrymander*, and *lobby* were all once considered political slang, but are now used routinely in serious speaking and writing.

An exact definition of slang is difficult to pin down. In some ways, it's easier to say what slang isn't. Although sticklers for correct speech sometimes label all nonstandard usages slang, many don't fit that category. For instance, regionalisms like *disremember* are not part of the larger vocabulary, but they're not slang. Nor are colloquialisms like *I guess so* and *sure*, or standard expressions like *fight fire with fire*. Colloquial language is informal, but not edgy or challenging. It's part of ordinary speech, while slang is meant to create an effect.

Slang is also not the same thing as jargon. Jargon is the specialized language of a group with a common interest or occupation. The technical language of computer programmers, for instance, includes dozens of terms like *backend*, *hardcode*, *CSS*, and *object-oriented programming*, as well as more familiar words like *byte* and *server*. None of these qualify as slang. Because jargon provides a shorthand way of talking about a topic, it's opaque to non-specialists, but that's not its purpose. Some jargon, of course (like *byte* and *server*), makes it into the larger vocabulary, at which point it is usually considered standard English, not slang.

Slang words are created through some of the same processes as other words. More often than not, slang adopts words that already exist, but gives them an expanded, narrowed, or allusive meaning. Word coining in general shows creativity, but slang has an extra edge. It is irreverent, disruptive, often humorous. Slang has been called the poetry of the people, and it shares some features of poetry, such as rhyme (*drunk as a skunk*), hyperbole (*dead drunk*), and metaphor (*antifreeze* for alcohol).[2]

The origin of the word *slang* is not entirely clear. The earliest known examples appear in the mid-eighteenth century and are all connected with the criminal classes. These uses indicate that *slang* described activities like fraud or theft rather than speech. For instance, *stand slang* meant to receive stolen goods.[3] (The secret vocabulary of the underworld was historically called *thieves' cant* or *argot*.) At some point, the meaning of *slang* transferred from criminal activities to criminal speech. Gradually, it broadened to cover other forms of nonstandard, colloquial speech as well. Webster's 1828 dictionary defines slang as "low, vulgar, unmeaning language."

The verb *to slang*, meaning to harangue someone with abusive or insulting language, appeared around the beginning of the nineteenth century. It's still current in the British expression *slanging match*. The Americanism *slang-whanger* for a careless, foolish talker first appeared around 1809. It was sometimes used as an insulting word for newspaper editors, but usually applied to politicians. Bartlett's *Dictionary of Americanisms* defines *slang-whanging* as "political cant."

As might be predicted from the word's original meaning, the earliest records of American slang focus on the secret language of criminals, beggars, vagabonds, and others who lived outside mainstream society. Usually, these lists were part of larger narratives, almost always written by outsiders. They indicate that early Americans still used many of the same terms as the English. That's not surprising. During the seventeenth and eighteenth centuries, more than a quarter of a million immigrants arrived from the British Isles, including tens of thousands of indentured servants, as well as convicts sent to expand the workforce.[4] These groups spoke various vernaculars, including criminals' cant. Once they were in the country, their language became part of American speech.

Probably the first dictionary of American criminal slang was *Vocabulum, or Rogue's Lexicon*, published in 1859 by George Matsell, a chief of police in New York. His list relies heavily on *A Classical Dictionary of the Vulgar Tongue*, a 1785 collection of English slang by Francis Grose.[5] (John Russell Bartlett's *Dictionary of Americanisms* also draws on this source.) Examples of terms that appear in both Matsell and Grose include *to sham Abraham* 'to pretend sickness', *balsam* 'money', *dub lay* 'robbing houses by picking the locks', *mab* 'a prostitute', *rhino* 'money', and *used up* 'killed'. Both lists also include a small number of words that are more familiar, such as *to fence* (stolen goods), *jump bail*, and *to pop* meaning to pawn something.

By the time *Tramping with Tramps* by Josiah Flynt appeared in 1899, underworld language included many more Americanisms. Flynt collected his material by mingling with vagabonds while tramping around the country. In his introduction to the word list "A Tramp's Jargon," he emphasizes that knowing the specialized language is crucial to fitting into this closed group. He writes, "The 'tenderfoot' in tramp life, the beginner, is recognized by his ignorance of the 'lingo.'" Flynt describes how he prepared himself for life on the road by studying expressions in dictionaries and listening to casual street slang, only to realize that the language of "regular tramps" went far beyond any slang known to outsiders.[6] He also noted that the vocabulary changed frequently, with some words remaining popular for only a few years.

Although the vagabonds that Flynt met sometimes used slang and colloquialisms from the general vocabulary, they preferred talking to each other in their own coded speech. That way, they could converse without revealing their subject matter to nearby policemen or other bystanders. For example, this opening to a story is barely comprehensible to those outside the life: "I was batterin' [begging] one moon [night] . . . an' a stiff [fellow] 'e says: 'Blokey, squeal it at that house over there—it's a priest, he'll scoff [feed] ye.'"[7]

Tramps shared many words with criminals, since both of them tended to have trouble with the law. Some examples of American word inventions used by both groups include *bull* 'policeman' (also *cop* and *flattie*), *cooler* 'jail cell', *elbow* 'detective', *revolver* 'repeat offender', and *square it* 'reform'. A handful of terms have entered the mainstream, for instance, *mooch*, *meal ticket*, *hit the road*, *rube*, and *crook*. Most, however, stayed inside the closed circle until replaced with a newer term.

Secret languages such as tramps' and criminals' talk escape into the wider world when other people get interested in them for some reason. As described in Chapter 3, one impetus for the wider distribution of criminal slang was the onset of Prohibition in 1920. News coverage of bootlegging introduced middle-class Americans to the language of organized crime. Lists of "racketeer" speech started appearing in magazines and readers learned words like *bull* and *flattie*, along with new terms like *hood* and *trigger man*. Likewise, the language of tramps became more familiar to other Americans during the 1930s, when the Depression swelled the numbers of homeless men on the road. Linguists also began collecting the words of various closed groups around this time, making them better known as well as preserving them.[8]

The language of drug addicts and dealers shows a similar trajectory. Until the mid-twentieth century, there are very few records of drugs-related slang. One early researcher, writing in 1936, noted, "Addicts are almost fanatically clannish and tend to keep the argot well within their own fraternity."[9] Drug terms began filtering out to the general public during the 1950s when the Beats (a group of writers that included Allen Ginsburg and Jack Kerouac) and their followers embraced mind-altering drugs as part of their rebellion against conventional mores. That trend carried over into the 1960s, when hippies adopted several Beat terms, along with an interest in illicit drug taking. Increasing societal concern over drug-addicted teenagers also led to articles listing current drug slang so parents and teachers could more easily recognize it. Terms like *mainline*, *get a fix*, *dealer*, *pusher*, *reefer*, (drug) *bust*, *hophead*, and *buzz*, which had been part of the narcotics subculture for decades, suddenly entered the common vocabulary, along with dozens of terms for marijuana and other common drugs. During the 1980s, the popularity of cocaine added words like *coke*, *blow*, and *nose candy* to the mainstream word store.

Even so, these widely known terms represent only the tip of the iceberg. Within the world of illegal drugs, there are dozens of words that outsiders never hear unless they work in law enforcement or at drug treatment centers. A 2017 report by the Drug Enforcement Agency, Houston Division, lists six pages of slang and code words for amphetamines, cocaine, marijuana, fentanyl, heroin, LSD, and other illicit drugs. The list for cocaine alone includes over 200 terms. The report's authors warn that "due to the dynamics of the ever-changing drug scene," the lists will inevitably be outdated before long.[10]

Language innovation that flows from the edges of the culture to the mainstream is not limited to criminals or entirely closed-off groups. Starting with the twentieth century, several other communities have contributed inventive words and phrases to the general vocabulary, although these are usually only a percentage of the terms that they keep for themselves. These include youth culture, African American music culture, and very recently, the denizens of various corners of the Internet.

## Youth Slang: Long Ears, Dweebs, Freaks, and Dudes

Young people have been a major source of popular slang since the early decades of the twentieth century. Youth slang is similar to the language of closed groups in that it's a way of identifying as an insider. However, the need for secrecy is not as much a factor, so the language of teenagers tends to slip more easily into the mainstream vocabulary. Youth slang was not a separate category before the twentieth century because teenagers were not a distinct group before that time. Young people went straight from being children to being adults. Many left school for work by age 14, or even earlier, if they were from the poorer classes. The slang and colloquialisms they used depended on their location and daily activities, and would not have been limited to people their own age. The exception was college students, a small, privileged group who formed a closed circle with similar interests and experiences.

The topics that early college slang covered are very similar to the topics of current college slang. Most dealt with attending classes and studying (or not), and interacting with various classmates and teachers.

College students were all male until the end of the nineteenth century and most entered college a few years earlier than is typical today. For these reasons, some topics, such as dating and drinking, generated little or no slang.[11]

Much nineteenth-century college slang was specific to an individual college and most of it only lasted through a few generations of students. Slang words having to do with classes and studying include *barney* (recite badly), *fish* (get favors from the instructor), *pole* (study hard), and *rake* (recite perfectly). Examples of words to describe fellow students are *long ear* (a serious person), *short ear* (a boisterous person), *squirt* (a show-off), *smooth* (well-dressed), and *blood* (excellent). A few words did have staying power—*cram*, *flunk*, and *drag* for a bore are still part of the language. *Haze* with its modern meaning was used at Harvard and probably other schools as well. The word originally meant to frighten or punish.

Spirits were forbidden on most campuses, but of course students sometimes sneaked them in anyway. The few alcohol-related words that have been preserved are mostly from the mainstream, for instance, *tight*, *soaked*, and *stiff*. A *smile* was a small amount of spirits, just enough to elevate someone's mood, and *spoony* was very drunk. There were also a large number of slang words for "privies" or outhouses. Some examples include *lem*, *temple*, *burt*, *bank*, *No. 10*, *Joe*, and *Cousin John*.

More recent studies of college student slang show that it still revolves around classes, common activities, and attractive or unattractive fellow students. Because outhouses are no longer a feature of college campuses, that category has disappeared, while words for dating and romance have been added, since students now come in all genders and enter college at an older age. Slang for drinking and getting drunk is also more plentiful.

Slang historian Connie Eble, one of the first scholars to study student slang, collected nearly twenty years' worth of slang terms from the University of North Carolina at Chapel Hill between 1972 and 1993. Most of those words, predictably, didn't stay current long. Of the 200 or so words collected in 1972, only twelve were still being used in 1987. Several are still familiar, suggesting that they have become part of mainstream slang. A few are probably specific to UNC. The twelve words are *bad* (for good), *bummer*, *slide* (easy class), *wheels*, *cool*, *do* (as an all-purpose verb), *gravy* (easy), *get real*, *pound* (drink heavily), *threads*, *shit* (as an expletive), and *tough* (good or attractive).

A core of slightly more recent slang has also been long-lived. This includes academics-related words (*ace* for doing well on a test and *bomb* for failing), words expressing approval (*sweet, excellent, awesome, killer*), and descriptors for classmates (*clueless, the pits, dork, dweeb, nerd*). *Hook up* is still used to mean connect with romantic partners. Some words for drunk are still reasonably current, such as *wasted, blitzed, buzzed*, and *trashed*.[12]

Widespread teenage slang not limited to college students arose during the 1930s when teenagers emerged as an identifiable social group. Teenagers gained new status partly because the time gap between childhood and serious adult life had widened. Young people typically attended school until age 18, and a greater number than ever went on to college. Radio, the movies, and television nationalized popular culture, encouraging teenagers to develop common interests. Improved communications also helped spread teenagers' slang throughout the country, although much of it still varied from region to region or school to school. Magazine articles appeared regularly with lists of the latest teen words, probably somewhat random and not entirely current, but still giving adult readers a flavor of youth speech.[13]

Mainstream teen slang is more focused on social activities than on school. Slang from the early decades includes words for unappealing people, such as *goof* (silly), *fuddy-duddy* (stodgy), *screwball* (crazy), *drip* (boring), and *square* (boring and conventional). Funny people were a hoot and nice people were good eggs. *Nerd* was in use by the 1950s. Examples of still recognizable slang verbs are *cramp someone's style, blow your top, bust loose, horse around, fade out*, and *clue in*. A good party was a blast and a half, worth getting all dolled up for. Two common exclamations of agreement were *you and me both* and *and how!*

Dancing was a popular way to socialize. Dancing energetically to swing or jazz was called jitterbugging or doing the jitterbug, originally part of jazz slang. Beginning in the 1920s, having the jitters meant being extremely nervous or jumpy, and could also mean having the shakes after drinking too much. That meaning extended naturally to the swoops and jumps of the jitterbug. Other words for dancing were *cut a rug, drag a hoof*, and *mop*. Words for dance parties were *shindig* and *hop*.

Dancing also took place at juke joints, casual roadhouses where people could eat and drink as well as dance, and records played on a juke box. *Juke* came into English from the African American creole language called Gullah (see Chapter 6). Probably, it is based on a word for disorderly in the West African language of Wolof.

The 1960s, when the first of the Baby Boomers came of age, saw the advent of a more subversive and oppositional form of youth slang. The term *baby boom* usually covers the years from 1946 to 1964, when the birth rate in the United States sharply increased. The term *Boomer* to refer to children born during the boom first appeared in print in 1963 as the oldest Boomers started entering college. Because the Boomer cohort is so large, its members had a major impact on late-twentieth-century American culture, including the vocabulary.

Opposition to the Vietnam War and a rejection of 1950s norms and expectations led many young people to embrace the counterculture, or an alternative lifestyle, two terms in use since the late 1960s. Establishment types who disapproved of the movement labeled its followers *hippies*. The word evolved out of *hip* and *hipster*, terms used by jazz musicians of the 1930s to mean someone sophisticated and up-to-date. Although *hippie* started out as a term of derision, hippies themselves quickly embraced the label.

The early hippie movement centered in the San Francisco Bay area and spread from there across the country. It inspired a variety of slang terms, nearly all of them standard words used in new combinations or with new meanings. A surprising number have since entered mainstream English. The hippie motto was "sex, drugs, and rock and roll." Words related to drug taking were the most plentiful. *Trip* meant a drug experience and taking a trip, which could be good or bad, was called tripping out. A *bummer* was originally a bad LSD trip before it broadened into any negative experience. Other terms include *blissed out* (a good trip), *acid* (LSD), *downer* (originally a depressant), *flip out*, *space out*, *freak out* (all originally drug-related experiences), *head shop* (for drug paraphernalia), *acid head*, and *pot head*. Some of the more lasting words for marijuana include *pot*, *dope*, *grass*, *joint*, and *reefer*.

Most rock and roll terms were borrowed from the jazz era, including *rock and roll* itself, which originally meant to energetically play and dance to jazz and swing. One new word was *groupie* to name the young girls who followed touring rock bands around. Additions to the terminology of sex include *get it on* for making love and *free love* to mean sex without commitment. Other hippie terms that have entered the mainstream, usually with expanded meanings, include *blow it*, *blow your cool*, and *blow your mind* (which could also be drug-related), *drop out*, *cop out*, *put down*, and *turn on*. *Turn on* could have both drug- and sex-related meanings, but *turn on to* just meant to get someone interested in something. *Vibrations*, intuitive feelings about a person or thing, was shortened to *vibes*, which could be good or bad. *Man* became popular as a form of address, although it had been around since at least the 1950s.

*Freak* also came into prominence during the 1960s. It had had the meaning of someone physically or mentally odd since the nineteenth century, and the alternative meaning of an enthusiast for some activity beginning in the early twentieth century. During the 1940s, a freak could also be a jazz player with an appealing, but unorthodox musical style. In the 1960s, *freak* started out as a term for hippies, presumably referencing their oddness, then gradually became a popular way to describe an enthusiast for anything, for instance, a clothes freak or an exercise freak.

Besides the hippies, two groups of young Californians had a big impact on American slang—surfers and Valley girls. In many cases, the two overlapped, with Valley girls (young teens living in the San Fernando Valley) borrowing surfing slang and then funneling it to the larger teenage world. Surfing culture first caught the attention of teenagers across the country thanks to the music of the Beach Boys, along with "beach" movies like the 1959 *Gidget* and the 1963 *Beach Party*. Surfers are very much a closed group, so only a small selection of surfing jargon ever spread beyond the surfing world. Some examples are *wipe out, stoked, epic, full-on, awesome, bitchin'* as a positive descriptor, and *brah* (the Hawaiian Pidgin version of *bro*) as a form of address.

The most successful surfer word is *dude*.[14] *Dude* is an excellent example of a word that has survived over the centuries by shifting and expanding its meaning. It may be a shortening of *doodle*, a word from Early Modern English for a foolish fellow (likely the meaning of *doodle* in *Yankee Doodle*). In the nineteenth-century United States, it gained the connotation of a showy dresser. *Duded up* for dressed up first appeared in the 1890s. In the American West, *dude* was a common way to describe newly arrived Easterners (hence *dude ranch*). By the mid-twentieth century, it had broadened to designate men generally, with the same sort of connotation as *guy*.

*Dude* use reached its peak among surfers and the young people whose language they influenced. To surfers, dudes were fellow surfers or others they considered friends. When *dude* was adopted more broadly, it kept both its friend and its guy meanings. By the 1980s, *Dude* was a common form of address, and *Dude!* was being used as a general exclamation of surprise, interest, approval, solidarity, or other strong feelings, without necessarily addressing a particular person. The word probably got a boost from the 1992 movie *Wayne's World*, featuring two dudes who were best friends. In recent times, the meaning of *dude* has broadened again to encompass young women as well as men.

It's likely that *dude* expanded its range because of its adoption by Valley girls, who helped popularize a number of surfer words like *awesome*. The girls of the San Fernando Valley were introduced to the rest of the country in the 1982 song "Valley Girl," by musician Frank Zappa and his then-teenaged daughter Moon Unit. While much Valley girl speech has now disappeared from the slang vocabulary, or never really arrived there (such as *billys* for dollars), several of their favorite words are now widespread. These include *airhead*, *bummed* (from hippie *bummer*), *grody*, *lame*, *slimeball*, *totally*, *for sure*, and *as if*. Valley girls were also among the first to habitually use *like* for emphasis (*I was like so bummed*) (more on *like* in Chapters 8 and 9).

The youth slang of recent generations has mainly addressed relationships and attitudes, both the speakers' own and other people's. The young people of the 1990s are known as Generation X from the title of a 1991 novel by Douglas Coupland. In some ways the antithesis of the hippie generation, they were perceived as disillusioned and directionless, and some of their slang expresses this attitude. One example is *McJob* for a low-paying, unfulfilling job, a back-formation from *McDonald's*. A similar back-formation is *McMansion*, a "starter" mansion that new earners could afford. *Bite*, a verb meaning to be really bad, was heard as early as the 1970s, but gained popularity with Gen X, as did the word *slacker*, which had been around since the late nineteenth century. A catchphrase of the time that's still heard is *yada yada yada* with the meaning of et cetera. Comedian Lenny Bruce used it in the 1960s, but it reached a wider audience through a 1997 episode of the television series *Seinfeld*. *Whatever* as a vague referent also became common, although the usage wasn't new.

The slang of the Millennials (also called Gen Y), who entered adulthood around the year 2000, and Generation Z, who were born around that date, runs together to a certain extent. It's too early to know which words and phrases will succeed in the long term, but if they have held on over a generational gap, they are promising candidates. Some are close to mainstream already, while others may be unintelligible to older generations. Some possibilities include *extra* (over the top), *lit* (amazing, exciting, also drunk), *salty* (upset or irritated), and *thirsty* (overeager).

## Jazz, Hip-Hop, and Rap: Cool and Fresh

Beginning in the twentieth century, African American musical culture has had a substantial influence on both mainstream and countercultural youth slang. Before that time, there is little record of African American slang. The segregation of Black Americans meant their slang vocabulary was unlikely to reach a larger pool of English speakers and, if it did, was unlikely to be preserved in writing. (That's true of earlier African American speech generally; see Chapters 2 and 6.) Following the typical path of closed-group languages, the situation began to change in the early twentieth century when Black jazz musicians started to perform for White audiences, and later, White musicians also started playing jazz.

Jazz came out of New Orleans around the turn of the century, the successor to blues and ragtime. It shifted north to Chicago and other large cities in the decades following World War I, when tens of thousands of African Americans moved from the rural South to northern and midwestern cities in search of work. The rise of the Big Band sound during the twenties, followed by swing and bebop, added crossover appeal. By the 1930s, listening and dancing to jazz music had become part of the broader culture, especially for young people. Most musicians' jargon never moved beyond the small circle of people who actually made music, but some words were adopted by fans and then by the general public.

*Jazz* itself started as a slang word, but not from the musical world. The first uses in print come from baseball, and mean something like pep or energy. A sports article in the *Los Angeles Times* for April 2, 1912, quoted a pitcher saying, "I got a new curve this year. . . . I call it the Jazz ball because it wobbles and you can't do anything with it." A March 16, 1913, article about the Seals baseball team in the *San Francisco Bulletin* explained *jazz* in inimitable sportswriter style: "What is the 'jazz'? Why it's a little of that 'old life', the 'gin-i-ker', the 'pep', otherwise known as the enthusiasalum." The word had obviously been circulating for a while, but was still new enough that the *Bulletin* writer thought he had to explain it to his readers.

A year or two later, instances of *jazz* with a musical meaning popped up in Chicago. Sometimes the word was spelled *jass*. One example is the name of the Chicago-based Original Dixieland Jass Band. An early musical use in print comes from the July 11, 1915, *Chicago Sunday Tribune*: "The 'blues' had done it. The 'jazz' had put pep into the legs that had scrambled too long for the 5:15." The ultimate origins of the word are obscure. One theory is that it derives from *jasm*, a variant of *jism*, a nineteenth-century word for energy or strength that could also be slang for semen. As possible supporting evidence, *jazz* started being used as slang for sex in the early twentieth century. Other extended meanings are *jazzy* to mean highly decorative, and *jazz* as a substitute for *stuff*, as in *all that jazz*.

*Cool* is probably the most lasting and commonly used jazz contribution to slang. The word first described a restrained style of playing (in contrast to hot jazz). It was in use to mean stylish or excellent by the 1930s, and while it has since had ups and downs in popularity, it has never really gone away. Similar terms are *hip* and *hipster* and their variants, *hep* and *hepster*, all in use from the 1930s to describe someone who was cool, "with it," culturally sophisticated. *Dig* with the sense of understand or appreciate also came into use at about the same time. *Funky* is an old word that meant strong-smelling or spoiled as early as the seventeenth century. In jazz parlance, it meant soulful or down-to-earth jazz music. By the 1960s, it had gained the meaning of stylish or hip, but in a quirky way.

A few of the more technical music-making words also achieved wider familiarity. Examples include *jam* for a musical session, *cornball* or *corny* for saccharine music, and *riff* meaning to improvise. By the 1950s, *riff* could mean to improvise on any topic. Jive, a type of swing, could also be a word for nonsense or misleading or false talk, as well as a verb meaning to mislead or kid someone. *Send* meant to thrill the audience, then to arouse enthusiasm more generally (*That music really sends me*). *Go to town* and *cook with gas*, both meaning to play inspired music, took on the added meaning of doing anything energetically and well.

*Groovy*, now associated mainly with hippies, started life in the 1930s jazz world. Being in the groove or feeling groovey (with an *e*) meant playing your best, seemingly without effort. In the 1960s, the hippie counterculture adopted it as a general expression of approval. *Groovin'* meant enjoying yourself in a relaxed way. Later, many conventional teenagers started using the terms as well. *Groovy* was out of fashion by the late 1970s, although it enjoyed a brief revival among college students during the first years of the twenty-first century.

Jazz slang survived into the 1950s partly through the Beats and the beatnik movement they inspired. (The suffix *-nik*, from Yiddish and Russian, was popular during the 1950s to denote someone with a particular characteristic. *Nogoodnik*, for example, was one briefly popular *-nik* word.) The slang of beatniks borrowed largely from jazz terms, such as *cool* and *cool cat*, *hep cat*, *hipster*, *dig*, and *send*, as well as lesser-known words like *bread* for money. These same words were later passed on to hippies, extending their life still further, while musical terms like *riff* and *jam* got picked up by rock musicians.

Several terms from jazz also carried over into hip-hop. Hip-hop burst onto the music scene in 1973. It started with block parties in the Bronx, where disc jockeys created musical mixes from two record turntables, using techniques like sampling (taking excerpts from different records) and scratching (moving a record back and forth). Other important elements of hip-hop are rap (lyrics spoken rhythmically over the music), breakdancing, graffiti, and fashion. The name *hip-hop* is credited to rapper Keith "Cowboy" Wiggins, who repeatedly chanted "hip hop" in his early performances. *Rap* probably evolved from the talk seriously meaning of the hippie era (as in *Let's rap*).

Hip-hop owns a rich and copious vocabulary, but most of it has not spread much beyond Hip-Hop Nation itself. *Cool*, *funky*, *bad*, *jive*, and *blitzed* meaning drunk are still around from earlier times. Other familiar terms include *dis* (belittle), *homeboy*, *homegirl*, or *homey* (close friend), *chill* (relax), and *word up* (I agree or I mean it). Other fairly widespread terms are *def* (from *death*, but meaning cool), *fresh* (also cool), *fly* (cool and sophisticated), *dope* (excellent), *down with* (agreeable to), *good to go*, and *high five*. *Whattup* and the clipped version *'sup* are also fairly common. At least some of these words and phrases are either on their way to the permanent lexicon or have already arrived.[15]

## LGBTQ: The Language of Gay Liberation

An example of a group whose language has moved into the mainstream as attitudes of the larger society have shifted is that of the LGBTQ community (lesbian/gay/bisexual/transgender/queer or questioning).

There is little record of gay and lesbian slang before the twentieth century. Secrecy was imperative because same-sex relationships were illegal in most parts of the country until the late twentieth century and the advent of the Gay Liberation movement. So-called sodomy laws, although dormant, were still on the books in many places until 2003, when the U.S. Supreme Court ruled in *Lawrence v. Texas* that most such laws were unconstitutional. Early-twentieth-century writers on the subject emphasize that one important purpose of gay slang was "keeping in secrecy from the out-group that which is clear to the in-group."[16] Coded language identified in-group members to each other without revealing their status to others who might be within hearing distance.

The first glossaries of gay slang were usually incorporated into books on the subject of homosexuality, both by insiders and outsiders, usually doctors or sociologists.[17] Very few of the words collected would ever have been generally known. Two exceptions that are now familiar are *in drag* and *camp* as an adjective.

The word *gay* meaning homosexual was part of the gay lexicon long before it entered the general vocabulary. Over the twentieth century, it has evolved from a secret word to widely known slang to standard English, reflecting the political and cultural shifts of the past several decades. *Gay* is an old word, first attested in writing in the thirteenth century. It meant cheerful or lighthearted. It also had a secondary meaning of very well dressed. (Compare *glad rags*, outdated slang for party clothes.) In the seventeenth century, *gay* developed an extended meaning of hedonistic, uninhibited, or promiscuous, suggesting light-hearted behavior that was not quite respectable. One use in this sense is the now-obsolete *gay dog* for a hedonistic man.

The word's first known uses in the United States to refer to homo-sexuality are from the 1920s, but *gay* with this meaning remained an underground term until the 1970s. Writing in 1951, one author argues for *gay* as a preferred term because it is virtually unknown outside of homosexual circles and does not have the negative connotations of a word like *queer*, used by outsiders as an epithet (more about the recla-mation of *queer* in the next chapter). He also suggests *straight* for het-erosexual, also a little-known use at the time. He argues that because *gay* and *straight* have other, more common meanings, they are "safe" code words when talking to strangers. If they're gay, they'll know what you mean; if they're straight, it will go over their heads.[18] Several decades later, this once-specialized meaning of *gay* has become the default. It is rarely, if ever, used in any of its other senses.

The nature of gay slang changed during the 1970s, after an event known as the Stonewall riots (or Stonewall uprising). In the early hours of June 29, 1969, police raided the Stonewall Inn, a gay bar in Greenwich Village. Such raids were common, but this time the bar's patrons fought back, triggering widespread rioting over the next several days. The Stonewall riots are widely considered the starting point of the Gay Liberation movement, as radicalized gay men and women were energized to fight for the right to live their lives openly, without fear of police harassment or arrest.

As the gay community gained visibility, and attitudes within the straight community began to change, gay slang was no longer primarily about secrecy. LGBTQ vocabulary served rather as a way of expressing identity and group membership. One of the first post-Stonewall collections of gay speech appeared in 1972, *The Queen's Vernacular* by Bruce Rodgers (later retitled *Gay Talk*), which included about 12,000 entries.[19] The word play of the title indicates a shift in perspective from earlier sociological studies of gay terminology to the celebration of gay culture through its slang.

Most of the terms collected in *The Queen's Vernacular* and other vocabulary lists remain insider slang, unknown to other groups, although there is some overlap between gay and straight slang for sexual activities, besides some common terms like *one-night stand* and *cruise*. One study conducted in 1970 shows that slang terms vary from group to group and region to region. Although a core vocabulary exists that's known to most gay people, other slang may be known to (or at least used by) only one gender or only people living in one area, for instance, San Francisco or the Southwest. These terms, according to the study's author, are "constantly changing . . . and are generally unknown to heterosexuals," two features (ephemerality and exclusivity) that define most slang.[20]

Since the 1970s, mainstream American English has absorbed a variety of words and expressions from the LGBTQ vocabulary. *Closeted, out, come out, gay pride, gay rights,* and *gay baiting* were all starting to be familiar by around 1970. *Transgender* appeared in the early 1970s and *cisgender* in the 1990s. Both prefixes have spawned variations like *trans-* or *cis-people, trans-* or *cis-man* or *woman,* and terms like *ciscentric* and *transphobic.*[21]

The discussion of African American English in the previous chapter touched on the issue of the broader culture adopting terms without recognition of where they came from. That same dynamic sometimes occurs with gay slang. For example, the expression *throw shade* originated with Harlem ballroom culture of the 1980s, where mainly Black and Latino transgender people took part in competitive performances. The term was first heard more widely in the 1990 documentary *Paris Is Burning*. The original meaning of *throw shade* was to insult someone obliquely, perhaps so subtly that the person wasn't even sure of being insulted. However, since the term has been widely adopted, the meaning has shifted to cover any type of insult and its origin is largely forgotten.[22]

Besides the wider adoption of words from the LGBTQ community, ways of talking about gender and sexuality also started to shift by the end of the twentieth century. *Sexual orientation* is now used instead of the earlier *sexual inclination* (which suggested a choice), and *same-sex* has replaced *gay* in some terms like *same-sex marriage*. *Gay* has also started to cover women as well as men. Terms like *non-binary*, *gender nonconforming*, *gender fluid*, and *intersex*, which aim for inclusivity, have appeared in recent decades, as well as expanded abbreviations, for example, LGBTQIA (adding *intersex* and *asexual*), sometimes ending with +.

While gay slang has in some respects remained the language of a closed group, it also continues to add to the general vocabulary, with many once little-known slang terms now included in the dictionary as standard American English. One possible reason that gender identity terms have become more familiar is that Facebook and dating apps now offer them as options when filling out profiles.

# The Internet: Emojis and Algospeak

Chapter 3 listed words and phrases that the Internet has added to the American vocabulary, but that's not the full extent of its linguistic influence. The online world is also shaping how we use language and, in doing so, creating new linguistic in-groups and out-groups. More people (especially young people) are having most of their conversations electronically these days. In some ways, texting, instant messaging, posting to discussion boards, and commenting on social media have taken the place of old-style chatting. Yet these electronically assisted communications are not exactly the same as conversing face-to-face. They fall into a linguistic gray area, much more casual than traditional letters or even emails, but with some of the built-in limitations and formality of the written word.[23]

Social media posters and texters use a variety of tactics to get around these limitations. Some are techniques that pre-Internet writers already used, such as repeated letters for emphasis or exaggeration (*whaaat? eeeuuw! hmmm*) and repeated or combined punctuation marks (*!!!* or*???* or*!?!*) to express shades of meaning. Typing in all capital letters for emphasis has also traditionally been used by authors of print books. When used in online communications, all caps is often deprecated as SHOUTING and considered rude, but caps are also used to express excitement or other strong emotions, or simply for emphasis (*That is SO crazy!*)[24]

Other techniques have evolved specifically online. One example is the lavish use of abbreviations like *u* for *you*, *cuz* for *because*, and *btw* for *by the way*. Abbreviations might have become popular partly because early cell phones weren't equipped with typewriter-style keyboards (the so-called QWERTY keyboard). Texters had to use the telephone keys to laboriously type out one letter at a time. This problem might also have encouraged the all lowercase style. Later, the microblogging site Twitter at first limited postings to 140 characters, so abbreviations were valuable for squeezing in the most words possible.

Users also figured out creative ways to use hashtags, the hash symbol (#) that indicates the subject of a post and allows people to search for certain subjects. (More about abbreviations and hashtags in Chapter 9.) Hashtags first identified groups (*#history202*), news items (*#bluewave*), or general topics (*#caturday*), but have spilled over into other kinds of electronic communication and can act as a kind of meta-commentary. For example, someone might add *#losingmymind* to the end of a text or an email. Another way to directly signal conversational aims is with a / symbol, borrowed from website coding, as in ending a statement with /*sarcasm* or /*joke*.

Skilled social media users have also figured out ways to make the kinds of gestures that people normally make while talking, like smiling :) and frowning :(, thus giving conversational partners more of a sense of the writer's state of mind. Typed emoticons were eventually reinforced with emojis, stylized icons for smiling, frowning, and much else, which became widely available on electronic platforms starting around 2014. As with words, emojis can also gain "slang" meanings, such as an hourglass to represent a shapely woman or a peach to mean someone's bottom. These features and the ones previously described have helped bring electronic speech closer to the spoken face-to-face kind.

Although the blossoming of texting and online messaging has raised concerns that Americans are becoming less literate, that appears not to be the case. According to one study of a group of teenagers, participants used standard spelling and sentence formation for the most part. Abbreviations accounted for less than 3 percent of the total word count. *You*, for example, was far more frequent than *u*. The group's messaging style was not exactly the same as their writing style, but it was slightly more formal than their spoken speech. They mixed styles to craft the tone they wanted to convey. A study of social media users showed that participants typically calibrated their styles to their target audiences. Messages aimed at smaller, more specific groups, such as a circle of friends, used more nonstandard terms (*dawg*, *chillin'*, smiley faces), while messages broadcast to a wider audience tended to stick to a more formal style.[25]

The Internet is affecting American English in other ways, too. The growth of content moderation filters on social media platforms, which use algorithms to identify and block content that breaks the posting rules, have inspired those platforms' users to get linguistically creative to evade the filters. "Algospeak" uses deliberate misspellings to try to fool the filters, such as *seggs* and *#stopthesteallll*. Algospeak also uses code words or emojis to refer to forbidden topics. For instance, *camping* has been used to signal abortion-related discussions, *unalive* as a euphemism for suicide, and the corn emoji as a substitute for the word *porn* in a kind of rhyming slang. As platforms began trying to combat misinformation about the COVID-19 pandemic, bloggers used substitute words for *pandemic* like *panini* and *panda*.[26]

While content filters work to block misinformation and hate speech, they can also cause problems for sites that discuss issues like women's health, where posters have to replace *sexual assault* with *SA* and *nipples* with *nip nops*. Content filters might also block words that can be used as insulting slang, for example, *cracker*, which can mean a country hick, when they are being used with their literal meaning. The result is that algospeak has become widespread across all sorts of platforms. One survey of social media users found that one-third of respondents used alternative terms to circumvent the filters.[27]

The explosion of specialized blogs, message boards, and other niche sites allows online and social media users to live in what is often referred to as an "information bubble," creating closed groups of like-minded participants. One example is the alt-right, short for *alternative-right*, a loosely connected network of far-right extremists that arose around 2010. The alt-right world originated almost entirely online. Its members connect through blogs, webzines, message boards, and other social media.[28] Alt-right communications make heavy use of slang, code words, and memes, partly to create group cohesion and partly to make their discussions hard for outsiders—and algorithms—to decipher.

Because their conversations deal mainly with inflammatory topics like White nationalism, racism, anti-feminism, and political violence, they need to write using language that evades content filters. Another point of specialized vocabulary is to allow insiders to identify themselves as part of the closed group. A skilled command of the many invented terms and memes marks a person as a true believer and in the know.

Some words were invented as shorthand for concepts that mainstream English doesn't have a term for, such as *femoids* to refer to women in a way that suggests a subhuman status, and *to fedjacket*, meaning to make a case that a poster on a comment board is really a federal agent. Sometimes existing terms are borrowed and given specialized meanings, such as *wrongthink*, which originated in George Orwell's 1949 novel *Nineteen Eighty-Four*, to refer to ideas that alt-righters believe are true but are being suppressed by the mainstream culture's "thought police." Alt-right posters also make heavy use of abbreviations and memes that are specific to their group. For example, the "glass of milk" emoji signifies those of Northern European descent (who are able to digest milk more easily than some ethnicities), and the abbreviation GEOTUS refers to former president Donald Trump (*God-Emperor-of-the-United-States*).

One of the limitations of existing mainly online is that it's fairly simple for outsiders to infiltrate alt-right conversations. That means it's more difficult to keep code words and phrases secret. The terms and emojis mentioned earlier were gathered from readily available articles written by mainstream journalists. Others that have been noted by the outside world and become familiar to people who follow the news (and even some who don't) include the Pepe the Frog meme, a cartoon and emoji associated with the alt-right; the term *cuck*, short for *cuckold*, an insult against insufficiently committed conservatives; S. J. W., a derisive reference to social justice warriors; and the slogan *You will not replace us*, directed at anyone not White. If alt-right language follows the same path as other closed-group languages, these terms will have fallen out of favor shortly after becoming public knowledge and will have been replaced with something new.

In some ways, slang and the language of closed groups still operate the way they always have, as a way to embrace a group identity, while at the same time protecting conversations from uninvited listeners. In other ways, the Internet has had a clear impact on these types of speech. Because vast networks of geographically distant people can be connected online, slang and linguistic trends spread much faster than in past times. At the same time, in-group sites are also much more accessible to outsiders who are looking for them. The more accessible a secret language is, the more often terms have to be replaced. Nonetheless, most closed-group language remains unfamiliar to the majority of speakers. It's still true that only a few words and phrases escape into the mainstream vocabulary. Slang and coded language, even in the interconnected online world, continue to evolve underground, touching the larger speech community only around the edges.

# 8

# The Social Life
# of American English

## Listening to Ourselves and Others

Language isn't only about words, sounds, and structures—it's also about how its speakers perceive and use it. Speech is a social act. Language change and variation take place almost entirely at a subconscious level, but how we talk, and how we view the way other people talk, can be affected by our conscious attitudes and our awareness of others' attitudes. Our way of talking can indicate that we identify with a particular group (or don't), or have embraced a certain belief set or way of life. Our judgment of other people's speech can be shaped by our attitude toward the speaker's cultural background or ethnicity, or our perception of someone's occupation or educational level, or our view of the region they come from.

Consciously or not, people send signals with their speech. We all vary our speech style in different situations. We use one type of language when socializing with friends, for instance, and another variety when making a presentation at work. Even people who typically follow accepted grammatical usage and mainstream pronunciations drop into the vernacular sometimes. Everyone says 'in' for -*ing* a certain amount of the time, and makes nonstandard grammatical choices in casual speech, such as using *real* for *very*. People who have moved away from a region might lose some of their more obvious regional speech traits, but readopt them when visiting back home or even talking with family on the telephone.[1]

Speakers tend to standardize their speech more when they are focused on what they're saying. As shown in Chapter 5, New Yorkers who typically omit r after vowels increase their r production in formal situations. People also aim for standardized pronunciations when they're asked to read aloud. In other situations, they may shift into a more vernacular mode as a way of signaling closeness with the people they're talking to, or projecting authenticity or toughness. Harvard-educated politicians who sprinkle their speech with "down home" words like *y'all* and drop the *g* from -*ing* are trying to show voters that they're just regular folks, same as their constituents. The Native American students who speak like typical college students in most campus situations, but slip into the "rez" accent when hanging out with other Native students, are using language to express intimacy with that group.

In the early 1960s, sociolinguist William Labov conducted a groundbreaking study that revealed how our identity and social circumstances can unconsciously influence the way we use language.[2] Labov looked at certain pronunciations typical of Martha's Vineyard, an island off the coast of Massachusetts. Many of the islanders traced their ancestry to the first British colonists of the seventeenth century. Traditionally, they made their living mainly by fishing and farming, but by the mid-twentieth century both industries were in decline. The economy was beginning to rely instead on tourism. Tens of thousands of summer visitors arrived every year, overwhelming the small permanent population.

Because the island was historically isolated from the mainland, Vineyarders preserved a number of archaic features of English. For example, they continued to pronounce their *r*'s after vowels and at the end of a word, in spite of being located in otherwise *r*-less New England. They also kept old-fashioned words like *bannock* (a cornmeal cake) and *studdled* (dirty or roiled to describe water). A distinctive island pronunciation was to "centralize" the first part of the back vowels in words like *bite* and *bout* by slightly raising the tongue. In this dialect, *right* sounds something like 'rate' [rəit] and *house* sounds closer to 'hoose' [həus].

The centralized pronunciation dwindled over time and by the early twentieth century was heard only sporadically. However, when Labov began his study in 1961, this sound had reversed course and was on the upswing. Younger people were beginning to use it more than their elders. Islanders between the ages of 30 and 45 centralized the *bite* and *bout* vowels more than three times as often as those over 60. Centralization was strongest among Anglo-Americans whose families had lived on Martha's Vineyard for several generations. It was also more common among young people who had left the island for school or other reasons and later returned than among those who never left.

Labov concluded that centralized pronunciation was a marker of identity for Vineyarders who wanted to distinguish themselves from the summer incomers and recent transplants from the mainland. This distinctive dialectal feature was strongly associated with fishermen, a respected group whose occupation had traditionally been the mainstay of the island's economy. Fishing represented the old days, when the island was independent from the mainland and not overrun with tourists. The young people who left and then returned most likely adopted speech patterns of the fishermen as a way of reasserting their status as natives.

Centralized pronunciation was not a deliberate choice. The islanders themselves were unaware of it as a noticeable feature of their speech and apparently didn't consciously control it. Nonetheless, the rate of centralized pronunciations could be correlated with the level of a speaker's commitment to the island. Young people who were planning to leave for school and jobs tended toward more standard speech, while those who planned to make their lives on the island talked more like traditional Vineyarders.

The story of Martha's Vineyard shows that language is a social as well as a purely linguistic process. We have seen examples of similar (largely unconscious) language choices in previous chapters. One reason why regional and ethnic dialect use varies from person to person is that, besides occupation, social class, level of education, and other external factors, whether and how people adopt these varieties depend partly on how they define themselves.

While nonlinguists generally don't have a conscious recognition of the linguistic details of their own or other people's speech, they do have opinions and reactions. These attitudes are another aspect of the social life of language. Chapter 4 described the early American embrace of grammar books that, with few exceptions, championed a form of English based on an idealized version of educated upper-class speech. Many generations of American schoolchildren memorized the rules in these books as a part of their basic education. These rules represented "good English," even though they didn't have much connection with how anyone really talked. For many people in the modern United States, the rules in such grammar books still represent the correct way to use English. Those who veer away from the rules are speaking "bad" English (often labeled "bad grammar," even when referring to word choice or pronunciation).

Many speakers think of their own language use as correct or accentless, and have a lower opinion of people from other regions, classes, or ethnicities. In studies that asked non-specialists (frequently, college students) to label the speech of various regions on maps or to mark the places with the best and worst English, respondents typically judged their own regional variety in positive ways, and believed that their speech was "normal" or "standard" compared with other parts of the country.

Exceptions to this tendency are people whose language has been stigmatized, for example, Southerners and New Yorkers. Most speakers from these regions are aware that their regional vernacular is considered less correct. Nonetheless, they often approve of their own speech for other reasons. Southerners who were surveyed described their dialect as sounding "friendly" and "trustworthy," in contrast to Northerners who, although they might have used more "correct" language or had a less noticeable accent, also sounded "cold" and "dishonest."[3]

Participants in language attitude studies often notice genuine patterns, but describe them in cultural rather than linguistic terms. For example, when residents of Washington state were asked to label the speech of Washingtonians, respondents from the western part of the state used terms like "hick," "cowboy," and "country" to describe eastern Washington speech. The fact that eastern Washington is a rural area where farming and livestock raising are major occupations no doubt contributed to these judgments. However, the dialect of the region does include some South Midland features such as saying 'tahm' for *time*, 'spayshul' for *special*, and 'warsh' for *wash*, so study participants might also have been interpreting speech patterns that they associated with rural or Southern speakers.[4]

A study that measured perceptions of California speech among Californians revealed the same mix of cultural and linguistic judgments. Most study participants divided the state into a northern half, starting around the Bay area, and a southern half, centering around Los Angeles. Northern California was the area most often labeled "normal" or "standard," while Los Angeles and San Diego were frequently identified as "Spanish." Respondents also identified regions by their most salient slang terms, such as *hella* for northern California and *dude* for the southern coastal part of the state. Quotative *like* (*I'm like, wow!*) was heavily associated with Los Angeles and Valley girls. Some people simply labeled areas with descriptions like "surfer speak" (southern California), "hippie talk" (the northernmost area of California, where marijuana is a significant crop), "upper-class" (the Bay area), and "Mexican" (southern and inland areas). While some of these descriptors are obviously based on ideas of a region's culture ("hippie talk"), others correspond to actual linguistic features, such as the common use of *hella* in northern California.[5]

It's worth noting that to people who live in other areas of the United States, Washington is usually considered part of the accent-free West, while the entire state of California is identified as a place of Valley girl/surfer dude language. Residents of these places have a much more complex picture of their state's language, although it may not be one that's linguistically accurate. Participants in the California study, for example, noticed that Spanish is a common language in the Los Angeles and San Diego areas, but failed to note, or at least didn't remark on, its use elsewhere in the state. Quotative *like* is still used as shorthand for Valley girl speech, but it's now common everywhere in the country, especially among people under 40 (more on the evolution of *like* in Chapter 9).

Dialects with easily identified features are the most stigmatized. Regions that diverge noticeably from what's considered mainstream are often singled out for criticism. For instance, Michigan students asked to rank the states in terms of where the best and worst English are spoken overwhelmingly ranked the southern states and New York City at the bottom. Like nearly everyone, they approved the most of their own language use, which they considered accentless and grammatically correct.[6]

Unlike in Great Britain, where the prestigious Received Pronunciation of the upper classes is easily recognizable, standard English in the United States is defined by its lack of obvious regional or class-related features. The Inland North is commonly considered the region with the most standard or mainstream speech. This is true even though, as was pointed out in Chapter 5, the Midland dialect probably includes more features shared by the majority of Americans (post-vocalic *r*, a lack of distinction between *cot* and *caught*), while the Inland North has developed the regionally distinctive Northern Cities Vowel Shift.

The notion that the North is the home of "General American" is based more on the longstanding cultural and economic dominance of the area than on any specific linguistic traits. Certain ways of talking have historically been marginalized, not because there's something wrong with the language itself, but because politically and economically dominant groups hold its speakers in low esteem. Southern speech is deprecated outside the South at least partly because the Confederacy lost the Civil War. The vernaculars of African Americans and other non-White ethnic groups and the speech of working-class or rural people from any region are held in low esteem usually because of racist or classist stereotypes.

Negative perceptions of someone's speech can have a profound impact on the speaker's life in terms of jobs, promotion, entry to social circles, and assumptions about their intelligence and sophistication. In spite of laws meant to protect people from discrimination based on national origin, there are many documented cases of people who do not speak English as a first language being rejected for employment based on their accent. The same is true for native speakers of American English who don't sound mainstream enough for those doing the hiring.[7] A review of court cases that included witnesses who spoke a deprecated dialect of English showed that these witnesses' statements were often mistranscribed in ways that twisted their meaning. Jurors also tended to reject such testimony on the grounds that they couldn't understand it, or simply that it made the witness less believable in their view. These issues sometimes determined the outcome of the trial.[8]

In spite of the disadvantages of speaking in ways deemed nonstandard, speakers of deprecated dialects do not always rush to bring their speech into line with expectations. One reason is that it's not easy for most people to change how they talk. While avoiding stereotyped usages like *yinz* or *might could* is relatively straightforward, changing ingrained pronunciation and grammar patterns acquired as part of our first language is much harder.

Besides, as we've seen, people have a variety of conscious and unconscious motivations for talking the way they do. Embracing a regional dialect is a way of showing loyalty to a place and asserting that you belong. In certain situations, nonstandard or obviously regional speech can convey street smarts, genuineness, insider status, identification with the speaker's audience, or another positive trait. Conversely, using more standardized speech might suggest snobbishness, phoniness, distance from your listeners, or some other negative message. Modern linguistics and educational research have gone some way to destigmatizing dialects and advocating for people's right to their own way of talking. However, language policing—self-policing as well as monitoring others' speech—is still very much an aspect of American language use.

## Monitoring Our Words

As the continuing popularity of eighteenth-century grammar rules indicates, attempts to police the language are an ongoing part of the story of American English. At the founding of the United States, no less a person than John Adams pressured the federal government to establish a department of language standardization. Adams wrote a letter to the president of Congress in 1780, urging him to form a "public institution for refining, correcting, improving, and ascertaining the English language." He argued, "It will have a happy effect upon the union of the States to have a public standard for all persons in every part of the continent." Congress didn't act on Adams's suggestion, but calls for an academy to regulate American speech continued sporadically throughout the nineteenth century.[9]

Americans have also cooperated in the language standardization project by working to reform and control their own speech. As described in Chapter 4, those on the lower rungs of society saw a command of elegant English as an essential first step toward improving their social and economic status. Until the mid-nineteenth century, grammar books were the main source of linguistic guidance, but in the tumultuous years after the Civil War, with its cultural and economic upheavals, Americans began to turn to style guides for advice and linguistic reassurance. Style guides (also called usage guides) explained which words and grammatical formulations were deemed acceptable and which were considered nonstandard or problematic in some way. They promised to help people rid their speech of usages considered lower-class or less educated.

The most popular style guide author of the postwar era was Richard Grant White. White's book *Words and Their Uses*, which appeared in 1870, was concerned with "the right use and abuse of words and idioms." Like many such guides, White's book is a grab-bag of the author's personal prejudices. He was particularly resistant to new words and word meanings. Some of White's complaints are about word uses that language critics still disapprove of today. Examples include *aggravate* to mean irritate (instead of make something worse), *decimate* as a synonym for wipe out (instead of killing one in ten people, its original Latin meaning), and using *lay* for *lie*. Others were temporary fads (e.g., *sample room* as a slang word for a tavern), or more often, they have since become uncontroversial. The latter include *dress* to mean a woman's frock rather than clothing generally, *dirt* for soil rather than as a synonym for filth, *ice water* for *iced water*, and the coinages *reliable*, *practitioner*, *gubernatorial*, and similar words based on existing words like *rely*, *practice*, and *governor*.

Partly because of style guides like White's, benchmarks grew up during the nineteenth century that are still sometimes used to measure whether people speak correct English. Some of these linguistic "shibboleths," or indicators of approved speech, were never a problem until style guides declared them so. One example is the ban on "split" infinitives, so-called because an adverb or *not* intrudes between *to* and the verb, for instance, *I want to not do any work today*, or *It's hard to truly understand it.*[10] (*To* is not actually part of the infinitive, which is simply an untensed verb. Sometimes infinitives appear without *to*, such as *move* in *He helped us move our furniture.*) *To*-infinitives with intervening adverbs and *not* appear in written English beginning in the fourteenth century, and were not traditionally considered unacceptable. One of the earliest criticisms of the usage is found in *A Plea for the Queen's English*, an advice book by Anglican clergyman Henry Alford that was popular in the United States. Alford wrote, "We ever regard the *to* of the infinitive as inseparable from its verb. And when we have already a choice between . . . 'scientifically to illustrate' and 'to illustrate scientifically' there seems no good reason for flying in the face of common usage."[11] After centuries of being normal and acceptable, adverbs between *to* and a verb now became a problem.

Although modern style guide authors are more flexible than Alford, most still believe writers should avoid putting an adverb between *to* and the verb as much as possible. For example, *The Elements of Style* by

William Strunk, Jr. and E. B. White says, "The construction should be avoided unless the writer wishes to place unusual stress on the adverb." *Garner's Modern English Usage* advises splitting infinitives when not doing so would result in an awkward phrase like *unfairly to deflect*, but to avoid the split when it is "easily fixed by putting the adverb at the end of the phrase, and the meaning remains the same." Style advisers like Patricia T. O'Conner, author of *Woe Is I*, who think the split infinitives rule is defunct and should be laid to rest, are in the minority.[12] Many Americans still look to style guides for advice about how to write standard English, so many Americans still try to avoid "splitting" infinitives.

Language self-policing often leads to stilted speech, or to people falling short of their own standards. Because some of the strictures found in grammar books and style guides have never been part of natural English usage, consistently following the rules is almost impossible. Some recommended usages sound right (if a little formal) in certain idiomatic formulas, for example, *It is I*, *This is she* (when answering the phone), or *Carol is taller than I*. However, applying the same rule in other sentences sounds odd, as in *The guy in the purple shirt in that picture is I* or *No other group was as well organized as they*.

Trying to apply these rules across the board can also result in what is sometimes called hypercorrection, that is, using a form that's considered more correct even in places where it's not called for. One typical substitution is to use *I* and other nominative-case pronouns in phrases that are the objects of verbs or prepositions. This formula is especially common in conjoined pronouns, as in *Let's keep this between you and I* or *That's a decision for she and her husband to make*. Another common hypercorrection is the use of *whom* and *whomever* in a subject position, for example, *She'll speak to whomever shows up*. (The relative pronoun here is the subject of the verb *shows*, so it should be *whoever*.)

Case confusion is not due entirely to the influence of grammar books. One famous example of using a subject pronoun after a preposition is from Shakespeare's play *The Merchant of Venice*: "All debts are cleerd betweene you and I." Such phrases have been possible since the beginnings of Modern English. In Old English, the order of words in a sentence was flexible, and relationships like the subject and object of the verb were indicated with varying word endings marking nominative or objective case. As Old English evolved into Middle and Early Modern English, such endings almost entirely disappeared. English speakers now interpret sentence relationships through word order. We know that a noun is the object of a verb because it follows that verb. Pronouns still have nominative and objective forms (*I/me*, *he/him*), but they aren't really necessary for understanding the sentence. If they appear in the wrong place (*she and I* after a preposition), it doesn't really matter.

One explanation for the increasing use of *and I* in phrases like *between you and I* is that it has become an idiom in English. *I* appears in objective-case position far more frequently than most other pronouns. (For instance, a phrase like *between he and they* is much less likely.) Whatever the reason for their popularity, the overuse of such forms as *and I* and *whomever* indicates that many American English speakers believe they need to "watch their grammar," and so reject more natural-sounding locutions like *between you and me* even when they're not only part of normal English, but also correct according to the rules of grammar and style. They have an idealized grammar in their minds, one that neither they nor other people can really follow.[13]

## Monitoring Other People's Words

As noted before, attitudes toward language variety and variations in grammar and usage have become considerably more open-minded since the late nineteenth century. The advent of modern linguistics, which demonstrated that all varieties of language are structured systems and that all language changes over time, along with the rising interest in regional dialects and vernacular speech, led to greater acceptance of variations in grammar and usage, at least at the level of casual speech. Nonetheless, many people remain committed to the idea that only one version of American English is correct—the one based on the rules found in traditional grammar books, even if those rules are obsolete and rarely followed in normal conversation. Many people resist the idea that linguistic styles change, that different situations call for different styles, and that other dialects have equal validity with what they view as standard speech. They oppose any attempts to broaden the definition of what counts as acceptable English. These conflicting attitudes sometimes trigger sensational public clashes over American language use.

One such uproar occurred in 1961 with the G. & C. Merriam Company's publication of *Webster's Third New International Dictionary of the English Language*. *Webster's Third* was an updating of *Webster's New International Dictionary*, which appeared in 1934. The press release revealed that the new dictionary had been thoroughly revamped. It included trendy new terms like *beatnik* and *fringe benefit*, as well as a new perspective on usage that better reflected "the current informality" of American language and culture. As an example of an updated entry, the press release featured a snippet from the definition of *ain't*, which says in part "used orally in most parts of the U.S. by many cultivated speakers."[14]

Newspapers immediately latched onto this description of *ain't* with headlines like "Saying Ain't Ain't Wrong" (*Chicago Tribune*). Although the dictionary had not yet been published, reviews appeared lamenting the degradation of American English and predicting a nationwide descent into illiteracy. The earliest, from the *Toronto Globe and Mail*, was portentously titled "The Death of Meaning." The reviewer accused the Merriam Co. of contributing to the collapse of standard English with a dictionary that "will comfort the ignorant, confer approval upon the mediocre, and subtly imply that proper English is the tool only of the snob."[15]

The appearance of *ain't* in the dictionary should not have come as a shock. The word had been included since Noah Webster's 1828 *American Dictionary of the English Language* (where it is described as "vulgar dialect"). Its appearance in *Webster's Second* had not caused any remark. However, the *Second* labeled *ain't* "*Dial.* or *Illit.*" (dialectal or illiterate). The *Third*, while noting that the word was "substandard" and "more common in less educated speech," also asserted that many educated people occasionally said "ain't I." It wasn't so much the word's inclusion that horrified reviewers, but the neutral description of its usage. If the word must be in the dictionary, they believed that it should be clearly condemned as bad grammar. To the dictionary's critics, *ain't* represented a more general problem with the volume. A number of other new and changing words that they deplored as illiterate or slangy were also listed without warning labels. These included new words formed with suffixes like *-ize* and *-wise* (*finalize, businesswise*), as well as new slang like *cool cats*.

As criticism of the volume built up, *The New York Times* editorial page felt moved to publish a scathing commentary. It started, "A passel of double-domes at G. & C. Merriam Co. . . . have been confabbing and yakking for twenty-seven years . . . and now they have finalized Webster's Third." There followed the usual complaints that *Webster's Third* had done Americans a disservice by including slang and deprecated usages without labeling them as wrong. Because Webster's dictionary was widely respected as an authority on American English, the *Times* editors believed that the publisher had a responsibility to the public to provide sound usage advice.[16]

The *Times* editorial drew a response from Philip G. Gove, the editor of *Webster's Third*. Gove pointed out that *finalize*, widely cited as an example of the Merriam editors' poor linguistic judgment, also appeared in *Webster's Second* without being labeled nonstandard. In fact, he noted, the word had been in frequent use since the 1920s in such reputable places as the *New Republic* and even the *Times* itself. That was enough to justify its inclusion in the dictionary. Gove concluded, "Whether you or I or others who fixed our linguistic notions several decades ago like it or not, the contemporary language of the Nineteen Sixties . . . is not the language of the Nineteen Twenties and Thirties."[17]

Gove's argument was that dictionary makers were not meant to decide which words were worthy of being an official part of American English or to determine what constitutes acceptable speech. Rather, their aim was to "describe the meanings and values of words as educated people use them today." Readers could judge from the examples given whether words were colloquial or more formal.[18]

Eventually, the furor over *Webster's Third* died down. Not all reviews were hostile. One sympathetic journalist, noting "the flurry of nitwitted commentary," pointed out that "the business of a dictionary is to report how words are used, and not to prescribe or proscribe meanings." It is both "stupid and futile" for the dictionary to try to outlaw words that style critics don't like.[19] However, many people continued to insist that *Webster's* should at least try to enforce a mainstream usage standard. Among editors and writers committed to the idea of a single unchanging standard, *Webster's Third* remained notorious for decades as an example of wrong-headed linguistic permissiveness.

A similar drama, with roots in the same beliefs about the existence of a preferred standard of English, played out when the Oakland, California, School Board passed a resolution concerning African American English on December 18, 1996, triggering what became known as the "Oakland Ebonics controversy." The resolution was a policy statement directing the superintendent of schools to devise a program that would help African American students improve their language skills. Using the recent coinage *Ebonics* (from *ebony* plus *phonics*), the School Board referred to research proposing that African American English was part of a creole system with roots in West African languages. (The term *Ebonics* encompasses not only African American English but also Caribbean creoles.) The Board resolved to recognize Ebonics as the "primary language" of many of their African American students and to begin "imparting instruction" using this language as a bridge to facilitating the students' eventual mastery of standard English.[20]

The School Board's goals were not at all radical. The resolution assumed that a command of mainstream English was necessary and desirable for their students. They believed that student outcomes would improve if teachers showed that they respected African American English as the home language of their students, but the eventual goal was to make students proficient in standard middle-class speech. The Board's main aim in defining Ebonics as a separate language rather than a dialect of American English was to be able to access some of the funds set aside for the teaching of English to students from non-English-speaking countries.

The Ebonics controversy was more complicated than the flap over *Webster's Third* because it brought together fraught issues of race and language use. However, the trajectory was similar in certain ways. Misleading headlines began to appear, for instance, "School District Elevates Status of Black English" (*The New York Times*) and "Oakland Schools Sanction 'Ebonics'" (*Philadelphia Inquirer*). Those who didn't read the articles carefully came away with the impression that Oakland was planning to teach in the language of Ebonics instead of in a mainstream dialect of English, or even more disturbing to many readers, to teach Ebonics to students.

The situation was made worse by the School Board's unfortunate wording in one paragraph that described Ebonics as "genetically based and not a dialect of English." It is unclear exactly what the Board meant by "genetically based," but the resolution was later amended to say that Ebonics had "origins in West and Niger-Congo languages." By that time, however, the damage was done. Several African American scholars and other public figures decried the plan as further marginalizing Black students and suggesting that their language capabilities were tied to their ethnicity. One newspaper article quoted linguist John McWhorter as saying, "It's an insult to the cognitive abilities of black children."[21]

Other public figures, such as politicians and educators, added their voices to the outcry, along with many other people who had not read the resolution and had no special knowledge of Ebonics or the issues involved. Some accused the Board of making a poorly disguised grab for funds that rightly belonged to bilingual education. President Bill Clinton announced that the Ebonics program would not be eligible for any such money. The issue got as far as a Senate subcommittee hearing chaired by Senator Arlen Specter of Pennsylvania, where two well-known sociolinguists, William Labov and Orlando Taylor, testified in favor of the School Board's plan. They reaffirmed that African American English is a systematic, rule-bound language variety, but their testimony didn't change many minds.

Public opinion remained firmly against the Oakland proposal. Similar to the furor over *ain't*, *finalize*, and other objectionable words, the main criticism of the School Board's resolution was that it respected the status of Ebonics as a valid form of speech with its own rules of grammar and pronunciation, even if these did not match the forms considered standard in American English. Just as style critics wanted *ain't* to be clearly labeled as bad English, opponents of Oakland's proposal wanted Ebonics to be clearly labeled substandard speech. Commenters often referred to it as slang or broken English. The School Board's goal, which was to help their students acquire mainstream English, was discounted, while discussion raged around whether Ebonics was a "real" language.

As with the controversy over *Webster's Third*, the outrage over Ebonics gradually subsided. One month after passing the initial resolution, the Oakland School Board passed an amended resolution. Besides clearing up the confusion over their description of Ebonics as "genetically based," they rephrased their statement to emphasize that their purpose was to "facilitate the acquisition and mastery of English language skills." They reiterated that they had never planned to teach Ebonics or to teach in it. They renamed their plan the Standard English Proficiency program and quietly began training teachers in how to work with their students on their speech and writing.[22] The term *Ebonics*, like *Webster's Third*, nevertheless remains a buzzword exemplifying foolishly permissive attitudes toward language use.

These two episodes reveal that many people have deeply held views about the value of an idealized speech standard, although it may not match the way they or anyone else actually uses language. They resist the idea that different ways of talking, including regional and ethnic varieties, are also valid. For these people, adherence to "good" grammar is a moral issue. Criticisms of both *Webster's Third* and Ebonics were often couched in moral terms, with references to sloppiness, laziness, decaying standards, and the new "anything goes" society.

Explanations of how dictionaries are put together or how children most easily learn language skills didn't persuade the critics to change their opinions. Many of the people weighing in had no special linguistic expertise, but nonetheless felt entitled to their views. Because language is such an intrinsic part of who we are as humans and as individuals, people are unwilling to defer to scholars when it comes to how to use it. People who have invested in learning the traditional rules laid down in grammar books and trying to apply them resist the idea that African American speech, vernacular usages, or strongly accented regional speech is just as rationally structured, expressive, and complex as the accepted standard.[23]

## Monitoring Women's Speech

The start of the women's movement for equal rights in the mid-twentieth century drew attention to another aspect of language monitoring: negative views about how women use language. Certain features of language use that are part of both men's and women's speech are noticed more in women and interpreted more negatively. A recent example of a vocal trend that has been noted and criticized in women, especially young women, is the shift in vocal register called vocal fry. Vocal fry (usually called creaky voice in linguistic descriptions) is speech pitched lower than the speaker's normal register. It's described as "fry" or "creaky" because of the rough vibrating or popping sounds that accompany the drop in pitch. In some languages, such as the indigenous Mexican language of Jalapa Mazatec, creaky voice is a meaningful part of the sound system. Adding creakiness to a consonant can change the meaning of a word.[24]

Occasional vocal fry is a natural occurrence in most people's speech. Mid-twentieth-century studies of British English speakers showed that men used vocal fry more than women, and the lowered pitch was associated with "hyper-masculinity," authority, and fearlessness.[25] In the past couple of decades, however, vocal fry has been on the rise among young American women. They use it more often than other groups, although it also occurs in the speech of men and women of all ages. It usually happens at the end of an utterance and may be a way to indicate that the speaker has finished talking.

In the early twenty-first century, articles began appearing in American newspapers and magazines, complaining about the tendency of young women to use vocal fry. The articles' authors speculated that it was meant to convey boredom, either with their conversational partner or with the world in general. Young women were cautioned that it made them sound immature and unserious, and told that they would never get good jobs if they didn't change their speech habits.[26]

The lowered pitch that signified authority when British men used it was judged differently when it became a noticeable part of young American women's speech. According to one experiment, people who listened to recordings of young women talking with vocal fry described the speakers as educated, upwardly mobile, professional, and urban, but also hesitant and nonaggressive.[27] It's unclear exactly why the use of vocal fry is on the rise. One suggestion is that it is simply a way for young women to lower their pitch range, possibly to sound more masculine and project more authority. Another idea is that movie actresses started using it to make their voices sound huskier and more desirable, and the trend caught on from there.

As with regional and ethnic dialects, gendered use of language varies from person to person and is influenced by social milieu, level of education, ethnicity, their specific circumstances, and other factors. There are more similarities than differences across gender groups, and many differences within groups. Some distinctions do exist between the speech patterns of women and men. (Recent research has also begun looking at the speech patterns of trans and non-binary people.) However, the way that others perceive women's speech doesn't always match the reality of how they actually talk.

The first linguist to address the issue of women's speech was Robin Tolmach Lakoff, in a 1975 book titled *Language and Woman's Place*.[28] Lakoff's purpose was to explore what language could tell us about the roles of men and women in American society. She argued that women talk differently at all levels, from intonation and word choice to syntactic structures. Women use a variety of tactics to soften their speaking style because they are encouraged from girlhood to "talk like a lady."

Lakoff made several observations about how women use language differently, relying largely on her own linguistic intuition. In the area of vocabulary, she noted that women use more euphemisms like *heck* and *go to the ladies' room*, as well as expressions like *dear me* and "gushy" words like *adorable* and *cute*. According to Lakoff, they also use more precise vocabulary when talking about culture, art, interior decoration, and other subjects that women are supposed to know about. For example, they may use color words like *mauve* and *magenta* when men would say *purple* or *red*. Women sometimes use men's words—for example, saying *cool* or *terrific* instead of *cute*—but men do not use women's words. Lakoff also claimed that women use tag questions (*That's sad, isn't it?*) and hedges (*That's kind of sad*) more often. She also noted that they use a rising intonation at the end of statements (uptalk) (*My name's Susan?*).

These are all ways of tempering speech so it's less direct and assertive, and perhaps more polite. However, these traits can also signal powerlessness and lack of confidence. Lakoff believed that the speech habits women are encouraged to adopt make them sound less competent and keep them in subordinate positions in their work and private life. On the other hand, if they adopt speech styles associated with men (speaking forcefully, using coarse or blunt language), they risk being criticized as over-aggressive and unladylike. Linguistic traits that are seen as positive in men are interpreted differently when women display them.

Later studies have shown that some of Lakoff's impressions of women's language use aren't entirely accurate. For example, women don't use more tag questions overall than men, although they may use them more in certain situations. Also, as later researchers pointed out, tag questions don't necessarily indicate powerlessness or hesitancy. They can be a way of asking for information (*You stay open until 10:00, right?*), or even asserting power over the hearer (*You won't try that again, will you?*). Some studies show that women tend to use tags more often than men to open a conversation (*Great movie, wasn't it?*), but men tend to use them more when seeking confirmation (*You saw that movie, didn't you?*).[29]

Similarly, studies of uptalk show that it does not always indicate a lack of confidence. For instance, in some situations it can signal that the speaker hasn't finished talking yet, or it can be an invitation to the listener to respond. One study of sorority women found that members with higher status used uptalk to soften requests and invite cooperation. (*I need you to do something for me?*)[30] Since the time of Lakoff's writing, uptalk has become much more common in the United States. Although it's popularly associated with young women (who are often criticized for it), Americans of all ages and genders sometimes make statements and answer questions with a rising intonation.

Lakoff's analysis of women's speech has been named the "deficit" approach because it implies that women's use of language is lacking certain features of men's language, which is seen as the norm. An alternative view is the "difference" theory proposed by sociolinguist Deborah Tannen, which claims that women and men have different conversational styles because they are raised in different cultures from childhood.[31] Boys play together in large, hierarchically structured groups, while girls typically play in small groups or pairs. Boys engage in competitive games, but girls play cooperatively, taking turns and making suggestions. Girls aim to fit in; boys try to stand out.

In this analysis, boys' and girls' separate social worlds result in different conversational tactics and expectations. Women's style is more cooperative and supportive, for instance, sympathizing with someone who's in distress by saying, "I know how you feel. That same thing happened to me." Men are more likely to offer practical advice or dismiss the other person's concerns as no big deal. Women have conversational exchanges, asking each other questions and discussing the answers. Men are more inclined to answer questions and then continue to talk, offering extra information rather than reciprocating with questions of their own. (Beginning in 2008, the new coinage *mansplain* started popping up on Internet comment sites to describe the tendency of some men to offer unsolicited facts and explanations.) Of course, not all men take the lecture approach to conversation, nor do all women use the cooperative style, any more than all Midlanders speak with the same accent. These are simply broadly identifiable trends.

Differing conversational patterns lead to misunderstandings and frustration between men and women. Both parties feel that the other is misinterpreting their intentions. Tannen suggested that men and women accept their conversational differences and learn to recognize each other's ways of using language, rather than expecting that either group will or should change. "Understanding the other's way of talking," she wrote, "is a giant leap across the communications gap between men and women."[32]

Like Lakoff, Tannen recognized that women's cooperative speech style often results in their being perceived as powerless, but women changing the way they talk won't solve that problem. That's because people's perceptions of speech depend partly on who's doing the talking. A speech trait that denotes confidence when men have it can be seen as a weakness in women. For example, an indirect, politely worded request might signal that a man has such unquestioned authority that he doesn't need to make demands. The same approach by a woman would be interpreted as a lack of authority or lack of confidence. Women who don't say much are assumed to be timid, while men who don't say much are admired as the "strong, silent" type. Women's supposed speech deficits are not so much a problem of how individual women use language as a systemic problem of women's conversational input being devalued, no matter how it's expressed.

Stereotypes of women's linguistic behavior are not always borne out by evidence, but two female speech traits are real. Women as a group use more grammatical forms associated with the prestige dialect than men do, and women also often lead the way in using new forms that are below the level of awareness (for instance, a shift in pronunciation). William Labov characterized this phenomenon as the Gender Paradox: "Women conform more closely than men to sociolinguistic norms that are overtly prescribed but conform less than men when they are not."[33]

One reason for women's increased use of standard grammar may be that the kinds of employment traditionally open to them, such as secretary, receptionist, store clerk, and flight attendant, involve dealing with the public. These jobs require a command of the agreed-upon linguistic standard. Men, on the other hand, have traditionally worked at many kinds of jobs that don't include public interactions, so don't call for any particular way of talking. Another idea is that standard grammar is associated with cultural refinement, which as Lakoff suggested, is supposed to be one of women's concerns. When marriage was the main way for women to achieve upward social mobility, refined and educated speech maximized their chances. A command of standardized speech is also connected with virtue and good behavior, which are expected more from girls. Using vernacular forms may be stigmatized as unladylike. Yet another factor might be that women in the business world feel more constrained to follow the conventions, while men in positions of power (politicians and CEOs, for instance) can afford to flout them by talking in a folksy or nonstandard way.

In some ways it seems counterintuitive that women also tend to adopt new usages earlier than men. One suggestion is that women make greater use of language to establish their social status because other avenues (like having a prestigious occupation) haven't been open to them in the past. One tactic is to adopt new, locally prestigious forms. For example, women in New York City were quicker to start pronouncing their *r*'s when that became trendy, and they pronounce them more consistently than men. However, women also adopt forms that are happening below the level of conscious awareness faster than men.

For example, a sound change happening in the Detroit area is the raising of the vowel sound in words with the *bite* vowel so it's closer to the vowel in *boy*. Words like *fight* and *right* sound like 'foit' and 'roit' in this dialect. A study of high school students in the area shows that working-class girls who are not planning to go to college—that is, who plan to stay in the area—use the sound much more frequently than either college-bound students or the boys in their circle. This pronunciation isn't prestigious—it's not consciously noticed—but it identifies its users as local. It also distinguishes the girls who use it from other social groups in their high school, such as college-bound students.[34]

One theory that would explain both women's greater use of standard forms and their quicker embrace of new ones is that women are more inclined than men to use language as a way to construct their social identities. Women may also feel freer than men to express themselves creatively though their language use.[35]

## Owning Our Words

Besides the differing ways that women and men use language, and how those are perceived, there are also differences in how people talk about women and men. Lakoff, writing in 1975, pointed out that females were called girls much longer than males were called boys. Male college students, for example, were often referred to as college men, while female students or the female friends of college men were called girls. She also noted that some gender-specific terms were positive in their male form, but negative or trivializing in their female form. Examples include *bachelor/spinster*, *governor/governess*, and *poet/ poetess*. *Master* usually has a positive meaning, such as expert or man in charge, for example, *He's a master of his craft*. (An exception is the slave owner connotation.) *Mistress* can signify the woman in charge of a household, but more commonly in modern times, it has the negative meaning of an illicit sexual partner. *Gentleman* has only a positive meaning, but *lady* can be demeaning when used in phrases like *lady doctor*, *little old lady*, and *my lady wife*.

Another language difference that reflects cultural attitudes is the existence of honorific titles that indicate a woman's marital status. All men, married or not, are called *Mr.*, but women are *Mrs.* if married and *Miss* if single. During the 1970s, feminists proposed *Ms.* as a title equivalent to *Mr.* that would apply to all women. *Ms.* was not a new invention. It had been around for decades as blend of *Miss* and *Mrs.* A 1952 pamphlet on how to simplify business letters advised, "Use abbreviation Ms. for *all women* addressees. This modern style solves an age-old problem."[36] *Ms.* started to become more widespread in the 1970s. The founding of *Ms.* magazine in 1971 no doubt helped publicize its use.

*Ms.* is now very common in the business world and is invariably offered as a choice on forms. However, it has not replaced *Miss* and *Mrs.*, as women's rights activists of the 1970s envisioned. A 2005 study of its use among college faculty and students revealed that professors used it fairly uniformly to refer to all women, but its use was much less regular among students. Some students were unclear about its intended meaning, assuming that it referred to a young unmarried woman. Nor did they see it as a neutral term. Women who used *Ms.* were viewed more positively in professional settings, and were judged to be more career-oriented and independent, but not as warm and approachable as women who went by *Mrs.* or *Miss*. Those who used *Ms.* were also predicted to be less likely to be interested in traditionally feminine activities like cooking.[37]

As cultural attitudes have changed, words referring to women have also begun to change accordingly. The use of *woman* and *women* has greatly increased and is now the most common way to refer to adult females. Although in formal contexts, *lady* and *ladies* may still be considered polite, they can also be seen as dated and patronizing. As more women have become doctors, their gender is not remarked on as often, but when it is, the usual phrase is *woman doctor* rather than *lady doctor*.[38]

Gender-neutral terms for various occupations have also become more common since women have started moving into jobs traditionally reserved for men and vice versa. Many are old terms that have gained popularity since the 1970s, such as *mail carrier* for *mailman*, *police officer* for *policeman*, *server* instead of *waiter* or *waitress*, *firefighter* for *fireman*, and *flight attendant* in place of *steward* or *stewardess*. Others, such as *foreperson* and *chairperson*, date from the 1970s. *Humankind* now often replaces *mankind*, and *synthetic* or *manufactured* is used instead of *man-made*.

People are clearly paying more attention to phrasing that can be seen as sexist. In 2016 a controversy emerged around the *Oxford English Dictionary*, an authoritative source for American as well as other varieties of English speech, and its inclusion of sexist usage examples. These included *rabid feminist* and *nagging housewife*, and examples that stereotyped gender roles, such as those for *doctor* that exclusively described doctors as male. (Usage examples are taken from print sources, so they reflect actual usages. However, lexicographers select which examples to use.) The dictionary's editors undertook an extensive review of usage examples and revised hundreds of entries, for example, replacing *rabid feminist* with *rabid ideologue*. In response to a petition, the dictionary also revised its definition of *woman* and added *derogatory* and *offensive* labels to some words referring to women.[39]

As was the case with *ain't*, which upset American usage purists, it's important that words used as slurs remain in the dictionary. Dictionaries are meant to be records of how the language is used, not how language monitors would like it to be used. However, as Oxford University Press lexicographer Katherine Martin noted, the dictionary can strike a balance: it can be "factually based, but not unintentionally cause harm."[40]

American English speakers are also thinking more about how they use pronouns. In particular, the use of *he* to refer to an indefinite antecedent that could include both males and females, such as *Everyone has his own ideas about grammar*, has been challenged. In earlier English, *they* was acceptable as a pronoun referent in such cases; it appeared widely in writing. However, beginning in the eighteenth century,

grammar and usage books rejected *they* on the theory that it was illog-
ical because words like *everyone* are grammatically singular (i.e., they
take singular verbs), although plural in meaning. *He* was proposed as a
more grammatically correct option that could cover all genders, just as
*man* has traditionally been used broadly to cover all humans.

In the wake of the women's movement, the use of *he* for groups
that potentially include women became more problematic. In spite of
the grammarians' decree that *he* covers everyone, most people assume
that men are being referred to when they read or hear indefinite *he*.
One possible alternative is *he or she*. However, there are certain types of
sentence structures where *he or she* sounds odd:[41]

- Everybody likes chocolate, doesn't he or she?
- Everybody was very polite because he or she was on his or her
  best behavior.
- Everyone was delayed by the traffic jam, so I was relieved when
  she or he arrived.

Singular *they* is much more natural in these types of sentences. (A third
possibility is to use *she* alone instead of *he*, which writers occasionally
choose to do. This usage has the same weakness as indefinite *he*, without the advantage of being considered traditional. Readers typically
assume it's a political statement.)

Usage guides usually advise writers to avoid the construction
whenever possible by using plural nouns, as in *Most people like chocolate,
don't they?* In spite of the strictures of editors and English teachers,
however, the use of singular *they* is on the rise, both in speaking and
writing. Studies show that American English speakers use singular *they*
more than other options in both formal and informal contexts. People
sometimes shift between *he or she* and *they*, possibly because repeated
uses of *he or she* sound awkward. Many participants in these studies
knew that *he* is the prescribed usage, and a minority used it for that
reason, but most chose *they* regardless, because it was more inclusive.
One or two pointed out that unlike *he or she*, it also covers people
who don't identify with the gender binary (more about this issue in
Chapter 9).[42]

Occasionally, invented gender-neutral pronouns are proposed, or
they arise naturally in some restricted location. For instance, *hoo*, which
evolved from an ancient Germanic pronoun, is sometimes used in the
West Midlands and Southwest of England to refer to both males and

females. Closer to home, children in Baltimore schools started using *yo* as a gender-neutral pronoun during the early twenty-first century, usually in the subject position. Typical examples are *Yo* [a classmate] *coming over after school* and *Yo* [the teacher] *handing out papers.*[43]

Two pronouns that transgender communities sometimes use are *ze* as a gender-neutral subject and *hir* as an object. *Ze* began appearing as a suggestion in magazines and newspapers as early as the mid-nineteenth century. The *Sacramento Bee* introduced *hir* in 1920, although the paper abandoned it a couple of decades later. Both words were originally introduced as ways to refer to people when their gender was unknown (e.g., with indefinite antecedents like *everybody*), but starting in the 1990s, they referred to people who didn't identify as either male or female. *Ze* and *hir* have gotten enough use to be included in the *Oxford English Dictionary*, but so far, neither these nor any other deliberately invented pronouns have gained widespread adoption.

When considering the possibilities for more gender-neutral language, Lakoff wrote, "Social change creates language change, not the reverse; or at best, language change influences changes in attitudes slowly and indirectly, and these changes in attitudes will not be reflected in social change unless society is receptive already."[44] Both things seem to be happening in American English. Attitudes toward women's place in American society are changing, and changes to American English are probably reinforcing, as well as reflecting, that fact.

Lakoff's rule also applies to terminology used by and about other groups. As attitudes toward those groups, and within them, evolve, language comes along. One example is the rehabilitation of the word *queer*, historically an unambiguous anti-gay insult. *Queer* is an old word with the broad meaning of strange, but has also been used as a derogatory term for gay people since the beginning of the twentieth century. The status of *queer* began to change as the result of post-Stonewall activism. Queer Nation, a gay rights organization founded in 1990, first embraced the word in the slogan, "We're here, we're queer, get used to it."

Embrace of an outsider slur was part of the Gay Liberation movement's rejection of traditional gay insider slang and "camp" speech on the ground that it tacitly accepted the larger culture's stereotype of who gay people were. As Bruce Rodgers, author of the gay lexicon *The Queen's Vernacular*, explained, many activists were "avidly opposed to this contrived lingo," which they saw as "another link" in the chain of oppression. To younger speakers in particular, the word *gay* seemed middle-class and assimilationist. *Queer* was purposely confrontational. Those claiming it were demanding to be accepted on their own terms.[45]

By the 1990s, *queer* had also gained status as the name of a scholarly approach to cultural study that challenges traditional ideas of gender and sexuality. It then became possible to queer various subjects, as in "queering Jane Austen." This use probably has helped to establish the word in the mainstream vocabulary. It is also increasingly being adopted as a reference (or self-reference) to someone whose gender identity doesn't conform to established categories.

*Queer* has currently overtaken *gay* as the preferred term in newspapers and magazines. However, opinions in the LGBTQ community over word choice still vary. Many older people prefer *gay* and *lesbian* as being more specifically about sexual orientation, while *queer* and *LGBTQ* (sometimes with additional terms like *asexual*) seem to them to be more about gender identity. Others, including many younger people, like the latter two terms for precisely that reason and because they feel more inclusive.[46]

Similar conversations are occurring around other terms. BIPOC, which stands for Black, Indigenous, and People of Color, has been around since at least 2013, but gained prominence during the anti-racism protests in the summer of 2020. Views on its use among people who fit into one of the categories are mixed. Some speakers like it because it is inclusive while still highlighting the unique experiences of Black Americans and Native Americans. Others find it problematic because it erases the distinctions between groups of people whose only similarity may be that they are not of western European extraction. In the words of one critic, podcast host Sylvia Obell, "When you blend us all together like this, it's erasure." As with people in the gay community who prefer not to use the term *queer*, another complaint about BIPOC is that it is a top-down invention, more popular among academics and writers than among the people it refers to. To quote Obell again, "We are asking for a lot of things, and being called BIPOC is not one of them."[47]

This dynamic is even more evident in the discussion surrounding *Latinx*, used as a gender-neutral term for those of Latin American origin, including Mexicans and Central Americans. It has also more recently been adopted specifically as a term for people with that heritage who don't identify as either male or female. *Latinx* first started appearing online around 2004. It is mainly used by activists and academics. Surveys show that the majority of Latin American Americans don't like it, and many who were questioned had never even heard the term. One Pew Research poll indicated that only 3 percent of respondents used it.[48]

One problem with *Latinx* is that it doesn't conform to the structure of Spanish. Spanish nouns have a feature called grammatical gender, which means that all nouns are either male or female (usually indicated through the word endings -*o* or -*a*), regardless of whether they have a physical gender. For example, the word for table, *la mesa*, is feminine. The *x* ending of *Latinx* goes against this system.

The perception that the word was imposed on Latinos from above, in some cases by people who don't belong to that ethnic category themselves, is also a stumbling block to its acceptance for many people. There is some evidence that *Latinx* (and an alternative, the gender-neutral *Latine*) originated with certain political groups in one or more Latin American countries in the 1990s. However, in the United States, many people nonetheless associate *Latinx* with college campuses. According to the surveys cited here, most Spanish speakers do not feel that it's a necessary part of their speech and it has not caught on as an organic feature of the language.[49]

This chapter highlights a theme that we have seen throughout the book, that language use marches in tandem with the larger culture. From the beginning, American English has reflected the linguistic, cultural, and ethnic backgrounds of the people who speak it, as well as the political and social history of the country as a whole. The shifts in how language is used and in what constitutes linguistic acceptability reflect, in part, the many conscious and unconscious linguistic decisions that we all make, both about how we talk and how we feel about the way others talk.

# 9

## American English Today

### Always More Words

The same forces of language change that have shaped and reshaped the language over the past four centuries are still at work, and as always, the vocabulary is in the vanguard. Hundreds of new words and expressions have come into the language just in the last decade or two. Taken together, they form a snapshot of recent cultural trends, revealing how Americans interact in the modern world, and what concerned them at a certain place and time. Some terms are passing fads that will slip out of use as soon as the situation that triggered them is forgotten, but others will find a place in the standard lexicon.

Social media and the Internet continue to provide a steady stream of new vocabulary, not only by contributing new terminology (*subtweet*, *retweet*, *podcast*, *vlog*), but as seen in Chapter 7, by inspiring new ways to use the language. Although abbreviations aren't as crucial as they were before the appearance of phones with keyboards, they have continued to proliferate and have taken on style connotations beyond their original purpose of saving time and space. Many of the most common ones express viewpoints or emotions: *fwiw* (for what it's worth), *imho* (in my humble opinion), *idc* (I don't care), *lmao* (laughing my ass off), *tl;dr* (too long; didn't read).

One of the earliest, *lol* (laughing out loud), is frequently used in a nonliteral sense as a kind of meta-commentary (e,g,, the response, *Lol, no*). Others, like *pwn*, a variant of *own* in the sense of to triumph over or utterly defeat, have taken on the status of insider slang. *Pwn* started life as a typographical error in a video game, but is now a word in its own right, listed in the *Oxford English Dictionary*. *Rlrt* (real-life retweet) creates a new conversational category, an in-person remark that is repeated in a tweet.

Hashtags, which indicate a topic by marking it with a hash symbol (#), have also influenced the vocabulary. Hashtags on popular or controversial topics sometimes jump from social media into the general vocabulary, becoming regular words. One example is the hashtag *#BlackLivesMatter* (or *#blacklivesmatter*, abbreviated *#BLM*) to protest the killings of African Americans in several high-profile cases.[1] The phrase first appeared in a 2010 tweet, but its use exploded after the 2013 trial and acquittal of George Zimmerman, a White man accused of shooting the Black teenager Trayvon Martin. The hashtag sparked the counter-hashtags *#alllivesmatter* and *#bluelivesmatter*. It also began to be used as a single word, as in the phrase *the* #BlackLivesMatter *movement*.

In 2014, the American Dialect Society added the category "most notable hashtag" to its Word of the Year competition, and *#BlackLivesMatter* won both the category and the overall word of the year. Other political hashtags that have gone viral include *#OccupyWallStreet* (economic inequality) and *#MeToo* (sexual harassment). *To hashtag* has also become a verb. The word *hashtag* itself is lately being said out loud as oral commentary, as in *hashtag confusing!* or *hashtag sorry not sorry!* People also sometimes say abbreviations like *lol* and *omg* (Oh my God) aloud, a development similar to the first step in *okay* becoming a word.

Politics remains a prolific source of new terms. Many are a flash in the pan, disappearing after a few news cycles, but other relatively recent terms appear to have more staying power. These tend to emphasize the increasing importance of personal identities to the way people participate in politics and also the country's increasing political polarization. *Red state* and *blue state* entered the vocabulary during the 2000 election, a reference to the colors that television networks used to mark the states according to whether they went for George W. Bush (red) or Al Gore (blue). The terms quickly caught on as shorthand for Republican- and Democratic-majority states. A little later, *purple state* was added to describe places that might be shifting from one color to the other. These terms have gone from simply indicating political affiliation to broadly representing lifestyle and belief systems, as people now make references to *blue-state types* and *red staters*.

Building on this color scheme are the terms *blue shift* and *red mirage*, two ways to describe the same phenomenon. Law scholar Edward Foley coined *blue shift* in 2013 in reference to the 2012 election, when some states that appeared to be going for John McCain early in the counting later shifted to Barack Obama.[2] The shift was due to the fact that votes cast in person, which generally favor Republican candidates, are counted first in many states. When absentee and provisional ballots are counted, the numbers begin to move toward the Democrats. News reporters began using the term *red mirage* during the 2020 election cycle to describe the early part of a blue shift, when vote counts appear to favor the Republican candidate. Both *red mirage* and *blue shift* became much more familiar in 2020 because the COVID-19 pandemic caused an unusually large number of people to cast absentee and provisional ballots, exaggerating the eventual shift.

Several other political terms have arisen, gained new meanings, or grown in popularity over the last couple of decades. *Identity politics* to describe political views based on a person's membership in a particular social, ethnic, or other group came into use in the 1970s, but grew in popularity during the early years of the twenty-first century. *Politically correct* to mean conforming to a dominant political philosophy was first used in the 1930s. Its meaning gradually shifted to the current one of rejecting opinions seen as discriminatory or offensive. It also spun off formations like *eco-correct* and *gender-correct*.

*Woke* in the sense of being alert to issues of racial injustice originated in the African American community during the 1930s. The first known use in print appeared in the title of a May 20, 1962, *New York Times* article by William Melvin Kelley, "If You're Woke, You Dig It." *Woke* with the broader meaning of being informed and enlightened about social justice issues started to become much more common in the early twenty-first century, probably owing, in part, to the hashtag *#StayWoke*. *Wokeness* and *unwoke* also entered the vocabulary around the same time.[3]

*Post-truth* to describe an era in which objective facts carry less weight than personal beliefs and emotions first appeared in the phrase "post-truth world" in a *Nation* article from January 6, 1992. It also became much more common after the year 2000. A related term, *fake news*, was used in the late nineteenth century to describe planted stories in the sensational newspapers, but during the 2016 election took on the new meaning of news that incorporates false or misleading information (or is said to do so). *Snowflake* as a label for people who are easily offended or hypersensitive also gained popularity during the 2016 election, usually as an insult against those on the political left. *Cancel culture* as a term for publicly withdrawing support for public figures who have behaved in a problematic way is yet another term that started appearing frequently in 2016, used mainly by people attacking what they saw as instances of the practice.

Singular events very often inspire a burst of linguistic creativity. One such event was the COVID-19 pandemic, first identified in December 2019. (COVID-19 or Covid-19 is short for Coronavirus disease 2019.) New and newly popular words and phrases ranged from terms related to dealing with viruses and pandemics to joking terms for pandemic-inspired social activities. As with all words invented in response to specific events and trends, many are already on their way out and others were never very familiar, but a few will no doubt be found useful enough to survive.[4] Meanwhile, they are a record of a moment that called for quite a bit of special vocabulary.

One of the earliest COVID-related terms in general use was the *Before Time* to refer to life before the pandemic. *Beforetime* with the now obsolete meaning of a previous time has been a word since at least the fifteenth century. It first occurred with the new meaning of the time before a cataclysmic event in an episode of the television series *Star Trek* that aired on October 27, 1966. During the episode, the show's stars beam down to a planet where all the adults have died of a plague. A young girl named Miri explains, "That was when they started to get sick in the Before Time. We hid, then they were gone."[5]

As the virus upended everybody's life, instances of *Before Time* and *Before Times* proliferated, first on Twitter and then in newspaper and magazine articles. The phrase evoked the nostalgia that people felt for ordinary pre-pandemic activities like hugging friends, dining in restaurants, and shopping without a mask. In an April 2020 *Atlantic* article, author Marina Koren wrote, "The days before the coronavirus swept across the country—the 'Before Time' as many have taken to calling it—feel like a bygone era."[6] The more hopeful term *After Time* has also appeared occasionally.

Words that were familiar to the medical community, but seldom heard outside it, entered the general vocabulary as the virus spread. These include *self-quarantine*, meaning to voluntarily isolate yourself to avoid infecting others, around since 1918; *superspreader*, meaning someone who infects an unusually large number of people, current from 1973; and *flatten the curve*, meaning to reduce the rate at which an infection spreads, cited from 2006. *Hygiene theater* as a term for pointless scrubbing and disinfecting was coined by the journalist Derek Thompson, who wrote, "COVID-19 [has inspired] businesses and families to obsess over risk-reduction rituals that make us *feel* safer but don't actually do much to reduce risk. This is hygiene theater."[7] When vaccines were approved for use, *herd immunity*, used since the early twentieth century to mean immunity through high levels of vaccination, became much more widely known. The term *anti-vaxxer* also became familiar to refer to people who rejected the vaccines.

Prior to COVID, *lockdown* was most often used to refer to the act of confining prisoners to their cells, but during the pandemic it meant government mandates that confined people to their homes except for essential business. *Essential worker* was the term for the health care workers, grocery store clerks, government employees, and others who continued to go to their jobs and work onsite. *Long hauler* originally meant a vehicle used to travel long distances, first cited in 1901, then a person who traveled long distances, especially a truck driver. During the pandemic, it started to mean someone who experienced the long-term aftereffects of COVID. The verb *to mask* has been around since Shakespeare's day, but *mask up* became much more common during 2020.

Wordsmiths soon started creating combinations based on *corona* or *COVID/Covid*. Examples include *coronapocalypse*, *coronasomnia*, *corona-coaster* (the ups and downs experienced during the pandemic), *coronaca-tion* (forced leave from work or school), *coronacut* (homemade haircut due to salons and barbershops being closed), and *coronababies* (children conceived during lockdown). *Covid* combinations include *covid beard* (grown during lockdown), *covid baking* (baking to keep busy while at home), and *covid 15* (pounds gained from comfort eating). *Covidiot* became popular as a term for someone who refused to socially dis-tance, wear a mask, or otherwise cooperate with restrictions. An alternative term was *moronavirus*. *Quarantine* also lent itself to several coinages, including *quarantaiment* (entertainment while quarantined), *quaranteam* (people you continue to see during quarantine, also known as a bubble), and *quarantini* (a drink enjoyed during virtual happy hour; another possibility is a *coronarita*).

Access to the Internet was even more crucial than usual while Americans were sheltering in place (current since the 1970s for finding a safe place in one's immediate surroundings during a tornado or other disaster). Many people were introduced to the videoconferencing program Zoom, first launched in 2012, and *to zoom* became a common verb. The verb *unmute*, around since the nineteenth century to mean releasing the sound of a musical instrument or electronic device, became much more common, as Zoomers everywhere reminded their fellow conference participants to turn on their computer's microphone. Obsessively roaming through all the bad news on the Internet inspired the words *doomscrolling* and *doomsurfing*.

Because the Internet was even more than usually the main mode of communication and news gathering for much of the population, COVID-related words spread very quickly. Controversy over causes of and treatments for the coronavirus, and later over the efficacy of vaccines, also led to creative ways to discuss these topics without running afoul of content filters. As mentioned in Chapter 7, *panda*, *panini*, *panorama*, and other *p*-words stood in for *pandemic*. On anti-vaccination sites, euphemisms like *pizza* and *Moana* stood in for Pfizer and Moderna, and vaccinated people were referred to as swimmers. These types of words were never widely known and won't last, but they indicate what is sure to be a continuing trend in American word invention—the interplay between language users and the technologies that try to moderate or censor written speech.

## Grammar Trends

Like the vocabulary, the grammar keeps evolving. Old words take on new grammatical roles as different ways of shaping sentences come into vogue. For instance, Americans keep adopting new ways to say *say*, each with slightly different characteristics. Quotative *go* (as in, *He goes, hey, that's great!, so I go, yeah, thanks*) was first heard among adolescents in the 1970s. Although mainly used in the present tense, past tense is also possible (*She went, no, thank you, and walked out*). One suggestion for how the usage evolved is that it comes from the common way of presenting imitative sounds with *go*, for example, *Cows go moo*.[8]

People who picked up quotative *go* in the 1970s continue to use it, but the next generation of adolescents adopted a new possibility, *all*. Quotative *all*, used in sentences of the form *She's all, do you like it?* originated, along with so many other linguistic trends, in California during the late 1980s. It's used mainly in the present tense (*I'm all* rather than *I was all*), and nearly always for reporting actual speech rather than thoughts. Over the next decade, quotative *all* spread across the country, but by 2005 it had reached the peak of its popularity. Although still sometimes heard, it's been giving way since the early 2000s to *like*.[9]

As mentioned in Chapter 8, quotative *like* is stereotypically associated with airheaded young women, especially Valley girls. However, since the early 1990s, this way of reporting speech has become common among young people generally, not only in California, but also around the country. While most studies indicate that young women use it the most, it's very widespread among young men as well. One survey even found that male participants used quotative *like* more than the females in the group. Older people also use it, although less frequently. *Like* has crossed ethnic boundaries as well, with some Black and Latino speakers adopting it, although at lower rates than White speakers.[10]

When *like* to introduce quoted speech first came to the attention of language critics, it was dismissed as a meaningless verbal tic that would most likely be a passing trend. As it turned out, quotative *like* has shown impressive staying power. One reason might be that it's such a versatile usage. It can be used with the past or present (*I was like, I don't think so, then he was like, okay, fine*). It can also introduce thoughts and reactions as well as reported speech. Compare *I'm like, oh no, don't ask to see my license*, which can be (and presumably would be) a report of the speaker's thoughts, to *I said, oh no, don't ask to see my license*, which could only have been spoken out loud. *Like* can even report non-speech sounds (*It was like, boom!*).

Quotative *like* also has the advantage of adding drama to a narrative. It is thought to have evolved from the longstanding use of *like* to focus some element of a sentence, as in *That movie was like really awful*. Introducing indirect speech with *like* extends that use. It lets speakers retain all the intensity of direct quotation while also allowing them to add their own point of view to the narrative. This flexibility is surely one more reason why *like* has been unexpectedly long-lived and may continue to stay around.

Another word that's been expanding its territory lately is *so*. The adverb *so* traditionally modifies adjectives or other adverbs:[11]

- She's so crazy.
- I was so very touched by your note.

During the late 1990s, uses of preverbal *so* expanded to modify words and phrases that can't usually be qualified or compared. These include nouns, verbs, and prepositional phrases. It can also occur before negatives:

- It's so not your business.
- He's so going to be sorry.
- Ella so hasn't changed.
- I'm so with you on that.

This way of using *so* is sometimes called GenX *so* because it first started appearing in the language of young people of Generation X, or drama *so* because it adds emphasis to a statement.

By the early 2000s, this usage was spreading. Like many linguistic innovations, young women produced it the most, but young men and older people also adopted it. One theory is that it derived from *so totally*. A similar use of *totally* to modify words that can't usually be qualified has been acceptable since the early nineteenth century (e.g., *That's totally false*). *So* might have been added for extra emphasis (*That's so totally false*), then later allowed to stand on its own.[12] It fits into the same verbal slot as modifiers like *really*, *definitely*, and *certainly*. While an older person would say, *You're certainly not getting my money*, a younger one would say, *You're so not getting my money*. This emphatic use of *so* may be a trend that will eventually go out of style, but for now it remains a popular way of forcefully underscoring a statement.

Another word that added to its repertoire in the early twenty-first century is *because*. In standard usage, *because*, which is traditionally identified as a conjunction, is either followed by *of* and a noun (*because of their courage*), or by a sentence (*because we needed to leave early*). Sometime during the 1990s, *because* started to be treated like a preposition, which can be followed directly by a noun.[13] This use of *because* became much more common with the rising popularity of Twitter and other social media, perhaps because it could encapsulate an idea with fewer characters than a full sentence would take.

Besides the fact that it saves characters, *because* + noun gives the sentence a humorous or ironic tone. *Because reasons* was the first combination to become popular and was established as a set phrase by 2010. *Because reasons* suggests that the reasons alluded to are too trivial and poorly supported to bother mentioning. When presented as part of the speaker's own logical processes, it works as a self-deprecating joke. A more standard phrasing, for example, *because of various reasons that I won't enumerate*, loses that edginess and sounds more serious.

Within a few years, *because* had branched out and was appearing with adjectives, interjections like *wow*, and words like *yes* and *no*. Some early examples include:

- Also, this is my current plan. It has seven steps because reasons.
- Completely stripped inside because race car.
- Almost lit this on fire. Because ugly.
- But don't, like, "follow" me, because ew.
- Is that another word for drunk? Because yes.

*Because reasons* and similar phrases share some of the typical hallmarks of slang. They are borderline ungrammatical and therefore disruptive and striking, and they set a light tone. Expressions like *because awesome* and *because science* also establish an in-group connection between the speaker and the hearers (or readers), another function of slang. These phrases stand in for a much longer explanation that the speaker doesn't have to make explicit because the intended audience already gets it. Although successful as slang, prepositional *because* so far has not gained a place in the standard dictionaries. It has lasted a while and may eventually enter the permanent vocabulary, but if it is like most slang, it will probably drop out of use.

Singular *they*, on the other hand, looks like it's becoming well entrenched in American English usage. This development might have been inevitable, given its already widespread use as a generic pronoun. However, the major impetus behind its official acceptance by style guides and publishers was the increasingly evident need for a gender-neutral pronoun. *Washington Post* copyeditor Bill Walsh announced in 2015 that the *Post* would begin using singular *they*, saying that he had been personally "rooting for" its adoption as a generic pronoun for years. What finally tipped the balance was "the increasing visibility of gender-neutral people." In the circumstances, "allowing *they* for a gender-nonconforming person is a no-brainer. And once we've done that, why not allow it for the most awkward of those *he or she* situations?"[14]

In 2017, both the *AP Stylebook* and the *Chicago Manual of Style* followed suit. Paula Froke, lead editor of the *Stylebook*, explained that the Associated Press made the change for two reasons: "Recognition that the spoken language uses *they* as singular and . . . we also recognize the need for a pronoun for people who don't identify as a he or a she."[15] The *Chicago Manual of Style* also allows *themself*, as in *The individual themself identifies as non-binary*. Both guides, however, are still uncomfortable with using *they* as a generic pronoun when gender identity isn't an issue. They prefer rephrasing the sentence, for example, by making the antecedent plural.

Dictionaries have also embraced the expanded uses of *they*. The *Oxford English Dictionary* lists both its generic and non-binary uses, as does Merriam-Webster's unabridged dictionary. Both dictionaries consider both uses of *they* acceptable (*Nobody has to do it if they don't want to* and *Mx. Jones found themself alone in the room*). In a 2019 usage note, Merriam-Webster's editors explained that they had adopted singular *they* based on the same criteria that they apply to every addition to the dictionary: "meaningful use, sustained use, and widespread use." Pointing to its many recent appearances in print and on social media, the editors concluded, "There's no doubt that it is an established member of the English language."[16]

## Dialectal Ebb and Flow

American dialects also continue to shift and form new patterns. In some cases, the sets of sounds that define a region are shrinking their range or starting to be heard less often, especially among younger speakers. In other cases, one or more features are spreading, although possibly not in a uniform way. Dialectal change, as always, is patchy and incremental.

The Northern Cities Vowel Shift, a defining trait of the Inland North, shows signs of leveling off or receding in some areas. As described in

Chapter 5, the Northern Cities Shift means that vowels typically pronounced with the tongue low in the mouth are said with the tongue higher and more forward than usual, which, in turn, pushes the higher vowels back and down. One of the earliest and most distinctive parts of the Shift, the raising and "gliding" of the low front vowel in words like *hat* and *cat*, so they sound something like 'he-yet' and 'ke-yet' [eə], seems to be waning. Some younger speakers don't exhibit the feature at all. Among other speakers, it's become more limited, only occurring before nasal consonants like *m* and *n*. That means, for instance, that the name *Ann* still sounds more like 'Ian', but *cat*, where the vowel isn't followed by a nasal, has the same pronunciation as in other regions. Other segments of the Shift are either failing to gain new speakers or are only expanding in a fragmented way.[17]

The Northern Cities Vowel Shift may be losing steam partly because sounding like you're from a northern city is viewed less favorably than it once was.[18] The Shift arose in urban areas of the North and upper Midwest during the mid-twentieth century when the economy was booming due to heavy industries such as auto making. In recent times, these industries have shrunk and the economy has declined. At the same time, the raised, gliding pronunciation of the *hat* vowel has become a stereotyped feature of the Inland North dialect. The dialect's speakers themselves consciously notice it, often with disapproval.

A survey of Syracuse, New York, residents asking for their perceptions of local speech indicated that many were aware of the pronunciation and had a negative view of it. One participant described the sound as "a hard vowel accent that I'd like to think I don't possess."[19] For younger people especially, the pronunciation conjured an image of someone who is less educated. The exception to this trend is blue-collar men, whose speech is much more likely to feature the hallmarks of the Shift than that of other speakers. This pattern supports the idea that the pronunciations of the Northern Cities Shift have become a way of identifying with a particular place and social group. Those who feel less attached to the area, such as college-bound students, are more likely to avoid the most obvious features of the local accent.

The Inland North is seeing some other changes as well. The area has been one of the places in the United States (along with the Southeast and New England) where speakers pronounce the *cot* [ɑ] and *caught* [ɔ] vowels differently, with the vowel of *caught* higher and more rounded.

However, many young urban speakers are beginning to merge the pronunciations so both have the low back vowel of *cot*, bringing their speech more in line with that of the Midland and West.[20]

The Southern Vowel Shift continues to fade in urban areas of the South. This is especially true for the later stages of the Shift, described in Chapter 5, when the vowels of *bait* and *bet* switch places or nearly so and pick up a glide (to become 'beh-ate' [bɛet] and 'bay-et' [beɛt]), as do the vowels of *bit* and *beat* (to become 'bee-it' [biɪt] and 'bih-eet' [bɪit]). The pronunciation of words like *time* and *ride* without a glide so they sound more like 'tahm' and 'rahd' [aː] is also becoming less common. As with the fading of the Northern Cities Shift, these changes are happening much more frequently among urban and suburban young people from white-collar backgrounds. Older people, rural people, and working-class people are more likely to retain some southern features. One recent study of Raleigh, North Carolina, speakers shows a fairly consistent absence of southern vowel sounds among young middle-class Raleigh natives. This trend is likely due, in part, to the large influx of people from other regions that started in the 1960s, which meant greater mingling between Raleigh natives and non-Southerners at school and work.[21]

The centralizing of the *bite* and *bout* vowels on Martha's Vineyard, discussed in Chapter 8, is also becoming less common, and for some of the same reasons.[22] The fishing tradition, once so central to the Vineyard identity, has all but died out. Commercial fishing is no longer considered a viable career option for young people. They are more focused on other possibilities, including some that will take them to the mainland. Also, Vineyarders no longer have the same feeling of resistance toward tourists and "summer people" that they expressed in the 1960s. In the words of one resident, "It is just part of Vineyard life."[23] As the islanders have grown less isolated from the mainland and more engaged socioeconomically with the rest of the country, their distinctive vowel sounds are no longer so prominent as a badge of identity. They are still heard, but less often.

In contrast with the vowels in other parts of the country, some parts of the California Vowel Shift are expanding across the West, although not uniformly. Different combinations of sounds are heard in different states.[24] (Some scholars have starting calling these vowel changes the Elsewhere Shift to contrast with the Northern Cities and Southern Shifts because they are now found in various western states besides

California.) One part of the California Shift that has become a general western sound is the pronunciation of the high back *boot* vowel more forward in the mouth, so *cool* sounds like 'kewl'. To a lesser extent, the midback vowel of *boat* is also moving forward, for a pronunciation something like 'bewt'. Besides California, this sound is heard in Oregon, Nevada, and Colorado, and sporadically in a few other western locations.

The California style of pronouncing the short front vowels lower and farther back in the mouth, so *bit* sounds like *bet* (*a lettle bet*), *bet* is moving back toward *but* (*Don't but on it*), and *bat* sounds almost like *bot* (*a baseball bot*), is also spreading. However, this pattern is only partial in most places outside California. For instance, Oregonians may push back the vowel of *bat* so it sounds more like *bot*, but pronounce the other vowels more in line with other dialects. Speakers in Colorado and Nevada pronounce the *bet* vowel lower (closer to *bat*) and the *bat* vowel farther back in the mouth (closer to *bot*), but the vowel in *bit* is less likely to be shifted. Washingtonians haven't developed the lowering and backing pattern so far. These vowel changes vary depending on the age and gender of the speaker. They tend to be more pronounced among younger speakers, especially young women.

A pronunciation shift that started in the Pacific Northwest is the raising of short vowels when they come before *g*, so *bag*, which normally has the same low front vowel as *bat* [æ], sounds closer to *beg* [ɛ] (or in some cases [e]). This pattern is heard in Oregon and western Washington, and seems to be spreading to northern California and perhaps other places in the West. Shifting vowels before *g* are common to various ethnic groups in the region, including Chinese Americans and Mexican Americans. Young women are leading the way in adopting these sounds, a sure sign of a change in progress. Along with the other western vowel shifts, raising before *g* is clearly part of a growing pan-western dialect.[25]

American dialects are continuing to evolve, which is what we expect dialects to do, but American English is not homogenizing overall. The traditional dialectal boundaries are still largely intact. Each region still owns a unique constellation of sounds, words, and grammatical structures that distinguishes it from the others, although the details may be changing. Chicagoans of today might not sound exactly like Chicagoans of fifty years ago, but they still sound different from Charlestonians and San Franciscans.

# American English in the World

In 1828, Noah Webster predicted that the American language would be spoken by *"three hundred millions of people"* within a couple of centuries. He expected American English to be spoken by more people than "any other language on earth," except perhaps Chinese, and to have more influence than British English. Others in the new republic thought the same. John Adams wrote in 1780, "English is destined to be in the next and succeeding centuries more generally the language of the world than Latin was in the last or French is in the present age. . . . The increasing population in America, and their universal connection and correspondence with all nations will . . . force their language into general use."[26]

To some extent, these predictions came true. There are currently about four times as many English speakers in the United States as there are in the British Isles. It's also clear that English has become a common global language over the past several decades. By some estimates, as many as 2 billion people around the world speak at least a little English.[27] English is the language of worldwide shipping and air traffic control, and the official language (or one of them) of a multitude of international organizations, from the European Union to OPEC. It is the main language of international business, and of the majority of scientific and scholarly journals. Protesters around the world carry signs written in English, knowing that these will be broadcast internationally and understood in most places. English is the default language of tourism. In practical terms, it's the most likely language for two speakers of different languages to have in common.

Webster and Adams were mistaken in one respect, though. The initial spread of English was not due to Americans. Until the twentieth century, the American version of the language had little impact outside its own borders, except for word coinages that crossed over to England. English first made it around the world thanks to the British Empire. By the eighteenth century, English settlers were established not only in the American colonies, but also in Canada (where English competed with French), and on various Caribbean islands (where English-based creoles eventually evolved). By the late nineteenth century, the British had extended their reach into every part of the globe, including

Asia, Africa, and the South Pacific. The English that took root in these regions was based on the speech of the British.

In areas where the British settled permanently in large numbers, such as New Zealand and Australia, English became the primary language of the country. In places where British residents were in a minority and usually not permanent, such as India, English became a second language for the educated, especially businesspeople and those in official positions. When these countries gained independence during the twentieth century, many chose to name English as an official language because it's a convenient common tongue where multiple local languages are spoken. (E.g., India is home to nearly two dozen recognized regional languages, but the official languages are English and Hindi.)

This situation did not change until after World War II, when the United States emerged as a political and economic power at the same time as the British Empire was breaking up. English remained a useful language to know, but now because of American rather than British influence. A knowledge of English was essential for diplomacy and international business dealings. After the war, large numbers of Americans started traveling in Europe for the first time, and some familiarity with English was also helpful for Europeans who ran hotels, restaurants, shops, and tours. The practicality of learning English gradually built on itself. Visitors to Europe from other non–English-speaking places, such as Japan, learned English because they could count on one or two people knowing a little wherever they went.

In the late twentieth century, Americans also started exporting their culture. American movies, television programs, and popular music traveled the globe, and international franchises like McDonald's and Starbucks introduced the world to American brands. In this way, many more people were casually exposed to American slang and advertising language. Most recently, the Internet and social media have further encouraged the spread of American English.[28]

While it's clear that America's cultural and political dominance has led to speakers of other languages choosing to learn English, it's less obvious that the English they're learning is specifically American. Much of the world's English instruction comes from textbooks published in England or from teachers who speak British English.[29] This is especially true in former British colonies. British English also remains prestigious in western Europe. Nonetheless, there's some indication that speakers of world Englishes are starting to accept some American vocabulary words.

One clue is trends in word choice. British and American vocabularies include dozens of alternative terms that refer to the same thing. Some examples are word pairs such as *lorry/truck, barrister/attorney, biscuit/cookie, number plate/license plate, torch/flashlight, off-licence/liquor store, mobile phone/cell phone, porridge/oatmeal,* and *rubbish/garbage.* In one recent study, researchers reviewed the tweets of people in several countries to see which word choices they made.[30] They found that Twitter users in most places tended to favor American terms. Exceptions were the former colonies of Australia, New Zealand, South Africa, and India, which showed a slight preference for British terms, although also using Americanisms. The survey also found that American spelling was widespread. (As mentioned in Chapter 1, Americans adopted several alternative spellings that Webster included in his 1828 dictionary, for example, *favor* instead of *favour, organize* instead of *organise,* and *theater* instead of *theatre.*)

Similarly, a review of English-language newspapers, magazines, radio, and television in Nigeria showed that Nigerians are beginning to choose American terms rather than their British equivalents, even though Nigeria is a former British protectorate. Examples include *cookie* (instead of the British *biscuit*), *elevator* (instead of *lift*), *gas* (*petrol*), *movies* (*films*), *pants* (*trousers*), and *vacation* (*holiday*). American expressions like *pass the buck* are also in use.[31]

Besides learning English, speakers of other languages have also adopted English words into their own vocabularies, although they make up only a small part of the word store of any other language. For instance, one recent survey of English loanwords in common use in France features 360 terms, with many Britishisms or words that are common to both British and American English. Obvious Americanisms include *rush hour, boss, cornflakes, chewing gum, jeans, hot dog, snowboard, start-up,* and *cool.* Expressions like *no stress, just do it,* and *fashion victim* are also on the list.[32]

Such borrowings have sparked controversy in many places, as communities work to preserve the integrity of their native languages. However, Americanisms are probably not as prevalent as it might at first seem. Most Americanisms come into other languages for the same reason that Americans adopted words like *raccoon, voodoo, filibuster, spaghetti,* and many others—because they name a novel object, trend, or idea. As terms like *chewing gum*, *jeans*, *rush hour*, and *fashion victim* suggest, the kinds of American words that find their way into other languages these days tend to come from American pop culture. Other examples of popular borrowings include *cheeseburger*, *hippie*, *gangster*, *jazz*, *motel*, *wild west*, *email*, and *wow*. As noted in Chapter 3, *okay* is now a word in numerous languages.

Adopted words often change their shape to better fit into the borrowing language, and sometimes narrow or change their meanings as well. Some examples are German *der Rowdy* (the hooligan) and *der Evergreen* (the golden oldie), and Spanish *básquetbol* (basketball) and *un cóctel* (a cocktail). Argentinian Spanish has *un shopping* (a shopping mall) and *un country* (a gated community). *Un call* in Italian refers specifically to a business phone call. American loanwords in Japanese change to fit Japanese pronunciation rules, as in *deeto* (date), *apato* (apartment), *sofutu wea* (software), and *besuboru* (baseball).[33]

The languages that continue to be most affected by American English are the varieties of English spoken natively in other places. The word exchanges between the United States and Great Britain over the centuries are too numerous to count. While eighteenth-century word watchers in England once complained about Americanisms sullying the purity of English, the most common fear in modern times is that American words and usages are swamping British English through television programs and other forms of popular culture, and pushing British words out. Round-up articles appear regularly in British newspapers listing common peeves. Some that are frequently mentioned include *apartment* for *flat*, *cookie* for *biscuit*, *movie* instead of *pictures* or *film*, *season* for *television series*, and pronouncing the letter Z as 'zee' rather than 'zed'. British English also absorbs expressions and alternative grammatical usages, for instance, *Can I get a coffee*, *reach out to*, *I'm good, thanks*, and even occasional baseball expressions like *step up to the plate*, although most English people don't know the rules of baseball.

The perception that Americanisms are taking over British English is overstated, however. When people hear a word or usage that grates on them, they start to notice its use, but it's often less of a trend than they think it is. Besides, the presence of an American word doesn't mean the absence of the British equivalent. Surveys that ask informants about their word use, or that keep track of certain words appearing in the British press, find a clear preference for British English. While young people do pick up some Americanisms from social media, they more often use local terms that are specific to their social group and neighborhood.[34]

A similar situation is true for the English of New Zealand and Australia. Like the British, language purists in these places often complain that Americanisms are diluting the native vocabulary. Many of the same terms that are seen as problematic in England are also frequently mentioned in New Zealand and Australia. These include *movies, cookie, elevator, flashlight* instead of *torch, guys* instead of *blokes*, and such expressions as *sign off on* rather than simply *sign* and *meet with* instead of *meet*.

Again, it appears that this issue is overblown. Scholarly studies show that most New Zealanders and Australians use the words and expressions of their own dialect nearly all the time. When they do choose Americanisms, these don't necessarily replace native words. More likely, they fill a gap in the vocabulary. Even word pairs that might be considered synonymous have slightly different connotations for their users. For example, *service station* (American) implied a wider range of services than *petrol station* for New Zealanders who were asked about those terms.[35]

Word sharing flows in both directions. While people in other English-speaking places are watching American television, Americans are watching British, Australian, and New Zealand programs, as well as working for global companies, and adopting words and expressions that are useful or simply appealing. Americans have embraced British English with such enthusiasm that the website *Not One-off Britishisms* (notoneoffbritishisms.com) has collected hundreds of Britishisms heard in America. Besides *one-off*, a random sampling of these includes *cheers, queue, brilliant, roundabout, twit, spot-on, go wonky*, and *gutted*. Australian slang also enjoys some popularity in the United States. Words and expressions that have become familiar include *barbie* (for *barbecue*), *good on ya, no worries, whinge, she'll be right*, and *beauty* as an exclamation.

Now that more young people are familiar with soccer, the phrase *score an own goal*, meaning to accidentally score against your own team, has become popular. *Be on a sticky wicket* (in a difficult situation) and *have a good innings* (a successful turn at bat), both British cricket terms, are also becoming more familiar to those who watch cable television sports. It's interesting to note that the first two have already been absorbed into political commentary, so are probably on their way to becoming part of the American vocabulary.

As the American language continues to evolve, the same processes of language change and language variety are still at work, although they may assume new guises. Novel interactions with technology, changing cultural and demographic trends, and American membership in the global community have all shaped the language in new ways. These influences will no doubt continue into the future.

# Afterword

## American English Tomorrow

The story of American English doesn't have an ending. As long as the language has native speakers, it will continue to evolve and grow. We can be sure that it will keep adding and subtracting vocabulary, inventing new slang, and slowly refining its vowel sounds. The only question is what form these changes and variations will take.

Although we can't predict the form of new words and expressions, or exactly where they will come from, history suggests that certain parts of the culture will continue to be heavy contributors. Politics will surely provide new slogans and slang terms, some of which might ensconce themselves in the language permanently. These might, however, arrive through different conduits. As described in previous chapters, much political discourse takes place online these days and probably will continue to do so, leading to more "insider language" creations that facilitate unmonitored discussions. The recent rise of cryptocurrency, the online payment system, may also add more words to the vocabulary if it becomes more established. *Bitcoin* and *blockchain* are fairly familiar, but terms like *decentralized autonomous organization* and similar jargon less so.

COVID-19 might also have a lasting impact on the language, especially if it becomes endemic. Brand names for vaccines against the virus (e.g., *Comirnaty* and *Spikevax*), may eventually become household words, and *get your jab* might be a familiar way to refer to getting a dose of one. The After Time (the post-pandemic years? the vaccine era?) will no doubt bring enough societal changes to call for a number of new terms, and a few of them will stay.

Personal identities will likely continue to be central to political and cultural life. One trend to watch for is the evolution of gender-neutral pronoun usage. Although singular *they* is much more broadly acceptable than it used to be, its use hasn't yet become universal, so it still has room to spread. Alternatively, another word could take hold and end up being the default. *Ze* and *hir* are both good candidates. Gender identity terms that are not widely known now, such as *agender* (not identifying with the gender binary), *pangender* (having multiple gender identities), and *two spirit* (Native American term for dual gender identity), might become more familiar also. On the other hand, recent political backlash against the LGBTQ community might eventually result in increased resistance to singular *they*, fewer gender-related words entering the mainstream vocabulary, or new negative terms being invented.

New words from other languages will also continue to enter American English as people from around the world continue to immigrate to the United States. For example, refugees from climate change might arrive in increasing numbers from the warmer places on the globe, such as sub-Saharan Africa. Like earlier immigrants, they will no doubt contribute new cultural ideas that will result in new terms.

Dialects will certainly continue to change in various ways. One robust trend to watch is the merging of the vowel in *caught* with the one in *cot*. This sound change is well on its way to becoming the dominant pronunciation throughout the country, so everyone may soon be treating *Don* and *dawn* like homonyms. Another trend to keep an eye on is the spread of "California-style" vowels across the West and beyond. Of course, these trends could stabilize or even recede over the next decade or two, as the Northern Cities Shift eventually did. We can't predict the ways that sound changes will develop. One thing we can say for sure, though. By 2100, Americans will be pronouncing certain words in ways that would sound as strange and confusing to present-day Americans as some modern pronunciations would sound to George Washington.

Although regional dialects will keep evolving in unpredictable ways, we can also say with a fair bit of confidence that the country's dialectal regions will keep their separate identities, and probably more or less their current boundary lines. The original streams of English that formed the basis for modern American speech took root in the seventeenth century and have remained identifiable through 400 years of migration and demographic change, so it's doubtful that they will drastically realign anytime soon. A heavy relocation from one part of the country to another due to the changing climate or a changing economic situation could shift the boundaries sometime in the future, but there's no sign of it so far. The country's ethnic dialects also show little sign of losing their individuality in the near future.

The ancient European language of Germanic splintered into dialects so different that they're no longer mutually understandable, and the same thing happened to other ancient languages. Could American English someday be one member of a related family of Englishes, rather than one dialect of a single language? That's an intriguing thought, but it seems unlikely.

The world's English varieties will definitely continue to develop new words and ways of talking that set them apart from other varieties, and they will probably lose some common traits. However, modern communication makes it much easier to stay connected with speakers worldwide than it was several thousand years ago. As long as English speakers keep reading each other's books and watching each other's television programs, the most probable scenario is that the different kinds of English will retain enough common words, grammatical features, and pronunciations to remain versions of a single language. At the same time, their speakers will keep borrowing useful items from each other. Americans will share the *cool*s and *okay*s of the future with the rest of the English-speaking world, and in return they'll gain tomorrow's alternatives to *no worries* and *spot on*.

# APPENDIX

AMERICAN VOWELS

| Example Word | Phonetic Symbol | Description |
|---|---|---|
| **Short (lax) vowels** | | |
| *bit* | ɪ | high front |
| *bet* | ɛ | midfront |
| *bat* | æ | low front |
| *about* | ə | midcentral |
| *book* | ʊ | high back |
| *but* | ʌ | midback unrounded |
| *bought* | ɔ | midback rounded |
| *bot* | ɑ | low back |
| **Long (tense) vowels** | | |
| *beat* | i | high front |
| *bait* | e | midfront |
| *boot* | u | high back |
| *boat* | o | midback |
| **Diphthongs** | | |
| *boy* | ɔi | midback with front upglide |
| *bite* | ɑi | low back with front upglide |
| *bout* | ɑu | low back with back upglide |

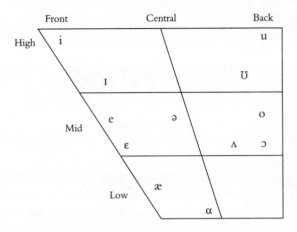

**Figure A.1** American Vowels by Tongue Position. This generic vowel chart shows the approximate position of vowel pronunciations for most American English speakers. The left side of the chart represents the front of a speaker's mouth, so the [i] sound is pronounced high and most forward in the mouth, with the tongue close to the palate and upper teeth. The lowest sound, [ɑ], is pronounced with the tongue retracted and held low in the mouth. The [o] sound is made with the tongue more retracted, but held about midway between the lowest point and the roof of the mouth. (See Chapter 1 for a description of early English vowels, the Great Vowel Shift, and the main differences between American and British vowels.)

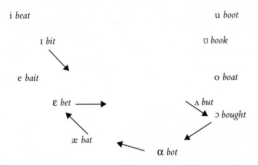

**Figure A.2** The Northern Cities Vowel Shift. The arrows show the direction of movement of displaced vowels, with the leftmost vowels of the chart representing the front of the mouth. The [ɑ] vowel of *bot* moves forward and slightly upward, and the [æ] vowel of *bat* also moves forward and up (and gains a glide so it sounds more like 'be-yet'). This movement pushes both the [ɪ] and [ʌ] vowels down and back, while the back vowel [ɔ] moves down and slightly forward. (See Chapter 5, the section titled "New England and the North," for a full explanation of the Northern Cities Vowel Shift.)

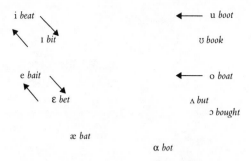

**Figure A.3** The Southern Vowel Shift. This chart shows stages 2 and 3 of the shift, after the vowel sound of *bite* (not shown) "deglides" to an 'ah' sound [aː]. In stage 2, the high front vowels of *beat* and *bit* seem to almost switch places, and in stage 3 the midfront vowels of *bait* and *bet* do the same. The chart also shows the forward movement of the long back vowels [u] and [o]. (See Chapter 5, the section titled "The South," for a full explanation of the Southern Vowel Shift.)

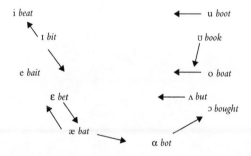

**Figure A.4** The California/Elsewhere Vowel Shift. This chart shows a general pattern of the short front vowels [ɪ], [ɛ], and [æ] being pronounced farther back and down in the mouth, with two exceptions. The upward arrow from *bat* represents the upward glide of the [æ] sound before *n* or *m* (so *band* sounds like 'be-and'), and the upward arrow from *bit* represents the upward movement of the [ɪ] sound in -*ing* (so it's pronounced more like 'een'). The short vowel [ɑ] is moving farther back and raising. Meanwhile, the back vowels [u], [o], and [ʌ] are being pronounced farther forward in the mouth, and the back vowel [ʊ] is moving forward and down. (See Chapter 5, the section titled "The West," for a full explanation of the California Vowel Shift.)

# Notes

INTRODUCTION

1. Josh Katz and Wilson Andrews, "How Y'all, Youse and You Guys Talk," *The New York Times*, December 21, 2013, https://www.nytimes.com/interactive/2014/upshot/dialect-quiz-map.html. The quiz was based on questions from the Harvard Dialect Survey. Also see Ben Zimmer, "About Those Dialect Maps Making the Rounds," *Language Log*, June 6, 2013, https://languagelog.ldc.upenn.edu/nll/?p=4676.

2. For an excellent in-depth introduction to the processes of language change, see Jean Aitchison, *Language Change: Progress or Decay?*, 4th ed. (Cambridge, UK: Cambridge University Press, 2013).

CHAPTER 1

1. Noah Webster, *An American Dictionary of the English Language,* vol. 1 (New York: S. Converse, 1828), viii.

2. The historical population figure is from the U.S. Census Bureau, "Annual Population Estimates of the United States, 1790–1970," in *Historical Statistics of the United States, Colonial Times to 1970*, 8. The latest population estimates can be found at the Census Bureau's website, www.census.gov, and at worldometers.info/population. According to the table "Detailed Languages Spoken at Home and Ability to Speak English for the Population 5 Years and Over for United States: 2009–2013," in the Census Bureau's American Community Survey, nearly 400 languages other than English are spoken in the United States, including over 150 Native American languages. However, the majority of the population speaks English as a first or only language.

3. *Notes on the Life of Noah Webster,* vol. 2, compiled by Emily Ellsworth Fowler Ford (New York, 1912), 309.

4. John Smith, "A Map of Virginia" [1612], in *Works 1608–1631*, part 1, edited by Edward Arber (Westminster, UK: Archibald Constable, 1895), 56.

5. A standard work on the history of English is Albert C. Baugh and Thomas Cable, *A History of the English Language,* 4th ed. (Englewood Cliffs, NJ: Prentice-Hall, 1993).

6. For a detailed explanation of the Great Vowel Shift, see Baugh and Cable, *A History of the English Language*, 232–34. Also see Edmund Weiner, "Early Modern English Pronunciation and Spelling," *Oxford English Dictionary* blog, https://public.oed.com/blog/early-modern-english-pronunciation-and-spelling/.

7. *Records of Salem Witchcraft*, vol. 1 (Roxbury, MA, 1864), 17, 32; vol. 2, 125, 208.

8. Charles H. Lincoln, ed., *Narratives of the Indian Wars, 1675–1699* (New York: Charles Scribner's Sons, 1913), 15, 16.

9. Examples are from the following: William Bradford, *Bradford's History of Plymouth Plantation 1606–1646*, edited by William T. Davis (New York: Charles Scribner's Sons, 1908), 77; Smith, "A Map of Virginia," 56; Thomas Morton, *The New English Canaan of Thomas Morton* [1637], edited by Charles Francis Adams, Jr. (Boston: John Wilson & Son, 1883), 149, 187.

10. Examples are from the following: John Smith, "A True Relation of Virginia" [1608], in *Works*, part I, 10; John Smith, "The Generall Historie of Virginia, New England, and the Summer Isles" [1624], in *Works*, part II, 642; Smith, "A Map of Virginia," 143; Bradford, *Plymouth Plantation*, 99, 374; Laura Wright, "Eight Grammatical Features of Southern United States Speech Present in Early Modern London Prison Narratives," in *English in the Southern United States*, edited by Stephen J. Nagle and Sara L. Sanders (Cambridge, UK: Cambridge University Press, 2003), 45.

11. Frederick J. Furnivall, ed., *Harrison's Description of England in Shakespere's Youth*, Part 1 (London: The New Shakespere Society, 1877), App. 1, lv.

12. Population figures are from Christian F. Feest, "Virginia Algonquians," in *Handbook of North American Indians*, vol. 15, *Northeast*, edited by Bruce G. Trigger (Washington, DC: Smithsonian, 1978), 256.

13. Virginia Algonquian belongs to the language subfamily called Eastern Algonquian. It is now extinct, as are most of the other sixteen or so related languages in this subfamily, although some (such as Wampanoag) are currently being revived. There are around thirty Algonquian languages altogether. Several in the Central and Plains subfamilies are still spoken. These include Ojibwe, Blackfoot, Cheyenne, Cree, and Mi'kmaq.

14. Smith, "A True Relation," 18–19. *Aroughcun* appears in Smith, "A Map of Virginia," 59; *Rarowcun* is in Smith, "The Generall Historie of Virginia, New England & the Summer Isles," 400.

15. Smith, "A True Relation," 25.

16. For an account of Powhatans in England, see Alden T. Vaughn, "Powhatans Abroad: Virginia Indians in England," in *Envisioning an English Empire: Jamestown and the Making of the North Atlantic World*, edited by Robert Appelbaum, and John Sweet (Philadelphia: University of Pennsylvania Press, 2005), 49–67.

17. See Smith, "A Map of Virginia," 44–46. This list and another one by writer and adventurer William Strachey are the only records we have of Virginia Algonquian.

18. Smith, "A Map of Virginia," 51.

19. It's unclear what the disease was. Smallpox, measles, and typhus are all possibilities. For more details about disease from early contacts with Europeans, see T. J. Brasser, "Early Indian-European Contacts," in *Handbook of North American Indians*, vol. 15, *Northeast*, 82–83.

20. Bradford, *Plymouth Plantation*, 114.

21. Edward Winslow, *Good Newes from New England* (London, 1624), 54; John Oldmixon, *The British Empire in America* (London, 1708), 395.

22. Roger Williams, *A Key into the Language of America* [1643] (Bedford, MA: Applewood Books, 1997), 2.

23. Quotations are from the following: Smith, "A True Relation," 9, 35; Bradford, *Plymouth Plantation*, 148.

24. Smith, "A Map of Virginia," 63; Smith, "The Generall Historie of Virginia," 886.

25. Francis Moore, *A Voyage to Georgia* (London: Jack Robinson, 1744), 23–24.

26. Francis L. Hawks, ed., *A Relation of Maryland* [1635] (New York: Joseph Sabin, 1865), 22–23.

27. Washington Irving, *A History of New York, from the Beginning of the World to the End of the Dutch Dynasty* [1809] (Philadelphia: David McKay, 1848), 311

28. See Harold Davis, "On the Origin of Yankee Doodle," *American Speech* 13 (April 1938): 93–96.

29. Population figures are taken from Eric Foner, *Give Me Liberty! An American History*, 2nd Seagull ed. (New York: Norton, 2009), 101, 131.

30. Thomas Jefferson's letter of instructions to Meriwether Lewis, June 20, 1803, is reprinted in Gunther Barth, ed., *The Lewis and Clark Expedition: Excerpts from the Journals Arranged by Topic* (Boston: Bedford/ St. Martin's, 1998), 18–22.

31. The most recent edition of Lewis and Clark's journals is *Journals of the Lewis and Clark Expedition*, edited by Gary E. Moulton (Lincoln: University of Nebraska Press, 1983–2001). It is available both in print and at http://lewisandclarkjournals.unl.edu.

32. John Walker, *A New Critical Pronouncing Dictionary of the English Language* [1791] (Burlington, NJ: D. Allinson, 1813), 53. Bracketed explanation added.

33. Gordon E. Bigelow, "More Evidence of Early Loss of [r] in Eastern American Speech," *American Speech* 30 (May 1955): 54–56; Noah Webster, *Dissertations on the English Language* (Boston: Isaiah Thomas, 1789), 110.

34. A review of the various theories of *r*-lessness in America can be found in John Hurt Fisher, "British and American, Continuity and Divergence," in *The Cambridge History of the English Language*, vol. 6, *English in North America*, edited by John Algeo (Cambridge, UK: Cambridge University Press, 2001), 75–77.

35. A number of other, less obvious pronunciation differences have arisen over the last three centuries. A brief list can be found in Edward Finegan, "American English and Its Distinctiveness," in *Language in the USA*, edited by Edward Finegan and John R. Rickford (Cambridge, UK: Cambridge University Press, 2004), 23–27. Also see Fisher, "British and American," 71–76, for some discussion. A recent book for general readers that looks at the differences between British and American English more broadly is Lynne Murphy, *The Prodigal Tongue: The Love-Hate Relationship between American and British English* (New York: Penguin, 2018).

36. Richard Owen, *The World*, December 12, 1754, quoted in Allen Walker Read, "British Recognition of American Speech in the Eighteenth Century," *Dialect Notes* VI (1933): 314.

37. Frederick Marryat, *A Diary in America*, vol. 2 (Philadelphia: Carey & Hart, 1839), 35.

38. Thomas Jefferson, *Notes on the State of Virginia* [1787] (Boston: Lilly and Wait, 1832), 67; *European Magazine and London Review* 12 (1787), 114.

39. Samuel Sewall to Stephen Sewall, 1680, quoted in *New England Historical and Genealogical Register* 24 (April 1870), 121.

40. Almira Larkin White, *Genealogy of the Descendants of John White* (Haverhill, MA: Chase Brothers, 1900), 36; James Flint, *Letters from America* (Edinburgh: W. & C. Tait, 1822), 251.

## CHAPTER 2

1. Quoted in Allen Walker Read, "The Assimilation of the Speech of British Immigrants in Colonial America," *Journal of English and Germanic Philology* 37 (January 1938): 72.

2. Quoted in Read, "Speech of British Immigrants," 73, 75, 76.

3. Noah Webster, *Dissertations on the English Language* (Boston: Isaiah Thomas, 1789), 105, 108, 110, 111. Webster reviewed pronunciation features of American English in Dissertation II and Dissertation III, 108–60.

4. Anne Royall, *Sketches of History, Life, and Manners in the United States* (New Haven, CT, 1826), 58, 229.

5. Anne Royall, *Letters from Alabama* (Washington, DC, 1830), 22.

6. John Witherspoon, *Pennsylvania Journal,* May 23, 1781, quoted in M. M. Mathews, *The Beginnings of American English* (Chicago: University of Chicago Press, 1931), 25.

7. Quoted in Mathews, *The Beginnings of American English*, 99–112.

8. Quoted in Allen Walker Read, "British Recognition of American Speech," *Dialect Notes* VI (1933): 323, 326.

9. Quoted in Robert J. Menner, "Two Early Comments on American Dialects," *American Speech* 13 (February 1938): 9.

10. Quoted in Read, "British Recognition," 322–23.

11. Jonathan Boucher, *Boucher's Glossary of Archaic and Provincial Words*, edited by Joseph Hunter and Joseph Stevenson (London: Black, Young and Young, 1832–33), ix.

12. Not all local dialects were English. Speakers of Celtic languages (Irish, Welsh, Cornish, and Scots-Gaelic), who once covered the British Isles, had been pushed into the corners of the territory by Anglo-Saxons and later Anglo-Normans, but they had not entirely adopted English. Many were monolingual in their own ancestral language well into the nineteenth century.

13. David Hackett Fischer, *Albion's Seed: Four British Folkways in America* (New York: Oxford University Press, 1989). Immigration statistics for the four groups are taken from pages 17, 28, 421, and 608–09.

14. Fischer's work has been criticized for overgeneralization and selective use of linguistic sources. See, for example, Michael Ellis, "On the Use of Dialect as Evidence: 'Albion's Seed' in Appalachia," *Appalachian Journal* 19 (Spring 1992): 278–97. For detailed discussions of the issues involved in pinpointing ancestral dialect areas, see Raymond Hickey, "Dialects of English and Their Transportation," in *Legacies of Colonial English*, edited by Raymond Hickey (Cambridge, UK: Cambridge University Press, 2004), 33–58, and Michael Montgomery, "British and Irish Antecedents," in *The Cambridge History of the English Language*, vol. 6, *English in North America*, edited by John Algeo (Cambridge, UK: Cambridge University Press, 2001), 86–153.

15. Hans Kurath, "The Origin of the Dialectal Differences in Spoken American English," *Modern Philology* 25 (May 1928): 387. Most modern dialectologists agree. See, for example, Walt Wolfram and Natalie Schilling, *American English: Dialects and Variation*, 3rd ed. (Chichester, UK: Wiley Blackwell, 2016). For a different perspective, see J. L. Dillard, *All-American English* (New York: Vintage, 1975). Dillard argues that American English grew out of a colonial "koiné," a common form of popular speech, with little reliance on British dialects.

16. For an explanation of the founder effect, see Salikoko Mufwene, "The Founder Principle in Creole Genesis," *Diachronica* 13 (1996): 83–134.

17. John Winthrop, *Life and Letters of John Winthrop, 1630–1649*, edited by Robert C. Winthrop (Boston: Ticknor & Fields, 1867), 19.

18. Fischer, *Albions's Seed*, 130.

19. Webster, *Dissertations*, 158–59.

20. *Records of Salem Witchcraft*, vol. 1 (Roxbury, MA, 1864), 176.

21. John Russell Bartlett, *Dictionary of Americanisms: A Glossary of Words and Phrases Usually Regarded as Peculiar to the United States* (New York: Bartlett & Welford, 1848, reprinted by John Wiley and Sons, 2003), 182.

22. See Fischer, *Albion's Seed*, 57, for further discussion.

23. Quoted in George Philip Krapp, *The English Language in America*, vol. II (New York: Frederick Ungar, 1925), 24.

24. Maximilian Schele de Vere, *Americanisms: The English of the New World* (New York: Charles Scribner, 1872), 427.

25. The first three examples are from Seba Smith, *Jack Downing's Letters* (Philadelphia: T. B. Peterson, 1845), 8, 30, 34. The last two are from Seba Smith, *The Life and Writings of Major Jack Downing of Downingville*, 2nd ed. (Boston: Lilly Wait, 1834), 59, 66.

26. Hugh Jones, *The Present State of Virginia* [1724] (New York: Joseph Sabin, 1865), 48.

27. Edward Duffield Neill, *History of the Virginia Company of London* (Albany, NY: Joel Munsell, 1869), 155, fn. 2.

28. This population figure is taken from Eric Foner, *Give Me Liberty! An American History*, 2nd Seagull ed. (New York: Norton, 2009), 60.

29. L. R. Dingus, "A Word List from Virginia," *Dialect Notes* 4 (1915): 177–78.

30. Krapp, *The English Language in America*, II, 34; Fischer, *Albion's Seed*, 260.

31. See Michael Montgomery, "Historical and Comparative Perspectives on *A*-Prefixing in the English of Appalachia," *American Speech* 84 (Spring 2009): 5–26.

32. Quoted in Krapp, *The English Language in America*, II, 269.

33. George Washington, *The Writings of George Washington*, II, collected and edited by Worthington Chauncey Ford (New York: G.P. Putnam's Sons, 1889), 235.

34. *The lamentable and true tragedie of M. Arden of Feversham in Kent* (London, 1592). For a discussion of the origins of *liketa* in England, see Laura Wright, "Eight Grammatical Features of Southern United States Speech Present in Early Modern London Prison Narratives," in *English in the Southern United States*, edited by Stephen J. Nagle and Sara L. Sanders (Cambridge, UK: Cambridge University Press, 2003), 53–55.

35. See Fischer, *Albion's Seed*, 257, 260–61.

36. Edgar W. Schneider, "The English Dialect Heritage of the Southern United States," in *Legacies of Colonial English*, 270. For late-developing features of southern English, see Guy Bailey, "When Did Southern American English Begin?," in *Englishes Around the World: Studies in Honour of Manfred Görlach*, vol. 1, *General Studies, British Isles, North America*, edited by Edgar W. Schneider (Amsterdam: John Benjamins, 1997), 255–75. See Fischer, *Albion's Seed*, 258, for some discussion of southwestern English pronunciation.

37. Royall, *Letters from Alabama*, 22.

38. Royall, *Letters from Alabama*, 122.

39. Quoted in Claude M. Newlin, "Philip Vickers Fithian's Observations on the Language of Virginia (1774)," *American Speech* 4 (December 1928): 110.

40. Jones, *Present State of Virginia*, 37, 43.

41. J. F. D. Smyth, *A Tour in the United States of America*, vol. 1 (Dublin: G. Perrin, 1784), 24.

42. Allen Walker Read, "The Speech of Negroes in Colonial America," *Journal of Negro History* 24 (July 1939): 250, 251, 253.

43. For a useful overview of the issues involved, see Salikoko S. Mufwene, "African-American English," in *The Cambridge History of the English Language*, vol. 6, 291–324.

44. William Penn, *A Further Account of the Province of Pennsylvania* (London, 1685), 2–3.

45. Fischer, *Albion's Seed*, 472–73.

46. William Penn, *William Penn's Own Account of the Lenni Lenape or Delaware Indians* [1683], rev. ed. (Moorestown, NJ: Middle Atlantic Press, 1970), 35.

47. Krapp, *The English Language in America*, I, 40.

48. James Parton, *The Life of Andrew Jackson*, vol. 1 (New York: Mason Brothers, 1860), 47.

49. Quoted in Alan Crozier, "The Scotch-Irish Influence on American English," *American Speech* 59 (Winter 1984): 317.

50. Michael Montgomery, "Solving Kurath's Puzzle: Establishing the Antecedents of the American Midland Dialect Region," in *Legacies of Colonial English*, 318.

51. For a good review of the possibilities, see Barbara Fennell, "Evidence for British Sources of Double Modal Constructions in Southern American English," *American Speech* 68 (Winter 1993): 430–37. For an overview of multiple modals generally, see Nick Huang, "Multiple Modals," *Yale Grammatical Diversity Project: English in North America*, 2011, http://ygdp.yale.edu/phenomena/multiple-modals.

52. William Goodell Frost, "Our Contemporary Ancestors in the Southern Mountains," *Atlantic Monthly* 83 (March 1899): 313, 316.

53. See, for example, Michael Montgomery, "In the Appalachians They Speak like Shakespeare," in *Language Myths*, edited by Laurie Bauer and Peter Trudgill (New York: Penguin, 1998), 66–76.

54. Bartlett, *Dictionary of Americanisms*, xxiv.

55. *Sketches and Eccentricities of Col. David Crockett of West Tennessee* (New York: J. and J. Harper, 1833), 164.

56. The first two quotations are from David Crockett, *An Account of Col. Crockett's Tour to the North and Down East* (Philadelphia: Carey & Hart, 1835), 5, 120. The third is from *Davy Crockett's Almanack* (Nashville, TN: Heirs of Colonel Crockett, 1837), 17. The last is from Emerson Bennett, *Mike Fink: Legend of the Ohio* (Cincinnati, OH: J.A. & U.P. James, 1853), 10. Other humorists whose books featured dialect representative of this region include Augustus Baldwin Longstreet, George Washington Harris, and Johnson Jones Hooper.

CHAPTER 3

1. For a detailed look at how new words are formed, see John Algeo, *Fifty Years among the New Words: A Dictionary of Neologisms 1941–1991* (Cambridge, UK: Cambridge University Press, 1991), 3–14.

2. A comprehensive list of these differences is offered in Marv Rubenstein, *American English Compendium: A Portable Guide to the Idiosyncrasies, Subtleties, Technical Lingo, and Nooks and Crannies of American English*, 4th ed. (Lanham, MD: Rowman & Littlefield, 2014), 169–314. Lynne Murphy also talks about differences in word choice throughout her

book *The Prodigal Tongue: The Love-Hate Relationship between American and British English* (New York: Penguin, 2018).

3. Allan Metcalf, *Predicting New Words: The Secrets of Their Success* (Boston: Houghton Mifflin, 2002), 149–66. Metcalf calls these FUDGE factors from the initial letter of each one.

4. J. S. Buckingham, *America: Historical, Statistic, and Descriptive*, vol. 3 (London: Fisher, 1841), 421.

5. A detailed investigation into the origin of *gerrymander* and the earliest examples of the word in print can be found in Elmer Cummings Griffith, *The Rise and Development of the Gerrymander* (Chicago: Scott Foresman, 1907), 16–22. Many versions of the *gerrymander* story wrongly attribute the original drawing to Gilbert Stuart.

6. The origin of *okay* was discovered by Allen Walker Read and described in a series of articles, beginning with "The First Stage in the History of 'O.K.,'" *American Speech* 38 (February 1963): 5–27. More recently, Allan Metcalf has written about the word in *OK: The Improbable Story of America's Greatest Word* (Oxford: Oxford University Press, 2011).

7. See Allen Walker Read, "Later Stages in the History of O.K.," *American Speech* 39 (May 1964): 83–101, and Metcalf, *OK: The Improbable Story*, Chapter 14, "The World—and England."

8. Benson J. Lossing, *Pictorial History of the Civil War in the United States*, vol. 3 (Hartford, CT: Thomas Belknap, 1877), 600.

9. D. W. Meinig, *The Shaping of America*, vol. 2, *Continental America, 1800–1867* (New Haven, CT: Yale University Press, 1993), gives a readable, detailed account of western expansion up to the end of the Civil War.

10. John E. Norcross, "Dollars: 'Bits:' 'Picayune,'" *Notes and Queries* 10S. viii (July 27, 1907): 63–64.

11. Population figures are taken from Eric Foner, *Give Me Liberty! An American History*, 2nd Seagull ed. (New York: Norton, 2009), 450, 568.

12. For a brief outline of Native American trading pidgins, see Suzanne Romaine, "Contact with Other Languages," in *The Cambridge History of the English Language*, vol. 6, *English in North America*, edited by John Algeo (Cambridge, UK: Cambridge University Press, 2001), 154–60.

13. For a discussion of typical features of pidgins, see Derek Bickerton, *The Roots of Language* (Ann Arbor, MI: Karoma, 1981).

14. Number of Chinese immigrants is given in Foner, *Give Me Liberty!*, 452.

15. Patricia W. Lipski, "The Introduction of 'Automobile' into American English," *American Speech* 39 (October 1964): 176–87, goes in-depth on the adoption of *automobile* as the preferred term for vehicles with combustion engines.

16. For the complete story of *scofflaw*, see Metcalf, *Predicting New Words*, 44–51.

17. See John Algeo, "Etymologies Unknown: *Boondoggle*," *American Speech* 59 (Spring 1984): 93–95.

18. See, for example, A. Grove Day, "How to Talk in Hawaii," *American Speech* 26 (February 1951): 26.

19. Quoted in Stuart Berg Flexner, *I Hear American Talking* (New York: Van Nosrand and Reinhold, 1976), 375.

20. A comprehensive look at the *-in* phenomenon can be found in Kelsie B. Harder, "Coinages of the Type of 'Sit-in,'" *American Speech* 43 (February 1968): 58–64.

21. Arthur Herzog, "It's the Innest, It's the Jet Set," *The New York Times Magazine*, October 28, 1962, 32.

22. John Witherspoon, *Pennsylvania Journal,* May 9, 1781, quoted in M. M. Mathews, *The Beginnings of American English* (Chicago: University of Chicago Press, 1931), 16.

23. John Pickering, *A Vocabulary, or Collection of Words and Phrases Which Have Been Supposed to Be Peculiar to the United States of America* (Boston: Cummings and Hilliard, 1816), 9.

24. John Russell Bartlett, *Dictionary of Americanisms: A Glossary of Words and Phrases Usually Regarded as Peculiar to the United States* (New York: Bartlett & Welford, 1848, reprinted by John Wiley and Sons, 2003), 33.

25. William A. Craigie and James R. Hulbert, eds., *A Dictionary of American English on Historical Principles*, vol. 1 (Oxford: Oxford University Press, 1938), v.

26. The numbers of entries are from Michael Adams, "The Making of American English Dictionaries, in *The Cambridge Companion to English Dictionaries*, edited by Sarah Ogilvie (Cambridge, UK: Cambridge University Press, 2020), 167.

27. Number of entries is from Frank Abate, Review of *Dictionary of American Regional English,* vol. V, *Dictionaries* 33 (2012), 245.

CHAPTER 4

1. George Washington, *The Writings of George Washington,* II, collected and edited by Worthington Chauncey Ford (New York: G.P. Putnam's Sons, 1889), 89–90; *Washington's Farewell Address to the People of the United States 1796* (Boston: Houghton Mifflin, 1913), 7.

2. Lincoln delivered the Cooper Union speech on February 27, 1860. It is posted at Abraham Lincoln Online: https://abrahamlincolnonline. org/lincoln/speeches/cooper.htm.

3. William Jennings Bryan's "Cross of Gold" speech, delivered to the Democratic Nominating Convention in Chicago on July 9, 1896, posted on History Matters: https://historymatters.gmu.edu/d/5354.

4. Laura Wright, "Eight Grammatical Features of Southern United States Speech Present in Early Modern London Prison Narratives," in *English in the Southern United States*, edited by Stephen J. Nagle and Sara L. Sanders (Cambridge, UK: Cambridge University Press, 2003), 44, 45.

5. Examples are taken from Noah Webster, *Dissertations on the English Language* (Boston: Isaiah Thomas, 1789), 210–13.

6. These examples are from David Hume, *Treatise of Human Nature*, vol. III (London: John Noon, 1739), 619; *Whitehall Evening-Post* (London), September 13–15, 1748; Edward August Kendall, *Travels Through the Northern Parts of the United States in the Year 1807 and 1808*, vol. I (New York: I. Riley, 1809), 169.

7. The first example is from John Smith, "A True Relation of Virginia" [1608], in *Works 1608–1631*, part 1, edited by Edward Arber (Westminster, UK: Archibald Constable, 1895), 10. The others are from John Smith, "A Map of Virginia" [1612], in *Works 1608–1631*, part I, 104, 44, 142, 46.

8. Noah Webster, *Dissertations on the English Language* (Boston: Isaiah Thomas, 1789), 201–13.

9. For an exploration of the historical use of *shall* and *will*, see Patricia A. Moody, "Shall and Will: The Grammatical Tradition and Dialectology," *American Speech* 49 (Spring–Summer 1974): 67–78.

10. The notice of the runaway servant is quoted in Allen Walker Read, "The Assimilation of the Speech of British Immigrants in Colonial America," *Journal of English and Germanic Philology* 37 (January 1938): 79. The Webster quotation is from *Dissertations*, 236–37. For examples of later writers, see Moody, "Shall and Will," 71.

11. John Algeo, *British or American English?* (Cambridge, UK: Cambridge University Press, 2006), 36.

12. For a list of verbs that were irregular in the eighteenth century, see Robert Lowth, *A Short Introduction to English Grammar*, new ed. (London: J. Dodsley, 1775), 88–102. A modern list may be found in Sidney Greenbaum and Randolph Quirk, *A Student's Grammar of the English Language* (Harlow, UK: Longman, 1990), 29–34. See Algeo, *British or American*, 12–19, for varying uses of the past tense.

13. For an overview of American and British tag questions, see Gunnell Tottie, "Tag Questions in British and American English," *Journal of English Linguistics* 34 (December 2006): 283–311.

14. *You all* and *y'all* have been extensively written about. A good overview of the scholarship on *y'all*, as well as double modals, discussed later, is Cynthia Bernstein, "Grammatical Features of Southern Speech: *yall*, *might could*, and *fixin to*," in *English in the Southern United States*, edited by Stephen J. Nagle and Sara L. Sanders (Cambridge, UK: Cambridge University Press, 2003), 106–18. For a good discussion of *yinz*, see Barbara Johnstone et al., *Pittsburgh Speech and Pittsburghese* (Berlin: Walter de Gruyter, 2015), 26–30.

15. Quotations are from Michael Montgomery, "The Structural History of *Y'all*, *You All*, and *You'uns*," *Southern Journal of Linguistics* 26 (April 2002): 20; Margaret Van Horn Dwight, *A Journey to the Ohio in 1810* (New Haven, CT: Yale University Press, 1912), 37. For the origins of *y'all* and *you'uns*, see Michael Montgomery, "The Etymology of *Y'all*," in *Old English and New*, edited by Joan H. Hall et al. (New York: Garland Press, 1992), 356–69.

16. S. Pardee, "Odd Southernisms: A Few Examples of Quaint Sayings in South Carolina," *The New York Times*, February 23, 1886, quoted in David B. Parker, "*Y'all*: Two Early Examples," *American Speech* 81 (2006): 111.

17. See Jan Tillery and Guy Bailey, "*Yall* in Oklahoma," *American Speech* 73 (Autumn 1998): 265, for numbers of speakers who say they use singular *y'all*. For arguments that *y'all* cannot be singular, see Gina Richardson, "Can *Y'all* Function as a Singular Pronoun in Southern Dialect?," *American Speech* 59 (Spring 1984): 51–59.

18. For spread outside the South, see Jan Tillery, Tom Wikle, and Guy Bailey, "The Nationalization of a Southernism," *Journal of English Linguistics* 28 (September 2000): 280–94.

19. Natalie Maynor, "Battle of the Pronouns: *Y'all* versus *You-Guys*." *American Speech* 75 (Winter 2000): 416–18.

20. A recent survey of modal use is Davide Zullo, Simone E. Pfenninger, and Daniel Schreier, "A Pan-Atlantic 'Multiple Modal Belt'?," *American Speech* 96 (February 2021): 8–9. See also Nick Huang, "Multiple Modals," *Yale Grammatical Diversity Project: English in North America*, 2011, http://ygdp.yale.edu/phenomena/multiple-modals.

21. Early studies of invariant *be* in southern speech include Guy Bailey and Natalie Maynor, "The Present Tense of *Be* in Southern Black Folk Speech," *American Speech* 60 (Autumn 1985): 195–213; Guy Bailey and

Natalie Maynor, "The Present Tense of *Be* in White Folk Speech of the Southern United States," *English World-Wide* 6 (1985): 199–216; Guy Bailey and Marvin Bassett, "Invariant *Be* in the Lower South," in *Language Variety in the South*, edited by Michael B. Montgomery and Guy Bailey (Tuscaloosa: University of Alabama Press, 1986), 158–79. A review of New England *be* is found in Adrian Pablé and Radosław Dylewski, "Invariant *Be* in New England Folk Speech: Colonial and Postcolonial Evidence," *American Speech* 82 (Summer 2007): 151–84.

22. Webster, *Dissertations*, 385. Examples are from Pablé and Dylewski, "Invariant *Be* in New England," 169. The Harriet Beecher Stowe quotation is from *Sam Lawson's Oldtown Fireside Stories* [1872] (Boston: Osgood, 1967), 139, quoted in Pablé and Dylewski, 170.

23. See Bailey and Maynor, "White Folk Speech," Bailey and Maynor, "Black Folk Speech," and Bailey and Bassett, "Invariant *Be* in the Lower South," all cited earlier. The listed examples are taken from the first two sources.

24. For the use of invariant *be* in the Carolinas, see Michael Montgomery and Margaret Mishoe, "'He Bes Took up with a Yankee Girl and Moved up There to New York': The Verb Bes in the Carolinas and Its History," *American Speech* 74 (Autumn 1999): 240–81. Examples are from page 246. For the non-use of invariant *be* among White speakers, see Patricia Cukor-Avila, "Co-existing Grammars: The Relationship between the Evolution of African American and White Vernacular English in the South," in *Sociocultural and Historical Contexts of African American English,* edited by Sonja L. Lanehart (Amsterdam: John Benjamins, 2001), 109.

25. Examples are taken from Lisa J. Green, *African American English: a Linguistic Introduction* (Cambridge, UK: Cambridge University Press, 2002), 48, 101.

26. For further discussion, see Green, *African American English*, 54. Also see Guy Bailey and Natalie Maynor, "Decreolization?" *Language in Society* 16 (December 1987): 457–69.

27. For some discussion, see Salikoko S. Mufwene, "African-American English," in *The Cambridge History of the English Language*, vol. 6, *English in North America*, edited by John Algeo (Cambridge, UK: Cambridge University Press, 2001), 291–324. See Derek Bickerton, *The Roots of Language* (Ann Arbor, MI: Karoma, 1981) for typical features of creoles.

28. A recounting of Lincoln's grammar studies may be found in M. L. Houser, *Abraham Lincoln, Student. His Books* (Peoria, IL: Edward J. Jacob, 1932). Many Lincoln biographies also touch on the subject.

29. For a history of grammar books in America, see Rosemarie Ostler, *Founding Grammars: How Early America's War over Words Shaped Today's Language* (New York: St. Martin's, 2015). See also Beth Barton Schweiger, "A History of English Grammar in the Early United States," *Journal of the Early Republic* 30 (Winter 2010): 533–55. Statistics on numbers of grammar books printed and sold are from Rollo Laverne Lyman, *English Grammar in American Schools before 1850* (Washington, DC: Government Printing Office, 1922), 77–82.

30. The introduction to *Grammars, Grammarians, and Grammar Writing in Eighteenth-Century England*, edited by Ingrid Tieken-Boon van Ostade (Berlin: Mouton de Gruyter, 2008) provides an overview of English grammar books.

31. Lyman, *English Grammar in American Schools*, 34–35.

32. Lowth, *A Short Introduction*, 162.

33. Lowth, *A Short Introduction*, 164.

34. Webster, *Dissertations*, 286–87.

35. Lyman, *English Grammar in American Schools*, 80.

36. Quotations are from Harriet Beecher Stowe, *Uncle Tom's Cabin* (London: Ingram, Cooke, 1852), 1; C. P. Bronson, *Elocution, or Mental and Vocal Philosophy* (Louisville, KY: Morton & Griswold, 1845), 367; Houser, *Abraham Lincoln, Student*, 10.

#### CHAPTER 5

1. George Goebel, "*Dictionary of American Regional English*," in *The Cambridge Companion to English Dictionaries*, edited by Sarah Ogilvie (Cambridge, UK: Cambridge University Press, 2020), 306–14 gives a brief history and description of the *Dictionary of American Regional English*. A summary can also be found at the dictionary's online website: https://www.daredictionary.com/dare/page/aboutdaresurvey/.

2. The Society's founding is described in Louise Pound, "The American Dialect Society: A Historical Sketch," *Publication of the American Dialect Society* 17 (April 1952): 3–28. Quotations here appear on pages 5 and 6.

3. George Davis Chase, "Cape Cod Dialect," *Dialect Notes* II, part V (1903): 289–303.

4. For some history of Hans Kurath and the linguistic atlases, see Craig M. Carver, *American Regional Dialects: A Word Geography* (Ann Arbor: University of Michigan Press, 1987), 2–3. See also the Linguistic Atlas Project website: http://www.lap.uga.edu/Site/About_Us.html.

5. The figure for quotations is from Goebel, "*Dictionary of American Regional English*," 309. The estimate of *Dialect Notes* listings is from the introduction to the *Dictionary of American Regional English*, vol. I, edited by Frederick G. Cassidy, Joan Houston Hall, and Luanne von Schneidemesser (Cambridge, MA: Harvard University Press, 1985), xi.

6. For a description of the Telsur Project, see William Labov, Sharon Ash, and Charles Boberg, *The Atlas of North American English: Phonetics, Phonology and Sound Change* (Berlin: Walter de Gruyter, 2006), 3–10.

7. Labov, Ash, and Boberg, *Atlas of North American English*, 3.

8. Brief essays covering every region, written for the general reader, are found in *American Voices: How Dialects Differ from Coast to Coast*, edited by Walt Wolfram and Ben Ward (Malden, MA: Blackwell, 2006). See also Allan Metcalf, *How We Talk: American Regional English Today* (Boston: Houghton Mifflin, 2000); Lee Pederson, "Dialects," in *The Cambridge History of the English Language*, vol. 6, *English in North America*, edited by John Algeo (Cambridge, UK: Cambridge University Press, 2001), 253–90.

9. For a detailed review of nineteenth-century settlement patterns, see D. W. Meinig, *The Shaping of America*, vol. 2, *Continental America, 1800–1867* (New Haven, CT: Yale University Press, 1993), Part II. The population of western New York is as recorded in Meinig, 225.

10. Eric Foner, *Give Me Liberty! An American History,* 2nd Seagull ed. (New York: Norton, 2009), 313.

11. Foner, *Give Me Liberty!*, 311.

12. Foner, *Give Me Liberty!*, 452.

13. Population statistics for San Francisco and Los Angeles are from the U.S. Census Bureau, "Population of the 100 Largest Urban Places: 1870," in *Population of the 100 Largest Cities and Other Urban Places in the United States: 1790–1990*.

14. Foner, *Give Me Liberty!*, 450.

15. About 236 people per square mile, significantly higher than the United States as a whole. See https://worldpopulationreview.com/regions/new-england-population.

16. For a study of increasing *r* use in Boston and New Hampshire, see Naomi Nagy and Patricia Irwin, "Boston (r): Neighbo(r)s Nea(r) and Fa(r)," *Language Variation and Change* 22 (2010): 241–78. See also Labov, Ash, and Boberg, *Atlas of North American English*, 47.

17. For a discussion of the *so don't I* structure, see Nick Huang and Jim Wood, "So don't I," *Yale Grammatical Diversity Project: English in North America*, 2011, http://ygdp.yale.edu/phenomena/so-dont-i.

18. George Philip Krapp, *The English Language in America,* vol. I (New York: Frederick Ungar, 1925), 40.

19. For some discussion see Timothy C. Frazer, "An Introduction to Midwest English," in *American Voices*, 101–05.

20. A detailed but highly technical explanation of the Northern Cities Vowel Shift may be found in Labov, Ash, and Boberg, *Atlas of North American English*, 187–205. Less technical descriptions can be found in many recent discussions of American regional variation, for example, Matthew J. Gordon, "Straight Talking from the Heartland (Midwest)," in *American Voices*, 108–10; Metcalf, *How We Talk*, 93–95; Rob Mifsud, "Vowel Movement: How Americans near the Great Lakes Are Radically Changing the Sound of English," *Slate*, August 22, 2012, https://slate.com/human-interest/2012/08/northern-cities-vowel-shift-how-americans-in-the-great-lakes-region-are-revolutionizing-english.html.

21. See, for example, Monica Nesbitt, "The Rise and Fall of the Northern Cities Shift: Social and Linguistic Re-organization of TRAP in 20th Century Lansing, Michigan," *American Speech* 96 (August 2021): 332–70.

22. The pioneering study of New York City pronunciation is William Labov, *The Social Stratification of English in New York City* (Washington, DC: Center for Applied Linguistics, 1966). A recent examination of New York City speech is Michael Newman, *New York City English* (Berlin: Walter de Gruyter, 2014). For discussions of *r*-pronunciation, see Newman, 46–52; also Labov, Ash, and Boberg, *Atlas of North American English*, 47.

23. See Labov, *The Social Stratification of English in New York City*, Chapter 3.

24. For some discussion of the recognizability of southern speech, and the widespread attitude that it contrasts with "standard" American speech, see Dennis Preston, "The South: The Touchstone," in Cynthia Bernstein, Thomas Nunnally, and Robin Sabino, eds., *Language Variety in the South Revisited* (Tuscaloosa: University of Alabama Press, 1997), 311–51.

25. The South is the most written about American linguistic region. Two relatively recent books that cover history and current issues are Bernstein, Nunnally, and Sabino, *Language Variety in the South Revisited*; and Stephen J. Nagle and Sara L. Sanders, eds., *English in the Southern United States* (Cambridge, UK: Cambridge University Press, 2003). A good brief introduction is Guy Bailey and Jan Tillery, "Sounds of the South," in *American Voices*, 11–16. For a discussion of dialectal features that did not appear until the late nineteenth century, see

Edgar Schneider, "Shakespeare in the Coves and Hollows? Toward a History of Southern English," in *English in the Southern United States*, 17–35. Also see Guy Bailey, "When Did Southern English Begin?," in *Englishes Around the World: Studies in Honour of Manfred Görlach*, vol. 1, *General Studies, British Isles, North America*, edited by Edgar W. Schneider (Amsterdam: John Benjamins, 1997), 255–75.

26. A detailed technical description of the Southern Vowel Shift may be found in Labov, Ash, and Boberg, *Atlas of North American English*, 242–54. Southern pronunciation is also examined in George Dorvill, "Sounding Southern: A Look at the Phonology of English in the South," in *English in the Southern United States*, 119–25, and Crawford Feagin, "Vowel Shifting in the Southern States," in *English in the Southern United States*, 126–40. An excellent, easy-to-follow discussion of southern pronunciation appears in Paul E. Reed, "Phonological Possibilities in Appalachian Englishes," in *Appalachian Englishes in the Twenty-First Century*, edited by Kirk Hazen (Morgantown: West Virginia University Press, 2020), 27–30.

27. See Feagin, "Vowel Shifting in the Southern States," 128.

28. See Labov, Ash, and Boberg, *Atlas of North American English*, 240–58, for a discussion of these features.

29. See Jim Wood et al., "Dative Country: Markedness and Geographical Varieties in the Southern Dative Construction," *American Speech* 95 (February 2020): 3–45, for an overview of the different types of indirect object usage. Personal and presentative datives (the first two types given as examples) are also discussed on the website of the Yale Grammatical Diversity Project, https://ygdp.yale.edu/.

30. A classic description of Charleston speech may be found in Raven McDavid, "The Position of the Charleston Dialect," *Publication of the American Dialect Society* 23 (1955): 23–49. See also Maciej Baranowski, "Doing the Charleston (South Carolina)," in *American Voices*, 28–35.

31. Several people discuss this issue. See, for example, Carver, *American Regional Dialects*, 180–83, and Labov, Ash, and Boberg, *Atlas of North American English*, 263. For a more detailed overview, see Timothy C. Frazer, "The Dialects of the Middle West," in *Focus on the USA*, edited by Edgar W. Schneider (Amsterdam: John Benjamins, 1996), 81–102.

32. Labov, Ash, and Boberg, *Atlas of North American English*, 263.

33. Noah Webster, *Dissertations on the English Language* (Boston: Isaiah Thomas, 1789), 110. For some discussion of the possibility that Scots-Irish speakers introduced or encouraged this pronunciation,

see Michael Montgomery, "British and Irish Antecedents," in *The Cambridge History of the English Language*, vol. 6, *English in North America*, edited by John Algeo (Cambridge, UK: Cambridge University Press, 2001), 138; also, George Philip Krapp, *The English Language in America*, vol. II (New York: Frederick Ungar, 1925), 141–43.

34. For a discussion of these forms, see Erica J. Benson, "Everyone Wants In: Want + Prepositional Adverb in the Midland and Beyond," *Journal of English Linguistics* 37 (March 2009): 28–60, and Erica J. Benson, "Need + Prepositional Adverb in the Midland: Another Feature Needs In," *Journal of English Linguistics* 40 (September 2012): 224–55.

35. For overviews of these forms, see Thomas E. Murray, Timothy C. Frazer and Beth Lee Simon, "Need + Past Participle in American English," *American Speech* 71 (Autumn 1996): 255–71, and Thomas E. Murray and Beth Lee Simon, "Want + Past Participle," *American Speech* 74 (Summer 1999): 140–64.

36. A detailed explanation of how *joint* became *jawn* may be found on the Merriam-Webster website at https://www.merriam-webster.com/words-at-play/jawn-meaning-origin. Another detailed discussion appears in Dan Nasowitz, "The Enduring Mystery of 'Jawn', Philadelphia's All-Purpose Noun," *Atlas Obscura*, March 24, 2016, https://www.atlasobscura.com/articles/the-enduring-mystery-of-jawn-philadelphias-allpurpose-noun.

37. Details of Pittsburgh speech can be found in Barbara Johnstone et al., *Pittsburgh Speech and Pittsburghese* (Berlin: Walter de Gruyter, 2015).

38. See Betsy Evans, "Seattletonian to Faux Hick: Perceptions of English in Washington State," *American Speech* 86 (Winter 2011), 392–93, for further discussion.

39. For some aspects of Utah speech, see David Eddington and Matthew Savage, "Where are the Moun[ʔə]ns in Utah?" *American Speech* 87 (Fall 2012): 336–49.

40. An early article on the California Vowel Shift is Leanne Hinton et al., "It's Not Just the Valley Girls: a Study of California English," in *Proceedings of the 13th Annual Meeting of the Berkeley Linguistics Society*, edited by John Aske et al. (Washington, DC: eLanguage, Linguistic Society of America, 1987), 117–28.. Also see Robert Kennedy and James Grama, "Chain Shifting and Centralization in California Vowels," *American Speech* 87 (September 2012): 39–56. A comprehensive but technical examination of evolving vowel sounds in the West may be found in *Speech in the Western States*, 3 vols., edited by Valerie Fridland et al., *Publication of the American Dialect Society* 101, 102, 105 (December 2016, December 2017, December 2020).

CHAPTER 6

1. Raven I. McDavid, Jr. and Virginia Glenn McDavid, "The Relationship of the Speech of American Negroes to the Speech of Whites," *American Speech* 26 (February 1951): 12.

2. For a detailed description of the acoustics involved, see Kalina Newmark, Nacole Walker, and James Stanford, "'The Rez Accent Knows No Borders': Native American Identity Expressed through English Prosody," *Language in Society* 45 (2016): 633–64.

3. Quoted in Newmark et al., "'The Rez Accent Knows No Borders,'" 635.

4. See Carmen Fought, *Chicano English in Context* (New York: Palgrave Macmillan, 2003), 16, 109–10.

5. Newmark et al., "'The Rez Accent Knows No Borders,'" 643.

6. This structure is described in John R. Rickford, with Christine Théberge-Rafal, "Preterite *Had* + Verb *-ed* in the Narratives of African American Preadolescents," in *African American Vernacular English* (Oxford: Blackwell, 1999), 34–60.

7. John McWhorter, *Talking Back, Talking Black* (New York: Bellevue Literary Press, 2017), 74–75.

8. Martha Austen, "'Put the Groceries Up': Comparing Black and White Regional Variation," *American Speech* 92 (August 2017): 298–320; Taylor Jones, "Toward a Description of African American Vernacular English Dialect Regions Using 'Black Twitter,'" *American Speech* 90 (November 2015): 403–40; Ian Clayton and Valerie Fridland, "Western Vowel Patterns in White and Native American Nevadans' Speech," in *Speech in the Western States*, vol. 3, *Understudied Varieties*, edited by Valerie Fridland et al., *Publication of the American Dialect Society* 105 (December 2020): 39–63.

9. Early studies include William Labov, *Language in the Inner City: Studies in the Black English Vernacular* (Philadelphia: University of Pennsylvania Press, 1972), and J. L. Dillard, *Black English: Its History and Usage in the United States* (New York: Random House, 1972). Rickford, *African American Vernacular English*, cited previously, brings together over two decades of the author's research on major issues. A more recent comprehensive study is Lisa J. Green, *African American English: A Linguistic Introduction* (Cambridge, UK: Cambridge University Press, 2002). For differences between Black and White speech, see also *Language Variety in the South: Perspectives in Black and White*, edited by Michael B. Montgomery and Guy Bailey (Tuscaloosa, AL: University of Alabama Press, 1986).

10. McDavid and McDavid, "Relationship of Speech," 6, 10.

11. Salikoko Mufwene has written extensively on this topic. Two useful essays are "Some Sociohistorical Inferences about the Development of African American English," in *The English History of African American English*, edited by Shana Poplack (Oxford: Blackwell, 2000), 233–63; and "The Shared Ancestry of African-American and American White Southern Englishes: Some Speculations Dictated by History," in *English in the Southern United States*, edited by Stephen J. Nagle and Sara L. Sanders (Cambridge, UK: Cambridge University Press, 2003), 64–81.

12. Cotton Mather, *Angel of Bethesda*, an unpublished medical treatise quoted in Allan Walker Read, "The Speech of Negroes in Colonial America," *Journal of Negro History* 24 (July 1939): 248.

13. J. F. D. Smyth, *A Tour in the United States of America* (Dublin: G. Perrin, 1784), 75; Daniel Horsmanden, *The New York Conspiracy* (New York: Southwick & Pelsue, 1810), 128, 331.

14. Quotations are from Harriet Beecher Stowe, *Uncle Tom's Cabin* (London: Ingram, Cooke, 1852), 18, 191. George Phillip Krapp's comment is from *The English Language in America*, vol. I (New York: Frederick Ungar, 1925), 262. Also see Tremaine McDowell, "The Use of Negro Dialect by Harriet Beecher Stowe," *American Speech* 6 (June 1931): 322–26.

15. Joel Chandler Harris, *Uncle Remus and His Legends of the Old Plantation* (London: David Bogue, 1881), 19.

16. George Phillip Krapp, "The English of the Negro," *American Mercury* II (1924), 190; Hans Kurath, *A Word Geography of the Eastern United States* (Ann Arbor: University of Michigan Press, 1949), 6.

17. Generally speaking, *be* can be left out of sentences in the same places where standard American English allows present-tense *be* to be reduced to *'s* or *'re*—*He's tall* or *You're out of the game.* Where reduced *be* doesn't occur, such as at the end of a sentence like *I don't know where he's*, neither does omission of *be*. (No one says, *I don't know where he.*) William Labov described this pattern in "Contraction, Deletion and Inherent Variability of the English Copula," *Language* 45 (December 1969): 715–62.

18. Proponents of the creolist theory include Dillard, *Black English*, and Rickford, *African American Vernacular English*. Also see John R. Rickford, "Prior Creolization of African American Vernacular English? Sociohistorical and Textual Evidence from the 17th and 18th Centuries," *Journal of Sociolinguistics* 1 (1997): 315–36.

19. See Derek Bickerton, *The Roots of Language* (Ann Arbor, MI: Karoma, 1981) for characteristics of creoles.

20. Many enslaved people in New York and New Jersey, in fact, spoke Dutch, not English.

21. Estimated percentage comes from Mufwene, "Shared Ancestry," 66.

22. Population estimate comes from Rickford, "Prior Creolization," 323, 327.

23. See Dillard, *Black English*, and Rickford, "Prior Creolization," both cited previously. For a comparison of the verb *to be* in African American English and Gullah (Sea Island Creole) and how it may affect the Creolist hypothesis, see Tracey L. Weldon, "Revisiting the Creolist Hypothesis: Copula Variability in Gullah and Southern Rural AAVE," *American Speech* 78 (Summer 2003): 171–91.

24. Writings that discuss the earlier English basis of African American English (called the neo-Anglicist hypothesis) include the essays in *The English History of African American English*; Edgar W. Schneider, *American Earlier Black English* (Tuscaloosa: University of Alabama Press, 1989); Guy Bailey, "The Relationship between African American and White Vernaculars in the American South," in *Sociocultural and Historical Contexts of African American English*, edited by Sonja L. Lanehart (Amsterdam: John Benjamins, 2001), 53–92; and Patricia Cukor-Avila, "Co-existing Grammars: The Relationship between the Evolution of African American and White Vernacular English in the South," in *Sociocultural and Historical Contexts of African American English*, 93–128. See also Salikoko S. Mufwene, "African-American English," in *The Cambridge History of the English Language*, vol. 6, 291–324.

25. The original handwritten narratives are stored in the Library of Congress. The most comprehensive published collection is George P. Rawick, ed., *The American Slave: A Composite Autobiography*, 19 vols. (Westport, CN: Greenwood, 1972). A number of collections from single states have also been published. For a discussion of discrepancies between the original interviews and the published interviews, see Edgar W. Schneider, "Earlier Black English Revisited," in *Language Variety in the South Revisited*, edited by Cynthia Bernstein, Thomas Nunnally, and Robin Sabino (Tuscaloosa: University of Alabama Press, 1997), 35–50. For some discussion of whether invariant *am* was a genuine African American usage, see John McWhorter, "Revisiting Invariant *Am* in Earlier African American Vernacular English," *American Speech* 95 (November 2020): 379–407.

26. See Laura Wright, "Eight Grammatical Features of Southern United States Speech Present in Early Modern London Prison Narratives," in

*English in the Southern United States*, edited by Stephen J. Nagle and Sara L. Sanders (Cambridge, UK: Cambridge University Press, 2003), 42.

27. Examples are taken from Wright, "Eight Grammatical Features," 38, 39, 40, 45, 47, 52.

28. An early discussion of how and to what extent the dialects are diverging may be found in Ralph W. Fasold et al., "Are Black and White Dialects Diverging?," *American Speech* 62 (Spring 1987): 3–80.

29. See Bailey, "Relationship between African American and White Vernaculars," 64–66.

30. For an exploration of this idea, see Donald Winford, "On the Origins of African American Vernacular English—A Creolist Perspective," parts 1 and 2, *Diachronica* 14 (1997): 305–44, 15 (1998): 99–154.

31. Margaret G. Lee, "Out of the Hood and into the News: Black Verbal Expression in a Mainstream Newspaper," *American Speech* 74 (Winter 1999): 369–88.

32. Geneva Smitherman, *Black Talk: Words and Phrases from the Hood to the Amen Corner*, rev. ed. (Boston: Houghton Mifflin, 2000), 2, 29.

33. William Bradford, *Bradford's History of Plymouth Plantation: 1606–1646*, edited by William T. Davis (New York: Charles Scribner's Sons, 1908), 110.

34. Statistic taken from R. David Edmunds, Frederick E. Hoxie, and Neal Salisbury, *The People: A History of Native America* (Boston: Houghton Mifflin, 2007), 101.

35. Nancy Shoemaker describes Native American whaling experiences in *Native American Whalemen and the World* (Chapel Hill: University of North Carolina Press, 2015). Edmunds et al., *The People*, is one of many sources for information about Native American slavery and indentured servitude. Allen Walker Read gives several examples of ads for runaways in "The English of Indians (1705–1745)," *American Speech* 16 (February 1941): 72–74.

36. Quotations are taken from Douglas Leechman and Robert A. Hall, "American Indian Pidgin English: Attestations and Grammatical Peculiarities," *American Speech* 30 (October 1955): 163–71.

37. Rudolf Kaiser has written about the various versions of the speech in "Chief Seattle's Speech(es): American Origins and European Reception," in *Recovering the Word: Essays on Native American Literature*, edited by B. Swann and A. Krupat (University of California Press, 1987), 497–536.

38. Quoted in Edmunds et al., *The People*, 322.

39. Alan Dundes and C. Fayne Porter, "American Indian Student Slang," *American Speech* 38 (December 1963): 270–77.

40. Population and numbers of speakers come from the U.S. Census Bureau: "Detailed Languages Spoken at Home and Ability to Speak English for the Population 5 Years and Over for United States 2009–2013"; and Tina Norris, Paula L. Vines, and Elizabeth M. Hoeffel, "The American Indian and Alaska Native Population: 2010," published January 2012.

41. Quoted in William L. Leap, *American Indian English* (Salt Lake City: University of Utah Press, 1993), 43.

42. Relatively little recent linguistic analysis has been done on Native American English (as opposed to Native American Indigenous languages). Leap's *American Indian English* provides a good general overview. Two recent articles also provide a review of later research along with their own findings: Alicia Beckford Wassink and Sharon Hargus, "Heritage Language Features and the Yakama English Dialect," in *Speech in the Western States*, vol. 3, *Understudied Varieties*, edited by Valerie Fridland et al., *Publication of the American Dialect Society* 105 (December 2020): 1–38; and Ian Clayton and Valerie Fridland, "Western Vowel Patterns in White and Native American Nevadans' Speech," in *Speech in the Western States*, vol. 3, 39–63.

43. Leap, *American Indian English*, 52.

44. Hamilton McMillan, *Sir Walter Raleigh's Lost Colony* (Wilson, NC: Advance Presses, 1888), 14. For an argument that Lumbees can trace part of their ancestry to the 1587 English settlement on Roanoke Island in what is now North Carolina (known as the Lost Colony), see Adolph L. Dial and David K. Eliades, *The Only Land I Know: A History of the Lumbee Indians* (Syracuse, NY: Syracuse University Press, 1996).

45. Lumbee English is discussed in detail in Clare J. Dannenberg, "Socio-linguistic Constructs of Ethnic Identity: The Syntactic Delineation of a Native American Indian Variety," *Publication of the American Dialect Society* 87 (December 2002): 1–106; and Chapter 9 of Walt Wolfram and Jeffrey Reaser, *Talkin' Tar Heel* (Chapel Hill: University of North Carolina Press, 2014).

46. Examples are taken from Clare Dannenberg and Walt Wolfram, "Ethnic Identity and Grammatical Restructuring: Be(s) in Lumbee English," *American Speech* 73 (Summer 1998): 139–59.

47. Statistic taken from U.S. Census Bureau, "Quick Facts California," 2019.

48. Manuel Godinez, Jr., "Chicano English Phonology: Norms vs. Interference Phenomena," in *Form and Function in Chicano English*, edited by Jacob Ornstein-Galicia (Rowley, MA: Newberry House, 1981), 43.

49. Carmen Fought's *Chicano English in Context* gives a broad overview of Chicano English. Most examples in this section are taken from her book.

50. Fought, *Chicano English in Context*, 66.

51. Norma Mendoza-Denton, *Homegirls: Language and Cultural Practice among Latina Youth Groups* (Malden, MA: Blackwell, 2008), Chapter 8.

52. Joyce Penfield, "Prosodic Patterns: Some Hypotheses and Findings from Fieldwork," in *Form and Function in Chicano English,* 49; Allan A. Metcalf, "The Study of California Chicano English," *International Journal of the Sociology of Language* 2 (1974): 55. See Fought, *Chicano English in Context,* 76, for a comparison with uptalk.

53. Timothy C. Frazer, "Chicano English and Spanish Interference in the Midwestern United States," *American Speech* 71 (Spring 1996): 72–85.

54. Walt Wolfram, Phillip Carter, and Beckie Moriello, "Emerging Hispanic English: New Dialect Formation in the American South," *Journal of Sociolinguistics* 8 (2014): 339–58.

55. Figure is from Viveka Velupillai, "Hawai'i Creole," in *The Survey of Pidgin and Creole Languages*, vol. 1, edited by Susanne Maria Michaelis et al. (Oxford: Oxford University Press, 2013), 252.

CHAPTER 7

1. "The Drinkers Dictionary" has been reprinted in numerous places. One source is Cedric Larson, "The Drinkers Dictionary," *American Speech* 12 (April 1937): 87–92. It was also posted on *Mental Floss* on January 17, 2014 (https://www.mentalfloss.com/article/29753/ben-franklins-200-synonyms-drunk). The list is usually attributed to Benjamin Franklin. However, a very similar list appeared a year earlier in the *New England Weekly Journal,* so Franklin may have simply copied it. See Joel S. Berson, "The Source for Benjamin Franklin's 'The Drinkers Dictionary' (and Was It Mather Byles?)," *American Speech* 81 (2006): 164–79.

2. Recent books that explore the nature of slang in depth include Michael Adams, *Slang: The People's Poetry* (Oxford: Oxford University Press, 2009); Julie Coleman, *The Life of Slang: a History of Slang* (Oxford: Oxford University Press, 2012); and Jonathon Green, *The Vulgar Tongue: Green's History of Slang* (Oxford: Oxford University Press, 2015). For a more detailed look at slang and poetic devices, see Jonathan E. Lighter, "Slang," in *The Cambridge History of the English Language*, vol. 6, *English in North America*, edited by John Algeo, (Cambridge, UK: Cambridge University Press, 2001), 224–25.

3. For more early expressions using *slang*, see Lighter, "Slang," 227–28.

4. The number of immigrants is taken from Eric Foner, *Give Me Liberty! An American History*, 2nd Seagull ed. (New York: Norton, 2009), 107.

5. George W. Matsell, *Vocabulum, or Rogue's Lexicon* (New York: George W. Matsell & Co., 1859); Francis Grose, *A Classical Dictionary of the Vulgar Tongue* (London: S. Hooper, 1785).

6. Josiah Flynt, *Tramping with Tramps: Studies and Sketches of Vagabond Life* [1899] (New York: Century, 1907), 381.

7. Flynt, *Tramping with Tramps*, 384.

8. An early prolific collector was the linguist David W. Maurer. Twenty of his articles are reprinted in David W. Maurer, *Language of the Underworld* (Lexington: University Press of Kentucky, 1981). Another good source for the slang of closed groups is *American Speech*, the journal of the American Dialect Society.

9. David W. Maurer, "The Argot of the Underworld Narcotic Addict," *American Speech* 11 (April 1936), 117.

10. *Drug Slang Code Words*, DEA Intelligence Report, April 2017, https://www.dea.gov/sites/default/files/2018-07/DIR-020-17%20Drug%20Slang%20Code%20Words.pdf.

11. Two sources of slang words are B. H. Hall, *A Collection of College Words and Customs* (Cambridge, MA: J. Bartlett, 1851) and Eugene H. Babbitt, "College Words and Phrases," *Dialect Notes* 2 (1900): 3–70. Connie Eble provides a useful analysis of categories of nineteenth-century college slang in *Slang and Sociability: In-Group Language among College Students* (Chapel Hill: University of North Carolina Press, 1996), 115–19.

12. See Eble, *Slang and Sociability*, 125–30, for lists of the most used slang.

13. An entertaining round-up of twentieth-century youth slang is Tom Dalzell's *Flappers 2 Rappers: American Youth Slang* (Springfield, MA: Merriam-Webster, 1996). Not much latter-day youth slang has been collected in book form, but three possibilities are Mary Corey and Victoria Westermark, *Fer Shurr! How to be a Valley Girl—Totally!* (New York: Bantam Books, 1982); Trevor Cralle, *The Surfin'ary: A Dictionary of Surfing Terms and Surfspeak* (Berkeley, CA: Ten Speed Press, 1991); Fab 5 Freddy, *Fresh Fly Flavor: Words & Phrases of the Hip-Hop Generation* (Stamford, CT: Longmeadow Press, 1992).

14. For a thorough exploration of *dude*'s history, see Richard A. Hill, "You've Come a Long Way, Dude," *American Speech* 69 (1994): 321–27. For a detailed examination of modern uses of *dude*, see Scott Kiesling, "Dude," *American Speech* 79 (2004): 281–305.

15. For a detailed discussion of the language of hip-hop, see H. Samy Alim, *Roc the Mic Right: The Language of Hip Hop Culture* (New York: Routledge, 2006).

16. Donald W. Cory, *The Homosexual in America: A Subjective Approach* (New York: Greenberg, 1951), 103. Cory's chapter on the language of homosexuals, "Take My Word For It," and several other early writings on gay slang may be found in *The Language and Sexuality Reader*, edited by Deborah Cameron and Don Kulick (London: Routledge, 2006).

17. For a review of early glossaries, see Gary Simes, "Gay Slang Lexicography: A Brief History and a Commentary on the First Two Gay Glossaries," *Dictionaries* 26 (2005): 1–159. For an excellent overview of the evolution of gay language use, see Pascale Smorag, "From Closet Talk to PC Terminology: Gayspeak and the Politics of Visibility," *Transatlantica* 1 (2008): 1–20. A book that focuses on gay men's conversational practices rather than vocabulary is William L. Leap, *Word's Out: Gay Men's English* (Minneapolis: University of Minnesota Press, 1996).

18. Cory, *The Homosexual in America*, 108–10.

19. Bruce Rodgers, *Gay Talk* [formerly *The Queen's Vernacular*] (New York: Paragon Books, 1972). Number of entries is from Green, *The Vulgar Tongue*, 287.

20. Julia P. Stanley, "Homosexual Slang," *American Speech* 45 (Spring–Summer 1970), 51.

21. A list of gender identity terms may be found in "Among the New Words," *American Speech* 89 (Winter 2014): 470–96.

22. For a discussion of *throw shade* and how it relates to linguistic appropriation, see John Paul Brammer, "The Difference between Appreciating and Appropriating Queer Culture," *Oprah Daily*, October 22, 2018, https://www.oprahdaily.com/life/a23601818/queer-cultural-appropriation-definition/.

23. For an excellent overview of how the Internet is changing the way we use language, see Gretchen McCulloch, *Because Internet: Understanding the New Rules of Language* (New York: Riverhead Books, 2019). For a study of different styles that teenagers employ when instant messaging and talking, see Sali Tagliamonte and Derek Denis, "Linguistic Ruin? LOL! Instant Messaging and Teen Language," *American Speech* 83 (Spring 2008): 3–34.

24. McCulloch, *Because Internet*, 115.

25. For percentage of abbreviations, see Tagliamonte and Denis, "Linguistic Ruin," 12. For use of regional and nonstandard terms, see Umashanthi Pavalanathan and Jacob Eisenstein, "Audience-Modulated Variation in Online Social Media," *American Speech* 90 (May 2014): 187–213.

26. Alexandra S. Levine, "From Camping to 'Cheese Pizza,' 'Algospeak' Is Taking Over Social Media," *Forbes*, September 19, 2022, http://for bes.com/sites/alexandralevine/2022/09/16/algospeak-social-media-survey/?sh=5b53828855e1; Taylor Lorenz, "Internet 'Algospeak' Is Changing Our Language in Real Time, from 'Nip Nops' to 'le Dollar Bean,'" *Washington Post*, April 8, 2022,https://www.washingtonpost.com/technology/2022/04/08/algospeak-tiktok-le-dollar-bean/.

27. Survey figure is from Levine, "From Camping to 'Cheese Pizza.'"

28. For a history of the alt-right, see Thomas J. Main, *The Rise of the Alt-Right* (Washington, DC: The Brookings Institution Press, 2018). For discussions of alt-right language, see Tim Squirrell and Nikhil Sonnad, "The Alt-Right Is Creating Its Own Language: Here's the Dictionary," *Quartz* October 30, 2017, https://qz.com/1092037/the-alt-right-is-creating-its-own-dialect-heres-a-complete-guide; also Liam Stack, "Alt-Right, Alt-Left, Antifa: A Glossary of Extremist Language," *The New York Times*, August 15, 2017, https://www.nytimes.com/2017/08/15/us/politics/alt-left-alt-right-glossary.html. An Internet search will also bring up numerous lists of alt-right slang and memes.

CHAPTER 8

1. Overviews of the research on style shifting and social varieties of English can be found in Walt Wolfram and Natalie Schilling, *American English: Dialects and Variation,* 3rd ed. (Chichester, UK: Wiley Blackwell, 2016), Chapters 6 and 10; and Susan Tamasi and Lamont Antieau, *Language and Linguistic Diversity in the US: An Introduction* (New York: Routledge, 2015), Chapter 6.

2. William Labov, "The Social Motivation of a Sound Change" [1963], in *Sociolinguistic Patterns* (Philadelphia: University of Pennsylvania Press, 1972), 1–42.

3. Dennis R. Preston has discussed these issues in "Where the Worst English Is Spoken," in *Focus on the USA*, edited by Edgar W. Schneider (Amsterdam: John Benjamins, 1996), 297–360, and in "Language Attitudes to Speech," in *Language in the USA*, edited by Edward Finegan and John R. Rickford (Cambridge, UK: Cambridge University Press, 2014), 480–92.

4. See Betsy Evans, "'Seattletonian' to 'Faux Hick': Perceptions of English in Washington State," *American Speech* 86 (Winter 2011): 383–414.

5. See Mary Bucholtz et al., "Hella Nor Cal or Totally So Cal? The Perceptual Dialectology of California," *Journal of English Linguistics* 5 (December 2007): 325–52. For the myths associated with quotative *like* use, see Alexandra D'Arcy, "*Like* and Language Ideology: Disentangling Fact from Fiction," *American Speech* 82 (Winter 2007): 386–419.

6. See Preston's articles, "Where the Worst English Is Spoken" and "Language Attitudes to Speech."

7. For an exploration of these issues, see Rosina Lippi-Green, *English with an Accent: Language, Ideology, and Discrimination in the United States*, 2nd ed. (London: Routledge, 2012).

8. John R. Rickford and Sharese King, "Language and Linguistics on Trial: Hearing Rachel Jeantel (and Other Vernacular Speakers) in the Courtroom and Beyond," *Language* 92 (December 2016): 948–88.

9. John Adams to the President of Congress, September 5, 1780, quoted in *The Works of John Adams*, vol. 7, edited by Charles Francis Adams (Boston: Little Brown, 1852), 249–50. For proposals to establish a language academy, see Allen Walker Read, "Projects for an Academy to Regulate Speech," *PMLA* 51 (December 1936): 1141–79.

10. For a historical review of split infinitives, see Moisés D. Perales-Escudero, "To Split or to Not Split: The Split Infinitive Past and Present," *Journal of English Linguistics* 39 (2011): 313–34.

11. Henry Alford, *A Plea for the Queen's English* (London and New York: Alexander Strahan, 1866), 188.

12. William Strunk, Jr., and E.B. White, *The Elements of Style*, 4th ed. (Boston: Allyn and Bacon, 2000), 58; Bryan A. Garner, *Garner's Modern English Usage*, 4th ed. (Oxford: Oxford University Press, 2016), 854; Patricia T. O'Conner, *Woe Is I: The Grammarphobe's Guide to Better English in Plain English*, 4th ed. (New York: Riverhead Books, 2019), 238.

13. For some discussion, see Richard K. Redfern, "Is *between you and I* Good English?" *Publication of the American Dialect Society* 78 (December 1994): 187–93.

14. The story of the furor surrounding the release of *Webster's Third* is told in David Skinner, *The Story of Ain't: America, Its Language, and the Most Controversial Dictionary Ever Published* (New York: Harper, 2012). For a shorter summary, see Chapter 8 of Rosemarie Ostler, *Founding Grammars: How Early America's War over Words Shaped Today's Language* (New York: St. Martin's, 2015). Reviews are collected in James Sledd and Wilma R. Ebbitt, *Dictionaries and That Dictionary: A Casebook on*

*the Aims of Lexicographers and the Targets of Reviewers* (Chicago: Scott, Foresman, 1962).

15. "The Death of Meaning," *Toronto Globe and Mail*, September 8, 1961.

16. "Webster's New Word Book," *The New York Times*, October 12, 1961.

17. "New Dictionary Defended," *The New York Times*, November 7, 1961.

18. Brooks Atkinson, "Webster Editor Disputes Critics; Says New Dictionary Is Sound," *The New York Times*, March 1, 1962.

19. Roy H. Copperud, "English as It's Used Belongs in a Dictionary," *Editor & Publisher*, November 25, 1961, 44.

20. The original and amended resolutions and several perspectives on the issue may be found in the *Journal of English Linguistics* 26 (June 1998). See also Enid Lee, *Ebonics: The Urban Educational Debate* (Blue Ridge Summit, PA: Multilingual Matters, 2005). For a brief analysis of the ensuing uproar, see Geoffrey Nunberg, "Double Standards," *Natural Language and Linguistic Theory* 15 (August 1997): 667–75. For a detailed discussion that goes into the historical background and the social implications of the response, see John Baugh, *Beyond Ebonics: Linguistic Pride and Racial Prejudice* (New York: Oxford University Press, 2000).

21. Peter Applebome, "School District Elevates Status of Black English," *The New York Times*, December 20, 1996.

22. Rene Sanchez, "After Ebonics Controversy, Oakland Seeks Viable Lesson Plan," *Washington Post*, April 19, 1998.

23. A number of popular but inaccurate beliefs about the nature of language are explored in *Language Myths*, edited by Laurie Bauer and Peter Trudgill (London: Penguin Books, 1998).

24. See, for example, Ikuko Patricia Yuasa, "A New Feminine Voice Quality for Young Urban-Oriented, Upwardly Mobile American Women?" *American Speech* 85 (Fall 2010), 315.

25. These studies are described in Yuasa, "A New Feminine Voice Quality," 317.

26. The vocal fry controversy is discussed in several posts on the linguistics blog *Language Log*, especially Mark Liberman, "Vocal Fry: 'Creeping in' or 'Still here?,'" December 12, 2011 (https://languagelog.ldc.upenn.edu/nll/?p=3626), and Mark Liberman, "Male Vocal Fry," July 23, 2015 (https://languagelog.ldc.upenn.edu/nll/?p=20155). The academic study that inspired several news articles on vocal fry is Lesley Wolk, Nassima B. Abdelli-Beruh, and Dianne Slavin, "Habitual Use of Vocal Fry in Young Adult Female Speakers," *Journal of Voice* 26 (2012): e111–16. A later study is Stephanie A. Borrie and Christine R. Delfino, "Conversational Entrainment of Vocal Fry in Young Adult

Female American English Speakers," *Journal of Voice* 31 (July 2017): 513. e26–32.

27. Yuasa, "A New Feminine Voice Quality," 329–30.

28. Lakoff's book was reissued with commentary by the author and others as Robin Tolmach Lakoff, *Language and Woman's Place: Text and Commentaries*, rev. and exp. ed., edited by Mary Bucholtz (Oxford: Oxford University Press, 2004).

29. A broad introduction to language and gender, including a discussion of Lakoff's book and subsequent research on her claims, is Penelope Eckert and Sally McConnell-Ginet, *Language and Gender* (Cambridge, UK: Cambridge University Press, 2003).

30. See Eckert and McConnell-Ginet, *Language and Gender*, 176. Also see Tamasi and Antieau, *Language and Linguistic Diversity*, 133, for a brief summary.

31. Deborah Tannen, *You Just Don't Understand: Women and Men in Conversation* (New York: William Morrow, 1990).

32. Tannen, *You Just Don't Understand*, 298.

33. William Labov, *Principles of Linguistic Change*, vol. 2, *Social Factors* (Malden, MA: Wiley-Blackwell, 2001), 292–93.

34. Penelope Eckert, *Jocks and Burnouts: Social Categories and Identity in the High School* (New York: Columbia University Teachers College Press, 1989).

35. Eckert and McConnell-Ginet, *Language and Gender*, 295–304.

36. National Office Management Association, *The Simplified Letter*, January 1952.

37. Janet M. Fuller, "The Uses and Meanings of the Female Title *Ms.*" *American Speech* 80 (Summer 2005): 180–206.

38. Janet Holman, "Power, *Lady*, and Linguistic Politeness," in Lakoff, *Language and Woman's Place*, 151–57.

39. Alison Flood, "Dictionary Row Prompts Oxford Dictionaries to Review Language Used in Definitions," *The Guardian*, January 25, 2016, https://www.theguardian.com/books/2016/jan/25/oxford-dictionary-review-sexist-language-rabid-feminist-gender; Alison Flood, "Fresh Call for Oxford Dictionaries to Change 'Sexist' Definitions," *The Guardian*, March 3, 2020, https://www.theguardian.com/books/2020/mar/03/fresh-call-for-oxford-dictionaries-to-change-sexist-definitions; Alison Flood, "No More 'Nagging Housewives': How Oxford Dictionaries Is Cleaning Up Sexist Language," *The Guardian*, March 6, 2020, https://www.theguardian.com/books/2020/mar/06/no-more-nagging-wives-how-oxford-dictionaries-is-cleaning-up-sexist-language.

40. The quotation from Katherine Martin appears in "No More 'Nagging Housewives.'"

41. See George Jochnowitz, "Everybody Likes Pizza, Doesn't He or She?," *American Speech* 57 (Autumn 1982): 198–203.

42. Two studies are Miriam Watkins Meyers, "Generic Pronoun Usage: An Empirical Study," *American Speech* 65 (Autumn 1990): 228–37; and Darren K. LaScotte, "Singular *They*: An Empirical Study of Generic Pronoun Use," *American Speech* 91 (February 2016): 62–80.

43. See Elaine M. Stotko and Margaret Troyer, "A New Gender-Neutral Pronoun in Baltimore, Maryland: A Preliminary Study," *American Speech* 82 (Fall 2007): 262–79.

44. Lakoff, *Language and Woman's Place*, 72.

45. Quotation is from Bruce Rodgers, *Gay Talk* [formerly *The Queen's Vernacular*] (New York: Paragon Books, 1972), 11–12..

46. See Smorag, "Closet Talk to PC Terminology," 5. For perspectives from both early and recent times, also see Alessandra Stanley, "Militants Back 'Queer,' Shoving 'Gay' the Way of 'Negro,'" *The New York Times*, April 6, 1991, https://www.nytimes.com/1991/04/06/nyregion/militants-back-queer-shoving-gay-the-way-of-negro.html; and Pamela Paul, "Let's Say Gay," *The New York Times*, October 23, 2022, https://www.nytimes.com/2022/10/23/opinion/queer-gay-identity.html?searchResultPosition=1.

47. Quoted in Sandra E. Garcia, "Where Did BIPOC Come From?," *The New York Times*, June 17, 2020, https://www.nytimes.com/article/what-is-bipoc.html, Also see Nicole Holliday, "bipoc," *American Speech* 96 (May 2021): 222.

48. Daniel Hernandez, "Pew Poll Finds Most Latinos Haven't Heard of 'Latinx': Only 3% Use the Term," *Los Angeles Times*, August 11, 2020. https://www.latimes.com/entertainment-arts/story/2020-08-11/latinx-pew-poll-latino-hispanic-identity.

49. For a history of the various terms suggested or adopted to identify Americans with Latin American ancestry, see David Bowles, "Mexican X Part X: What the Hex a 'Latinx'?" *Medium*, December 22, 2018, https://davidbowles.medium.com/mexican-x-part-x-what-the-hex-a-latinx-706b64dafe22.

## CHAPTER 9

1. "Among the New Words," *American Speech* 90 (February 2015), 89–90, traces the evolution of *#BlackLivesMatter* in detail.

2. Edward B. Foley, "A Big Blue Shift: Measuring an Asymmetrically Increasing Margin of Litigation," *Journal of Law and Politics* 27 (2013): 501–46.

3. See "Among the New Words," *American Speech* 92 (May 2017), 221–23, for more explanation and examples.

4. For a large collection of coronavirus-related terms, not only Americanisms, see Tony Thorne's website, Language and Innovation, https://language-and-innovation.com/2020/03/31/coronaspeak-the-language-of-covid-19-goes-viral/, and several subsequent postings. See also Nancy Friedman's blog, Fritinancy, https://nancyfried man.typepad.com/away_with_words/2020/03/words-of-the-week-coronacoinages.html, and several subsequent postings.

5. This line has been quoted in numerous places. One of them is a posting on the Merriam-Webster blog titled "Remembering How It Was in the Before Time," https://www.merriam-webster.com/words-at-play/before-times-covid-history-and-usage.

6. Marina Koren, "The New Cringeworthy," *The Atlantic*, April 17, 2020, https://www.theatlantic.com/science/archive/2020/04/coronavirus-pandemic-cringe/610180/.

7. Derek Thompson, "Hygiene Theater Is a Huge Waste of Time," *The Atlantic*, July 27, 2020, https://www.theatlantic.com/ideas/archive/2020/07/scourge-hygiene-theater/614599/.

8. Ronald R. Butters, "Narrative Go 'Say,'" *American Speech* 55 (Winter 1980), 306.

9. See John R. Rickford et al., "Intensive and Quotative *All*: Something Old, Something New," *American Speech* 82 (Spring 2007): 3–31.

10. The greater number of male users is reported in Carl Blythe, Jr., Sigrid Recktenwald, and Jenny Wang, "I'm Like, Say What?," *American Speech* 65 (Autumn 1990), 221. Two additional studies of quotative *like* are Suzanne Romaine and Deborah Lange, "The Use of *Like* as a Marker of Reported Speech and Thought: A Case of Grammaticalization in Process," *American Speech* 66 (Autumn 1991): 227–79; and, Patricia Cukor-Avila, "*She Say, She Go, She Be Like*," *American Speech* 77 (Spring 2002): 3–31.

11. Ulrike Stange has written two articles that offer broad coverage of *so*, including reviews of earlier studies: "'You're So Not Going to Believe This': The Use of GenX *So* in Constructions with Future *Going to* in American English," *American Speech* 92 (November 2017): 487–524; and "'He Should So Be in Jail': An Empirical Study on Preverbal *So* in American English," *Journal of English Linguistics* 49 (2021): 114–36.

12. Stange, "The Use of GenX *So*," 493.

13. See "Among the New Words," *American Speech* 89 (Spring 2014): 93–96, for examples and discussion of the various usages. Also see Michael Adams, "*Because Much?*," *American Speech* 92 (November 2017): 533–46. Examples are from "Among the New Words." Gretchen McCulloch also discusses the origin of this use of *Because* on her blog *All Things Linguistic*, https://allthingslinguistic.com/post/67507311833/where-because-noun-probably-came-from. Her book about the Internet is titled *Because Internet*, offering a real-life example.

14. Bill Walsh, "The Post Drops the 'Mike'—and the Hyphen in E-mail," *Washington Post*, December 4, 2015, https://www.washingtonpost.com/opinions/the-post-drops-the-mike--and-the-hyphen-in-e-mail/2015/12/04/ccd6e33a-98fa-11e5-8917-653b65c809eb_story.html.

15. Quoted in Merrill Perlman, "Style Books Finally Embrace the Single 'They,'" *Columbia Journalism Review*, March 27, 2017, https://www.cjr.org/language_corner/stylebooks-single-they-ap-chicago-gender-neutral.php.

16. "A Note on the Nonbinary 'They,'" https://www.merriam-webster.com/words-at-play/nonbinary-they-is-in-the-dictionary.

17. See, for instance, Corinne McCarthy, "The Northern Cities Shift in Chicago," *Journal of English Linguistics* 39 (2011): 166–87; and Monica Nesbitt, "The Rise and Fall of the Northern Cities Shift: Social and Linguistic Re-organization of TRAP in 20th Century Lansing, Michigan," *American Speech* 96 (August 2021): 332–70.

18. For example, see Nesbitt, "The Rise and Fall of the Northern Cities Shift," for discussion of the possible socioeconomic reasons for the decline of the Shift in Lansing, Michigan.

19. Nesbitt, "The Rise and Fall of the Northern Cities Shift," 8.

20. See Nesbitt, "The Rise and Fall of the Northern Cities Shift," and the citations listed there.

21. See Robin Dodsworth and Mary Kohn, "Urban Rejection of the Vernacular: The SVS Undone," *Language Variation and Change* 24 (2012): 221–45.

22. See Renée Blake and Meredith Josey, "The /ay/ Diphthong in a Martha's Vineyard Community: What Can We Say 40 Years after Labov?," *Language in Society* 32 (September 2003): 451–85.

23. Blake and Josey, "The /ay/ Diphthong in a Martha's Vineyard Community," 458.

24. *Speech in the Western States*, 3 vols., edited by Valerie Fridland et al., *Publication of the American Dialect Society* 101, 102, 105 (December 2016, December 2017, December 2020), is a collection of detailed, fairly technical articles exploring the shifting vowels of various western states.

25. Kara Becker, Anna Aden, Katelyn Best, and Haley Jacobson, "Variation in West Coast English: The Case of Oregon," in *Speech in the Western States*, vol. 1 (2016): 107–34.

26. Noah Webster, *An American Dictionary of the English Language,* vol. 1 (New York: S. Converse, 1828), viii; John Adams to the President of Congress, September 5, 1780, quoted in *The Works of John Adams*, vol. 7, edited by Charles Francis Adams (Boston: Little Brown, 1852), 250. Current population statistics for the United States and the United Kingdom may be found at worldometers.info/population/.

27. David Crystal, "Two Thousand Million?," *English Today* 93 (March 2008), 5.

28. Lane Crothers, *Globalization and American Popular Culture*, 3rd ed. (Lanham, MD: Rowman & Littlefield, 2013), reviews in detail the impact of American popular culture in other countries.

29. See, for example, David Crystal, *English as a Global Language*, 2nd ed. (Cambridge, UK: Cambridge University Press, 2003), 112–13.

30. Bruno Gonçalves et al., "Mapping the Americanization of English in Space and Time," *PLOS One* 13 (May 25, 2018): 1–15.

31. Herbert Igboanusi, "Knowledge, Use and Attitudes towards Americanisms in Nigerian English," *World Englishes* 22 (2003): 599–604.

32. Miriam Ben-Rafael, "French: Tradition versus Innovation as Reflected in English Borrowings," in *Globally Speaking: Motives for Adopting English Vocabulary in Other Languages*, edited by Judith Rosenhouse and Rotem Kowner (Clevedon, UK: Multilingual Matters, 2008), 58.

33. For some discussion of the kinds of English terms that are adopted into other languages, see British Council, "English Loanwords in European Language," *Voices*, September 25, 2019, https://www.britishcouncil.org/voices-magazine/english-loan-words-european-languages.

34. See Deborah Cameron, "Whingeing and Cringing," *Critical Quarterly* 47 (December 2005): 101–05.

35. Bernadette Vine, "Americanisms in the New Zealand English Lexicon," *World Englishes* 18 (1999): 13–22.

# Select Bibliography

Abbott, O. L. "The Preterite and Past Participle of Strong Verbs in Seventeenth-Century American English." *American Speech* 32 (February 1957): 31–42.

Abbott, O. L. "Verbal Endings in Seventeenth-Century America English." *American Speech* 33 (October 1958): 185–94.

Adams, Michael. "*Because Much?*" *American Speech* 92 (November 2017): 533–46.

Adams, Michael. *Slang: The People's Poetry*. Oxford: Oxford University Press, 2009.

Aitchison, Jean. *Language Change: Progress or Decay?* 4th ed. Cambridge, UK: Cambridge University Press, 2013.

Alexander, Henry. "Early American Pronunciation and Syntax." *American Speech* 1 (December 1925): 41–48.

Alexander, Henry. "The Language of the Salem Witchcraft Trials." *American Speech* 3 (June 1928): 390–400.

Alexander, Henry. "Verbs of the Vulgate in their Historical Relations." *American Speech* 4 (April 1929): 307–15.

Algeo, John. *British or American English? A Handbook of Word and Grammar Patterns*. Cambridge, UK: Cambridge University Press, 2006.

Algeo, John, ed. *The Cambridge History of the English Language*. Vol. 6, *English in North America*. Cambridge, UK: Cambridge University Press, 2001.

Algeo, John. "Etymologies Unknown: *Boondoggle*." *American Speech* 59 (Spring 1984): 93–95.

Algeo, John. *Fifty Years among the New Words: A Dictionary of Neologisms 1941–1991*. Cambridge, UK: Cambridge University Press, 1991.

Alim, H. Samy. *Roc the Mic Right: The Language of Hip Hop Culture*. New York: Routledge, 2006.

Austen, Martha. "'Put the Groceries Up': Comparing Black and White Regional Variation." *American Speech* 92 (August 2017): 298–320.

Babbitt, Eugene H. "College Words and Phrases." *Dialect Notes* 2 (1900): 3–70.

Bailey, Guy. "When Did Southern American English Begin?" In *Englishes Around the World: Studies in Honour of Manfred Görlach*. Vol. 1, *General Studies, British Isles, North America*, edited by Edgar W. Schneider, 255–75. Amsterdam: John Benjamins, 1997.

Bailey, Guy, and Natalie Maynor. "Decreolization?" *Language in Society* 16 (December 1987): 457–69.

Bailey, Guy, and Natalie Maynor. "The Present Tense of *Be* in Southern Black Folk Speech." *American Speech* 60 (Autumn 1985): 195–213.

Bailey, Guy, and Natalie Maynor. "The Present Tense of *Be* in White Folk Speech of the Southern United States." *English World-Wide* 6 (1985): 199–216.

Bartlett, John Russell. *Dictionary of Americanisms: A Glossary of Words and Phrases Usually Regarded as Peculiar to the United States.* New York: Bartlett & Welford, 1848, reprinted by John Wiley and Sons, 2003.

Bauer, Laurie, and Peter Trudgill, eds. *Language Myths.* London: Penguin Books, 1998.

Baugh, Albert C., and Thomas Cable. *A History of the English Language.* 4th ed. Englewood Cliffs, NJ: Prentice-Hall, 1993.

Baugh, John. *Beyond Ebonics: Linguistic Pride and Racial Prejudice.* New York: Oxford University Press, 2000.

Benson, Erica J. "Everyone Wants In: Want + Prepositional Adverb in the Midland and Beyond." *Journal of English Linguistics* 37 (March 2009): 28–60.

Benson, Erica J. "Need + Prepositional Adverb in the Midland: Another Feature Needs In." *Journal of English Linguistics* 40 (September 2012): 224–55.

Bernstein, Cynthia, Thomas Nunnally, and Robin Sabino, eds. *Language Variety in the South Revisited.* Tuscaloosa: University of Alabama Press, 1997.

Bickerton, Derek. *The Roots of Language.* Ann Arbor, MI: Karoma, 1981.

Bigelow, Gordon. "More Evidence of Early Loss of [r] in Eastern American Speech." *American Speech* 30 (May 1955): 154–56.

Blake, Renée, and Meredith Josey. "The /ay/ Diphthong in a Martha's Vineyard Community: What Can We Say 40 Years after Labov?" *Language in Society* 32 (September 2003): 451–85.

Blythe, Carl, Jr., Sigrid Recktenwald, and Jenny Wang. "I'm Like, Say What?" *American Speech* 65 (Autumn 1990): 215–27.

Borrie, Stephanie A., and Christine R. Delfino. "Conversational Entrainment of Vocal Fry in Young Adult Female American English Speakers." *Journal of Voice* 31 (July 2017): 513.e26–32.

Bradford, William. *Bradford's History of Plymouth Plantation 1606–1646.* Edited by William T. Davis. New York: Charles Scribner's Sons, 1908.

Bucholtz, Mary, Nancy Bermudez, Victor Fung, Lisa Edwards, and Rosalva Vargas. "Hella Nor Cal or Totally So Cal? The Perceptual Dialectology of California." *Journal of English Linguistics* 5 (December 2007): 325–52.

Butters, Ronald R. "Narrative Go 'Say.'" *American Speech* 55 (Winter 1980): 304–07.

Cameron, Deborah. "Whingeing and Cringing." *Critical Quarterly* 47 (December 2005): 101–05.

Carver, Craig M. *American Regional Dialects: A Word Geography.* Ann Arbor, MI: University of Michigan Press, 1987.

Cassidy, Frederick G., Joan Houston Hall, and Luanne von Schneidemesser, eds. *Dictionary of American Regional English.* 6 vols. Cambridge, MA: Harvard University Press, 1985-2013.

Coleman, Julie. *The Life of Slang: A History of Slang*. Oxford: Oxford University Press, 2012.

Craigie, William A., and James R. Hulbert, eds. *A Dictionary of American English on Historical Principles*. 4 vols. Oxford: Oxford University Press, 1938.

Crothers, Lane. *Globalization and American Popular Culture*. 3rd ed. Lanham, MD: Rowman & Littlefield, 2013.

Crozier, Alan. "The Scotch-Irish Influence on American English." *American Speech* 59 (Winter 1984): 310–31.

Crystal, David. *English as a Global Language*. 2nd ed. Cambridge, UK: Cambridge University Press, 2003.

Crystal, David. "Two Thousand Million?" *English Today* 93 (March 2008): 3–6.

Cukor-Avila, Patricia. "*She Say, She Go, She Be Like.*" *American Speech* 77 (Spring 2002): 3–31.

Dalzell, Tom. *Flappers 2 Rappers: American Youth Slang*. Springfield, MA: Merriam-Webster, 1996.

Dannenberg, Clare J. "Sociolinguistic Constructs of Ethnic Identity: The Syntactic Delineation of a Native American Indian Variety." *Publication of the American Dialect Society* 87 (December 2002): 1-106.

Dannenberg, Clare, and Walt Wolfram. "Ethnic Identity and Grammatical Restructuring: Be(s) in Lumbee English." *American Speech* 73 (Summer 1998): 139–59.

Davis, Harold. "On the Origin of Yankee Doodle." *American Speech* 13 (April 1938): 93–96.

Day, A. Grove. "How to Talk in Hawaii." *American Speech* 26 (February 1951): 18–26.

Dillard, J. L. *All-American English*. New York: Vintage, 1975.

Dillard, J. L. *Black English: Its History and Usage in the United States*. New York: Random House, 1972.

Dingus, L. R. "A Word List from Virginia." *Dialect Notes* 4 (1915): 177–93.

Dodsworth, Robin, and Mary Kohn. "Urban Rejection of the Vernacular: The SVS Undone." *Language Variation and Change* 24 (2012): 221–45.

Dundes, Alan, and C. Fayne Porter. "American Indian Student Slang." *American Speech* 38 (December 1963): 270–77.

Eble, Connie. *Slang and Sociability: In-Group Language among College Students*. Chapel Hill: University of North Carolina Press, 1996.

Eckert, Penelope. *Jocks and Burnouts: Social Categories and Identity in the High School*. New York: Columbia University Teachers College Press, 1989.

Eckert, Penelope, and Sally McConnell-Ginet. *Language and Gender*. Cambridge, UK: Cambridge University Press, 2003.

Eddington, David, and Matthew Savage. "Where Are the Moun[ʔə]ns in Utah?" *American Speech* 87 (Fall 2012): 336–49.

Evans, Betsy. "'Seattletonian' to 'Faux Hick': Perceptions of English in Washington State." *American Speech* 86 (Winter 2011): 383–414.

Fennell, Barbara. "Evidence for British Sources of Double Modal Constructions in Southern American English." *American Speech* 68 (Winter 1993): 430–37.

Finegan, Edward, and John R. Rickford, eds. *Language in the USA*. Cambridge, UK: Cambridge University Press, 2004.

Fischer, David Hackett. *Albion's Seed: Four British Folkways in America*. New York: Oxford University Press, 1989.

Flexner, Stuart Berg. *I Hear American Talking*. New York: Van Nostrand and Reinhold, 1976.

Foner, Eric. *Give Me Liberty! An American History*. 2nd Seagull ed. New York: Norton, 2009.

Ford, Emily Ellsworth Fowler, comp. *Notes on the Life of Noah Webster*. 2 vols. New York, 1912.

Fought, Carmen. *Chicano English in Context*. New York: Palgrave Macmillan, 2003.

Frazer, Timothy C. "Chicano English and Spanish Interference in the Midwestern United States." *American Speech* 71 (Spring 1996): 72–85.

Fridland, Valerie, Tyler Kendall, Betsy E. Evans, and Alicia Beckford Wassink, eds. *Speech in the Western States*. Vol. 1, *The Coastal States*. Publication of the American Dialect Society 101 (December 2016).

Fridland, Valerie, Alicia Beckford Wassink, Tyler Kendall, and Betsy E. Evans, eds. *Speech in the Western States*. Vol. 2, *The Mountain West*. Publication of the American Dialect Society 102 (December 2017).

Fridland, Valerie, Alicia Beckford Wassink, Lauren Hall-Lew, and Tyler Kendall, eds. *Speech in the Western States*. Vol 3, *Understudied Varieties*. Publication of the American Dialect Society 105 (December 2020).

Fuller, Janet M. "The Uses and Meanings of the Female Title *Ms.*" *American Speech* 80 (Summer 2005): 180–206.

Goebel, George. "*Dictionary of American Regional English*." In *The Cambridge Companion to English Dictionaries*, edited by Sarah Ogilvie, 306–14. Cambridge, UK: Cambridge University Press, 2020.

Gonçalves, Bruno, Lucía Loureiro-Porto, José J. Ramasco, and David Sánchez. "Mapping the Americanization of English in Space and Time." *PLOS One* 13 (May 25, 2018): 1–15.

Grandgent, C. H. "From Franklin to Lowell: A Century of New England Pronunciation." *PMLA* 14 (1899): 207–39.

Green, Jonathon. *The Vulgar Tongue: Green's History of Slang*. Oxford: Oxford University Press, 2015.

Green, Lisa J. *African American English: A Linguistic Introduction*. Cambridge, UK: Cambridge University Press, 2002.

Griffith, Elmer Cummings. *The Rise and Development of the Gerrymander*. Chicago: Scott Foresman, 1907.

Grose, Francis. *A Classical Dictionary of the Vulgar Tongue*. London: S. Hooper, 1785.

Hall, B. H. *A Collection of College Words and Customs*. Cambridge, MA: J. Bartlett, 1851.

Harder, Kelsie B. "Coinages of the Type of 'Sit-in,'" *American Speech* 43 (February 1968): 58–64.

Hickey, Raymond, ed. *Legacies of Colonial English*. Cambridge, UK: Cambridge University Press, 2004.

Hill, Richard A. "You've Come a Long Way, Dude." *American Speech* 69 (1994): 321–27.

Hinton, Leanne, Birch Moonwomon, Sue Bremner, Herb Luthin, Mary Van Clay, Jean Lerner, and Hazel Corcoran. "It's Not Just the Valley Girls: a Study of California English." In *Proceedings of the 13th Annual Meeting of the Berkeley Linguistics Society*, edited by John Aske, Natasha Beery, Laura Michaelis, and Hana Filip, 117–28. Washington, DC: eLanguage, Linguistic Society of America, 1987.

Houser, M. L. *Abraham Lincoln, Student. His Books*. Peoria, IL: Edward J. Jacob, 1932.

Igboanusi, Herbert. "Knowledge, Use and Attitudes towards Americanisms in Nigerian English." *World Englishes* 22 (2003): 599–604.

Jochnowitz, George. "Everybody Likes Pizza, Doesn't He or She?" *American Speech* 57 (Autumn 1982): 198–203.

Johnstone, Barbara, Daniel Baumgardt, Maeve Eberhardt, and Scott Kiesling. *Pittsburgh Speech and Pittsburghese*. Berlin: Walter de Gruyter, 2015.

Jones, Hugh. *The Present State of Virginia* [1724]. New York: Joseph Sabin, 1865.

Jones, Taylor. "Toward a Description of African American Vernacular English Dialect Regions Using 'Black Twitter.'" *American Speech* 90 (November 2015): 403–40.

Kaiser, Rudolf. "Chief Seattle's Speech(es): American Origins and European Reception." In *Recovering the Word: Essays on Native American Literature,* edited by B. Swann and A. Krupat, 497–536. Oakland: University of California Press, 1987.

Kennedy, Robert, and James Grama. "Chain Shifting and Centralization in California Vowels." *American Speech* 87 (September 2012): 39–56.

Kiesling, Scott. "Dude." *American Speech* 79 (2004): 281–305.

Krapp, George Philip. *The English Language in America*. 2 vols. New York: Frederick Ungar, 1925.

Krapp, George Phillip. "The English of the Negro." *American Mercury* II (1924): 190–95.

Kurath, Hans. "The Origin of the Dialectal Differences in Spoken American English." *Modern Philology* 25 (May 1928): 385–95.

Kurath, Hans. *A Word Geography of the Eastern United States*. Ann Arbor: University of Michigan Press, 1949.

Labov, William. "Contraction, Deletion and Inherent Variability of the English Copula." *Language* 45 (December 1969): 715–62.

Labov, William. *Language in the Inner City: Studies in the Black English Vernacular*. Philadelphia: University of Pennsylvania Press, 1972.

Labov, William. *Principles of Linguistic Change.* Vol. 2, Social Factors. Malden, MA: Wiley-Blackwell, 2001.

Labov, William. *The Social Stratification of English in New York City.* Washington, DC: Center for Applied Linguistics, 1966.

Labov, William. *Sociolinguistic Patterns.* Philadelphia: University of Pennsylvania Press, 1972.

Labov, William, Sharon Ash, and Charles Boberg. *The Atlas of North American English: Phonetics, Phonology and Sound Change.* Berlin: Walter de Gruyter, 2006.

Lakoff, Robin Tolmach. *Language and Woman's Place: Text and Commentaries,* rev. and exp. ed., edited by Mary Bucholtz. Oxford: Oxford University Press, 2004.

Lanehart, Sonja L., ed. *Sociocultural and Historical Contexts of African American English.* Amsterdam: John Benjamins, 2001.

Larson, Cedric. "The Drinkers Dictionary." *American Speech* 12 (April 1937): 87–92.

LaScotte, Darren K. "Singular *They*: An Empirical Study of Generic Pronoun Use." *American Speech* 91 (February 2016): 62–80.

Leap, William L. *American Indian English.* Salt Lake City: University of Utah Press, 1993.

Lee, Enid. *Ebonics: The Urban Educational Debate.* Blue Ridge Summit, PA: Multilingual Matters, 2005.

Lee, Margaret G. "Out of the Hood and into the News: Black Verbal Expression in a Mainstream Newspaper." *American Speech* 74 (Winter 1999): 369–88.

Leechman, Douglas, and Robert A. Hall. "American Indian Pidgin English: Attestations and Grammatical Peculiarities." *American Speech* 30 (October 1955): 163–71.

Lippi-Green, Rosina. *English with an Accent: Language, Ideology, and Discrimination in the United States.* 2nd ed. London: Routledge, 2012.

Lipski, Patricia W. "The Introduction of 'Automobile' into American English." *American Speech* 39 (October 1964): 176–187.

Lowth, Robert. *A Short Introduction to English Grammar.* New ed. London: J. Dodsley, 1775.

Lyman, Rollo Laverne. *English Grammar in American Schools before 1850.* Washington, DC: Government Printing Office, 1922.

McCarthy, Corinne. "The Northern Cities Shift in Chicago." *Journal of English Linguistics* 39 (2011): 166–87.

McCulloch, Gretchen. *Because Internet: Understanding the New Rules of Language.* New York: Riverhead Books, 2019.

McDavid, Raven. "The Position of the Charleston Dialect." *Publication of the American Dialect Society* 23 (April 1955): 23–49.

McDavid, Raven I., Jr., and Virginia Glenn McDavid. "The Relationship of the Speech of American Negroes to the Speech of Whites." *American Speech* 26 (February 1951): 3–17.

McDowell, Tremaine. "The Use of Negro Dialect by Harriet Beecher Stowe." *American Speech* 6 (June 1931): 322–26.

McWhorter, John. "Revisiting Invariant *Am* in Earlier African American Vernacular English." *American Speech* 95 (November 2020): 379–407.

McWhorter, John. *Talking Back, Talking Black.* New York: Bellevue Literary Press, 2017.

Mathews, M. M. *The Beginnings of American English.* Chicago: University of Chicago Press, 1931.

Matthews, William. "Early New England Words." *American Speech* 15 (October 1940): 225–31.

Maurer, David W. *Language of the Underworld.* Lexington: University Press of Kentucky, 1981.

Maynor, Natalie. "Battle of the Pronouns: *Y'all* versus *You-Guys.*" *American Speech* 75 (Winter 2000): 416–18.

Meinig, D. W. *The Shaping of America.* Vol. 2, *Continental America, 1800–1867.* New Haven, CT: Yale University Press, 1993.

Mencken, H. L. *The American Language.* 4th ed. [1936]. New York: Alfred A. Knopf, 2000.

Mendoza-Denton, Norma. *Homegirls: Language and Cultural Practice among Latina Youth Groups.* Malden, MA: Blackwell, 2008.

Menner, Robert J. "Two Early Comments on American Dialects." *American Speech* 13 (February 1938): 8–12.

Metcalf, Allan A. *From Skedaddle to Selfie: Words of the Generations.* Oxford: Oxford University Press, 2016.

Metcalf, Allan. *How We Talk: American Regional English Today.* Boston: Houghton Mifflin, 2000.

Metcalf, Allan A. *OK: the Improbable Story of America's Greatest Word.* Oxford: Oxford University Press, 2011.

Metcalf, Allan. *Predicting New Words: The Secrets of Their Success.* Boston: Houghton Mifflin, 2002.

Metcalf, Allan A. "The Study of California Chicano English." *International Journal of the Sociology of Language* 2 (1974): 53–58.

Meyers, Miriam Watkins. "Generic Pronoun Usage: An Empirical Study." *American Speech* 65 (Autumn 1990): 228–37.

Montgomery, Michael. "The Etymology of *Y'all.*" In *Old English and New,* edited by Joan H. Hall, A. N. Doane, and Dick Ringler, 356–69. New York: Garland Press, 1992.

Montgomery, Michael. "Historical and Comparative Perspectives on *A*-Prefixing in the English of Appalachia." *American Speech* 84 (Spring 2009): 5–26.

Montgomery, Michael. "The Structural History of *Y'all, You All,* and *You'uns.*" *Southern Journal of Linguistics* 26 (April 2002): 19–27.

Montgomery, Michael B., and Guy Bailey, eds. *Language Variety in the South: Perspectives in Black and White.* Tuscaloosa: University of Alabama Press, 1986.

Moody, Patricia A. "Shall and Will: The Grammatical Tradition and Dialectology." *American Speech* 49 (Spring–Summer 1974): 67–78.

Moulton, Gary E., ed. *Journals of the Lewis and Clark Expedition.* Lincoln: University of Nebraska Press, 1983-2001.

Mufwene, Salikoko. "Some Sociohistorical Inferences about the Development of African American English." In *The English History of African American English,* edited by Shana Poplack, 233–63. Oxford: Blackwell, 2000.

Murphy, Lynne. *The Prodigal Tongue: The Love-Hate Relationship between American and British English.* New York: Penguin, 2018.

Murray, Lindley. *English Grammar Adapted to the Different Classes of Learners.* York, UK: Wilson, Spence, and Mawman, 1795.

Murray, Thomas E., Timothy C. Frazer, and Beth Lee Simon. "Need + Past Participle in American English." *American Speech* 71 (Autumn 1996): 255–71.

Murray, Thomas E., and Beth Lee Simon. "Want + Past Participle." *American Speech* 74 (Summer 1999): 140–164.

Nagle, Stephen J., and Sara L. Sanders, eds. *English in the Southern United States.* Cambridge, UK: Cambridge University Press, 2003.

Nagy, Naomi, and Patricia Irwin. "Boston (r): Neighbo(r)s Nea(r) and Fa(r)." *Language Variation and Change* 22 (2010): 241–78.

Nesbitt, Monica. "The Rise and Fall of the Northern Cities Shift: Social and Linguistic Re-organization of TRAP in 20th Century Lansing, Michigan." *American Speech* 96 (August 2021): 332-70.

Newman, Michael. *New York City Speech.* Berlin: Walter de Gruyter, 2014.

Newmark, Kalina, Nacole Walker, and James Stanford. "'The Rez Accent Knows No Borders': Native American Identity Expressed through English Prosody." *Language in Society* 45 (2016): 633–64.

Nunberg, Geoffrey. "Double Standards." *Natural Language and Linguistic Theory* 15 (August 1997): 667–75.

Ornstein-Galicia, Jacob, ed. *Form and Function in Chicano English.* Rowley, MA: Newberry House, 1981.

Ostler, Rosemarie. *Founding Grammars: How Early America's War over Words Shaped Today's Language.* New York: St. Martin's, 2015.

Pablé, Adrian, and Radosław Dylewski. "Invariant *Be* in New England Folk Speech: Colonial and Postcolonial Evidence." *American Speech* 82 (Summer 2007): 151–84.

Palmer, Colin A., ed. *Encyclopedia of African American Culture: The Black Experience in the Americas.* Vol. 3. Farmington Hills, MI: Macmillan Gale, 2006.

Penn, William. *A Further Account of the Province of Pennsylvania.* London, 1685.

Penn, William. *William Penn's Own Account of the Lenni Lenape or Delaware Indians* [1683]. Rev. ed. Moorestown, NJ: Middle Atlantic Press, 1970.

Pickering, John. *A Vocabulary, or Collection of Words and Phrases Which Have Been Supposed to Be Peculiar to the United States of America.* Boston: Cummings and Hilliard, 1816.

Pound, Louise. "The American Dialect Society: A Historical Sketch." *Publication of the American Dialect Society* 17 (April 1952): 3–28.

Read, Allen Walker. "Projects for an Academy to Regulate Speech." *PMLA* 51 (December 1936): 1141–79.

Read, Allen Walker. "The Assimilation of the Speech of British Immigrants in Colonial America." *Journal of English and Germanic Philology* 37 (January 1938): 70–79.

Read, Allen Walker. "British Recognition of American Speech in the Eighteenth Century." *Dialect Notes* VI (1933): 313–34.

Read, Allen Walker. "The English of Indians (1705–1745)." *American Speech* 16 (February 1941): 72–74.

Read, Allen Walker. "The First Stage in the History of 'O.K.'" *American Speech* 38 (February 1963): 5–27.

Read, Allen Walker. "Later Stages in the History of O.K." *American Speech* 39 (May 1964): 83–101.

Read, Allen Walker. "The Speech of Negroes in Colonial America." *Journal of Negro History* 24 (July 1939): 247–58.

Redfern, Richard K. "Is *between you and I* Good English?" *Publication of the American Dialect Society* 78 (December 1994): 187–93.

Reed, Paul E. "Phonological Possibilities in Appalachian Englishes." In *Appalachian Englishes in the Twenty-First Century*, edited by Kirk Hazen, 20–35. Morgantown: West Virginia University Press, 2020.

Rickford, John R. *African American Vernacular English*. Oxford: Blackwell, 1999.

Rickford, John R. "Prior Creolization of African American Vernacular English? Sociohistorical and Textual Evidence from the 17th and 18th Centuries." *Journal of Sociolinguistics* 1 (1997): 315–36.

Rickford, John R., and Sharese King. "Language and Linguistics on Trial: Hearing Rachel Jeantel (and Other Vernacular Speakers) in the Courtroom and Beyond." *Language* 92 (December 2016): 948–88.

Rickford, John R., Thomas Wasow, Arnold Zwicky, and Isabelle Buchstaller. "Intensive and Quotative *All*: Something Old, Something New." *American Speech* 82 (Spring 2007): 3–31.

Riess, Steven A., ed. *Sports in America from Colonial Times to the Twenty-First Century*. New York: Routledge, 2015.

Rodgers, Bruce. *Gay Talk* [formerly *The Queen's Vernacular*]. New York: Paragon Books, 1972.

Romaine, Suzanne, and Deborah Lange. "The Use of *Like* as a Marker of Reported Speech and Thought: A Case of Grammaticalization in Process." *American Speech* 66 (Autumn 1991): 227–79.

Rosenhouse, Judith, and Rotem Kowner, eds. *Globally Speaking: Motives for Adopting English Vocabulary in Other Languages*. Clevedon, UK: Multilingual Matters, 2008.

Royall, Anne. *Letters from Alabama*. Washington, DC, 1830.

Royall, Anne. *Sketches of History, Life, and Manners in the United States*. New Haven, CT, 1826.

Schele de Vere, Maximilian. *Americanisms: The English of the New World*. New York: Charles Scribner, 1872.

Schneider, Edgar W. *American Earlier Black English*. Tuscaloosa: University of Alabama Press, 1989.

Schneider, Edgar W., ed. *Focus on the USA*. Amsterdam: John Benjamins, 1996.

Schweiger, Beth Barton. "A History of English Grammar in the Early United States." *Journal of the Early Republic* 30 (Winter 2010): 533–55.

Simes, Gary. "Gay Slang Lexicography: A Brief History and a Commentary on the First Two Gay Glossaries." *Dictionaries* 26 (2005): 1–159.

Skinner, David. *The Story of Ain't: America, Its Language, and the Most Controversial Dictionary Ever Published*. New York: Harper, 2012.

Sledd, James, and Wilma R. Ebbitt. *Dictionaries and That Dictionary: A Casebook on the Aims of Lexicographers and the Targets of Reviewers*. Chicago: Scott, Foresman, 1962.

Smith, John. *Works 1608–1631*. 2 parts. Edited by Edward Arber. Westminster, UK: Archibald Constable, 1895.

Smitherman, Geneva. *Black Talk: Words and Phrases from the Hood to the Amen Corner*. Rev. ed. Boston: Houghton Mifflin, 2000.

Smorag, Pascale. "From Closet Talk to PC Terminology: Gay Speech and the Politics of Visibility." *Transatlantica* 1 (2008): 1–20.

Smyth, J. F. D. *A Tour in the United States of America*. 2 vols. London: G. Robinson, 1784.

Stange, Ulrike. "'You're So Not Going to Believe This': The Use of GenX *So* in Constructions with Future *Going to* in American English." *American Speech* 92 (November 2017): 487–524.

Stange, Ulrike. "'He Should So Be in Jail': An Empirical Study on Preverbal *So* in American English." *Journal of English Linguistics* 49 (2021): 114–36.

Stanley, Julia P. "Homosexual Slang." *American Speech* 45 (Spring–Summer, 1970): 45–59.

Tamasi, Susan, and Lamont Antieau. *Language and Linguistic Diversity in the US: An Introduction*. New York: Routledge, 2015.

Tannen, Deborah. *You Just Don't Understand: Women and Men in Conversation*. New York: William Morrow, 1990.

Thornton, Richard H. *An American Glossary*. 2 vols. Philadelphia: J.B. Lippincott, 1912.

Tieken-Boon van Ostade, Ingrid, ed. *Grammars, Grammarians, and Grammar Writing in Eighteenth-Century England*. Berlin: Mouton de Gruyter, 2008.

Tillery, Jan, and Guy Bailey. "*Yall* in Oklahoma." *American Speech* 73 (Autumn 1998): 257–78.

Tillery, Jan, Tom Wikle, and Guy Bailey. "The Nationalization of a Southernism." *Journal of English Linguistics* 28 (September 2000): 280–94.

Trigger, Bruce G., ed. *Handbook of North American Indians*. Vol. 15. Washington, DC: Smithsonian, 1978.

Vine, Bernadette. "Americanisms in the New Zealand English Lexicon." *World Englishes* 18 (1999): 13–22.

Webster, Noah. *An American Dictionary of the English Language*. 2 vols. New York: S. Converse, 1828.

Webster, Noah. *Dissertations on the English Language*. Boston: Isaiah Thomas, 1789.

Weldon, Tracey L. "Revisiting the Creolist Hypothesis: Copula Variability in Gullah and Southern Rural AAVE." *American Speech* 78 (Summer 2003): 171–91.

Wells, J. C. *Accents of English*. Vol. 1. Cambridge, UK: Cambridge University Press, 1982.

White, Richard Grant. *Words and Their Uses, Past and Present* [1870]. Rev. ed. New York: Sheldon & Co, 1876.

Winford, Donald. "On the Origins of African American Vernacular English— A Creolist Perspective," parts 1 and 2. *Diachronica* 14 (1997): 305–344; 15 (1998): 99–154.

Wolfram, Walt. "Towards a Description of A-Prefixing in Appalachian English." *American Speech* 51 (Spring–Summer 1976): 45–56.

Wolfram, Walt, and Jeffrey Reaser. *Talkin' Tar Heel*. Chapel Hill: University of North Carolina Press, 2014.

Wolfram, Walt, and Natalie Schilling. *American English: Dialects and Variation*. 3rd ed. Chichester, UK: Wiley Blackwell, 2016.

Wolfram, Walt, and Ben Ward, eds. *American Voices: How Dialects Differ from Coast to Coast*. Malden, MA: Blackwell, 2006.

Wolk, Lesley, Nassima B. Abdelli-Beruh, and Dianne Slavin. "Habitual Use of Vocal Fry in Young Adult Female Speakers." *Journal of Voice* 26 (2012): e111–e116.

Wood, Jim, Raffaella Zanuttini, Laurence Horn, and Jason Zentz. "Dative Country: Markedness and Geographical Varieties in the Southern Dative Construction." *American Speech* 95 (February 2020): 3–45.

Yuasa, Ikuko Patricia. "A New Feminine Voice Quality for Young Urban-Oriented, Upwardly Mobile American Women?" *American Speech* 85 (Fall 2010): 315–37.

Zullo, Davide, Simone E. Pfenninger, and Daniel Schreier. "A Pan-Atlantic 'Multiple Modal Belt'?" *American Speech* 96 (February 2021): 7–44.

# Index

*For the benefit of digital users, indexed terms that span two pages (e.g., 52–53) may, on occasion, appear on only one of those pages.*

*Please note: Figures are indicated by an italic f following the page number.*